Journeying in MacDougall Country

Second Edition

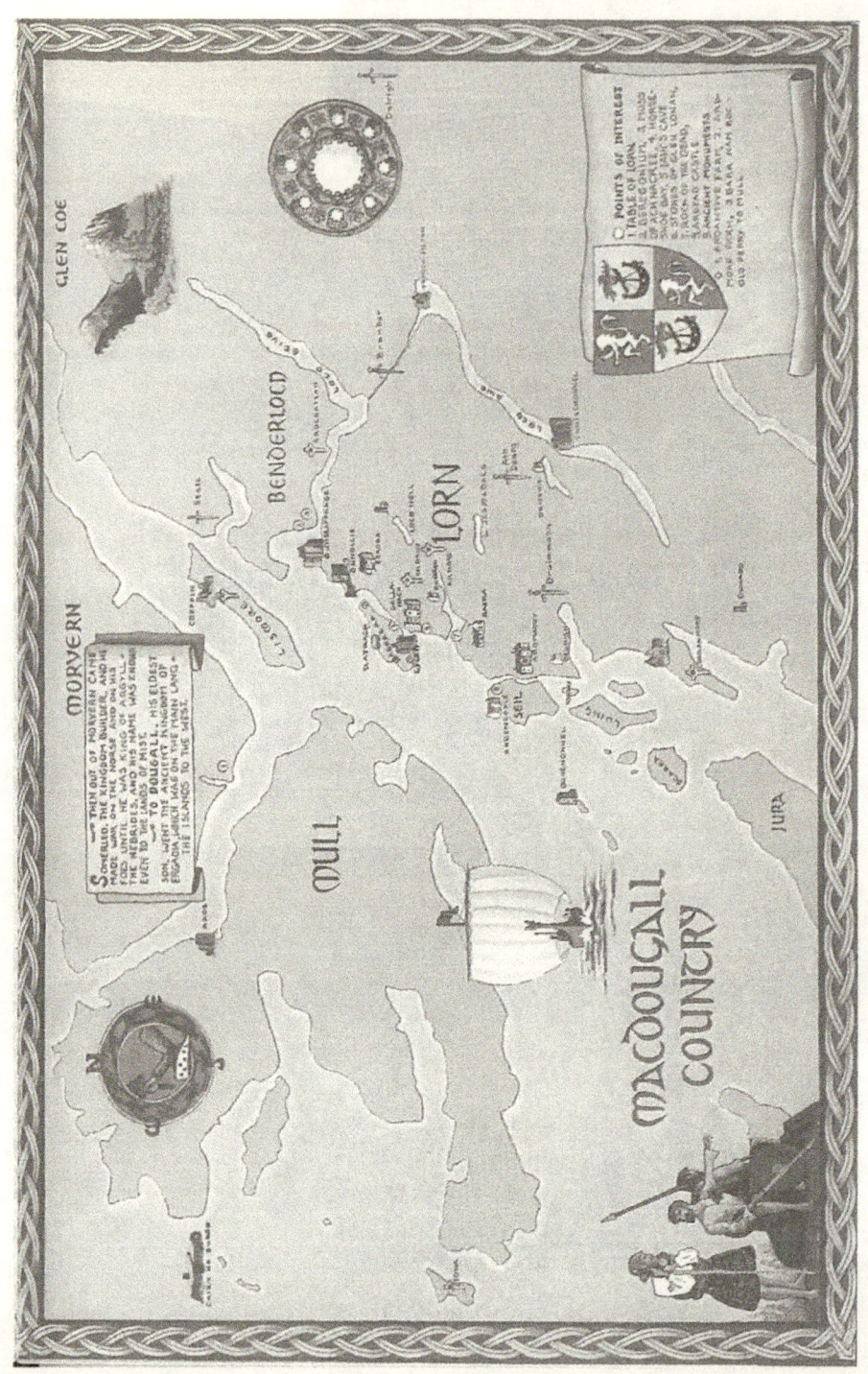

JOURNEYING IN MACDOUGALL COUNTRY

Second Edition

WALTER MARSHALL MACDOUGALL

Ionmhuin tír, an tír ud thoir,
Alba gona h-iongantaibh.

A lovely land, that land to the eastward
Alba with its wonders.

~ Lay of Deirdre

Clan MacDougall Society of North America, Inc.

Clan MacDougall Society of North America, Inc., Parkton 21120
www.macdougall.org

Copyright 1984, 2008 by Walter Marshall Macdougall

All rights reserved. No part of this book may be used or reproduced in any manner whatsoever without written permission, except in the case of brief quotations embodied in critical articles or reviews.

First edition published 1984. Second edition 2008

ISBN 978-0-6151-7789-2

Library of Congress Control Number: 2007908740

Illustrations: By Walter Marshall Macdougall, except where noted
Mendelssohn sketch: By permission of the Bodleian Library
Turner sketches: By permission of the Tate Gallery
Diagrams: By permission of The Royal Commission on the Ancient & Historical Monuments of Scotland
Photograph of Walter Macdougall by Pat McDougal, editor of *The Tartan*
Cover: MacDougall of Lunga tartan;
　"Barefoot MacDougall" by R.R. McIan;
　design by Joanne Masterson, BlueJ Projects
Formatting and editing: By Suzanne O. McDougal

This book is printed on acid-free paper.

Dedication

To my mother, Leah Parks Macdougall, and my father,
Arthur R. Macdougall, who lovingly encouraged their
children to see beauty and to cherish it,

and

Hope MacDougall of MacDougall and Jean MacDougall Hadfield
whose knowledge, wit, and kindness
brought joy and insight to this Highland journey.

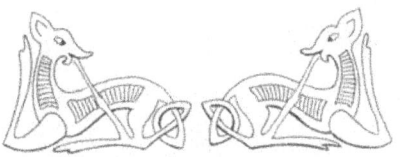

Contents

List of Diagrams ix

List of Maps ix

Foreward to the First Edition xi

Foreward to the Second Edition xii

Introduction to the First Edition xiii

Introduction to the Second Edition xv

THE JOURNEY
    Chapter 1 North to Oban 3
    Chapter 2 Dunollie 7
    Chapter 3 Ganavan 14
    Chapter 4 Kirk, Glenmore, Pulpit Hill, and McCaig's Tower 17
    Chapter 5 Lismore 22
    Chapter 6 On the Shore Road to Gallanach 27
    Chapter 7 The Old Track to Kilbride 31
    Chapter 8 The Islands and the Sea 37
    Chapter 9 Evening Atop Cnoc Carnach 43
    Chapter 10 Ardchattan, Brander, and Dalrigh 46
    Chapter 11 Dinner With the Chief 53
    Chapter 12 Glen Etive 56
    Chapter 13 The String of Lorn 63
    Chapter 14 Loch Awe, Melfort, and Degnish 67
    Chapter 15 Craignish and Lunga 73
    Chapter 16 Raera and Nether Lorn 81
    Chapter 17 Island of Kerrera 86
    Chapter 18 Dunstaffnage 92
    Chapter 19 Luncheon at Dunollie 98
    Chapter 20 Weather 100
    Chapter 21 Glen Lonan 105
    Chapter 22 Benderloch 111
    Chapter 23 Journey Epilogue 115

SUBSEQUENT SKETCHES
- Chapter 24 Blessed for a Second Time 119
- Chapter 25 Artists and MacDougall Castles.. 122
- Chapter 26 The Avenue.. 129
- Chapter 27 Pulpit Hill.. 131
- Chapter 28 Lismore 134
- Chapter 29 Gallanach 136
- Chapter 30 From Loch Gleann a' Bhearraidh to Gallanach.............. 141
- Chapter 31 Crossing Mull 143
- Chapter 32 Evening on Iona 148
- Chapter 33 Staffa.. 149
- Chapter 34 Loch Awe and the Islands of Inishail and Fraoch Eilean.. 153
- Chapter 35 Glencoe - a Second Look.. 158
- Chapter 36 Rannoch Moor and Glen Orchy 159
- Chapter 37 View Over Lunga House 160
- Chapter 38 Craignish... 162
- Chapter 39 Ardencaple House, Seil, and Luing 163
- Chapter 40 Tigh Cuil and the Stones of Duachy 168
- Chapter 41 A Day on Kerrera... 174
- Chapter 42 Dunollie's Eagle 180
- Chapter 43 Touched by the Mist 182

LORE OF LORN
- About the Notes... 184
- Antiquity of Lorn... 185
- Battles.. 196
- Cadets and Other Branches of Clan MacDougall............................... 203
- Castles and Houses 213
- Churches and Burial Grounds 233
- Chiefs of the Clan and Their Coats of Arms 239
- Flora and Fauna 249
- Physical Geology... 255
- Other Lore 264

Bibliography 268

Contact Information 271

Maps 272

Index.. 277

List of Diagrams

1. Architectural Decorative Designs 194
2. Arrow Slits and Gun Loops 195
3. Coeffin Castle, Floor Plan 218
4. Dunollie Castle, Floor Plan 220
5. Dunstaffnage Castle, Floor Plan 225
6. Gylen Castle, Floor Plan 227
7. Gylen Castle, Oriel Window 229
8. Ardchattan Priory, Floor Plan 233
9. Dunstaffnage Chapel, Windows 236
10. Arms of the MacDougall Chiefs 240

List of Maps

1. Northern Lorn 272
2. Central Lorn 273
3. Oban Area 274
4. Lismore 275
5. Dalrigh 275
6. Southern Lorn 276

Foreword to the First Edition

It is with great pleasure that I welcome the publication of Walter Macdougall's book, Journeying in MacDougall Country.

It makes a valuable addition to the few books written about the MacDougall Clan and country. He has gone to a tremendous amount of trouble to check the historical accuracy of his subject and has walked miles over the country he is writing about to see for himself the actual sites.

This beautifully written book should give tremendous pleasure to many who must feel gratitude to him for undertaking such a difficult task and for doing that task so well.

I wish the book every success.

Coline MacDougall of MacDougall

Coline MacDougall of MacDougall
Dunollie Castle
January 1984

Foreword to the Second Edition

I am privileged to be invited to write the foreword to this second edition of Walter Macdougall's book.

In re-reading <u>Journeying in MacDougall Country</u>, I am once again entranced by his genuine and deep love for the country of the MacDougalls.

This edition has been expanded by the rich addition of his subsequent journeys, the numbering of his chapters and by a series of symbols in the text, which are explained at the foot of each relevant page. He retains the number references which give us a wealth of extra information in the 'Lore of Lorn' section of the book.

Walter Macdougall's expansive knowledge of the relevant historic and other facts—which are so important to the backbone of this book—becomes richly enhanced by his emphatic and deeply thoughtful narrative. This exceptional mix of qualities make this edition, once again, a delight in store for many and a 'must read' for MacDougall Clansfolk.

Morag MacDougall of MacDougall

Morag MacDougall of MacDougall
Dunollie Castle
2007

Introduction to the First Edition

For thirty-five years, the author had dreamed of making a journey through the MacDougall Country of Lorn. During the summer of 1981, this dream became a reality. This little book is an abstract of the daily journal kept during this adventure in the land of our ancestors. To this text has been added maps, historical notes, and geographical facts to produce a guide that, it is hoped, will be useful to those planning a similar journey.

The author makes no apology for either his sentimentality or his enthusiasm be they the product of romantic fanasy, nostalgia, or something of more significance. If at times his sentiments appear excessive, the writer can only say that such extravagances seemed an upwelling from within—a surge of that mysterious continuum that may link past to present within our psyches. The author must admit that he feels we sail the same galleys of human experience as those from whom we sprang, no matter what new era rims our horizon. They from whom we came stand beside us at the steering oar with their plaids blowing in the age-old winds. In times of storm we feel their hand upon the oar, and in the cloud-blown day when the wind is fair and fresh we seem to hear their laughter and call for sail.

Archibald MacLeish in his poem "The Thrush on the Island of Bara" wrote, "I am remembering something," and then with caution born in our era of materialistic science, MacLeish corrects himself. "No, not remembering; it was told to me..." It cannot be that the memory of that thrush singing amidst the agony of the clearances lingers still. There is no known mechanics by which such a memory might be bequeathed nor an inborn recollection transmitted. Yet MacLeish seems unsure, nor is the author of this book certain, concerning the genesis of his own feelings.

It is a fact that our Highland ancestors felt a true sense of belonging to the glens and the mountains of their home. It is as though by holding their portion of Alba in their teeth, they and their children became part and parcel of the place they called their native own. By heart and by hand they grasped their bit of Scotland in filial grip until its falling waters sounded in their language and its bright mist diffused throughout their souls.

It is their tragedy—so often heard in the longing cry of their song and verse—that a people so united with headland, heath, and hearth should have been subjected by fate, both natural and contrived by men, to centuries of exodus.

There is no wonder that these Highlanders should have felt so strongly about these places from which they had been separated, even when the separation was voluntary and for the sake of their own material betterment. The marvel lies in our lingering attachment to the old clan lands—we who are their children's children and born on another continent. Are we the product of a conditioned romanticism and are our sentiments spurred by that human need for identity in a world grown too open and too complex, or do we by some unknown and inner means remember the call of our ancestral home?

The writer does not have the answer. He only testifies to how deeply he was moved on finding himself at last in MacDougall Country. It was in the evening's long-reaching rays that he arrived in Lorn—a moment when Etive's shores were set in amber and the Firth shone lavender under a purple cloud. He who was born in America and who had left so many dear connections four thousand miles away was close to Highland tears, and the words of an old saying came to mind: "All things come home at eventide."

Walter Marshall Macdougall
Milo, Maine
1984

Introduction to the Second Edition

To share the joy of discovering the land of our ancestors; to provide a guide for those planning an adventure in MacDougall Country; to suggest the interplay of history, a people, and a rugged, magnificent land were the objectives this book when it was written in 1984. They remain the primary goal for this second edition.

The first edition strove to paint verbal vistas, to recount the wonderful stories told, and to introduce the fine people met. The result was a text overflowing with adjectives. As one of my friends commented, "Your writing reminds me of that Scottish school of artist called the "Colorists." Certainly the book was best read in small portions at a time. In producing a new edition, we considered trimming descriptions and eliminating color descriptors, but in the end we decided that to do so would diminish the original exuberance—the total excitement and the honest attempt to revel in the magnificence of MacDougall Country.

Additional trips to Scotland coupled with expanding sources have made possible an enrichment of the original text in the form of "Subsequent Sketches." For the most part, these descriptions and reflections are contained in their own section within the new edition. However, in a few instances where further opportunity completed what I was unable to experience in my initial adventure, these extensions have been worked into the "Journey" text where they would be of greatest use to the reader and provide geographical and narrative continuity. Examples of such additions are the hike through Glen More near Oban or the visit to Ardencaple House on the Isle of Seil. Occasionally, as in the account of the train trip to Oban, details left out of the first edition have been inserted.

Serious readers will find the notes invaluable. There are footnotes at the bottom of many pages, referenced in the text by symbols; the pertinent longer notes located within the section "The Lore of Lorn" are referenced in the text by numbers.

The text is filled with the names of those who were important in this adventure. My appreciation and thanks deepens with the years for those who so kindly and wisely made my experiences, old and later, so memorable and meaningful. It is my hope that this account of my journey in MacDougall Country will, in some small way, add to the continuing memory of these fine folk in the annals of our Clan.

Of special importance in the creation of this second edition is Suzanne McDougal. Without her skill as an editor and her indomitable enthusiasm, this new edition would never have become a reality. My thanks also go to the Clan MacDougall Society of North America for underwriting this new publication.

Walter Marshall Macdougall
Milo, Maine
2007

THE JOURNEY

1981

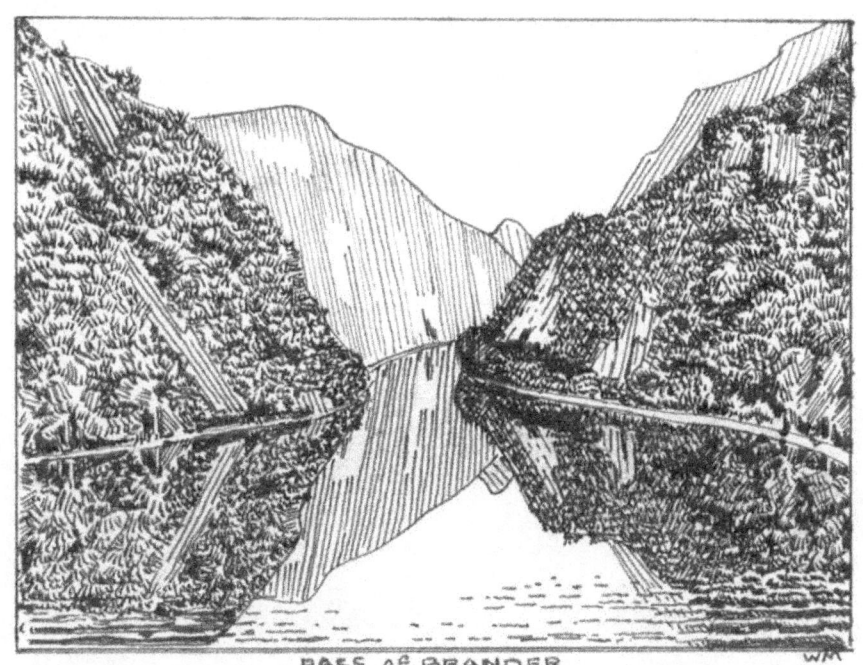

PASS OF BRANDER

Chapter 1
North to Oban

The train to Oban stands under the high girders and glass roof of Queen Street Station.* As I am early boarding, there is time to spread out a map and my lunch on one of the tables separating each pair of seats. Trains leave this station through a tunnel under the Glasgow streets, the red rear lights of each train disappearing through an arched portal in a massive stone wall—a passageway to a long-awaited adventure, it seemed to me. At last there comes the sharp trill of a trainman's whistle, doors bang shut, and beneath our feet traction motors surge. With quickening pace, we pass the glowing semaphore lamps and are suddenly enclosed in an outer darkness, surrounded by the echoing clatter of wheels clicking across the rail joints. The journey to Oban has begun!

The train emerges into the late afternoon sun. In the distance four high-rise towers, colored in bands of greens and oranges, reflect the late afternoon light. Closer to hand, the train is passing row on row of two-story houses crowded in clumps or strung together—all very much alike with chimney pots, lace curtains at the windows, exterior plumbing pipes, old red bricks or newer stucco gray or brown, and roofs of black slate or orange tile. Nearly all these houses have skylights, as if trying to catch all the sunlight there is.

The tracks follow an old canal green with water plants, and then we are on the "bonnie bank of Clyde." The hull of an old wooden boat with tattered traces of paint lies on its side in the mud. Beyond this wreck, patches of bright sunlight and the wind transform the muddy estuary into acres of dancing mirrors and polished silver.

I had anticipated fine scenery along the way to Oban but not the grandeur, apparent so soon beyond the Firth of Clyde. Just where the Highlands begin I am not sure. One senses their nearness at Dumbarton, where the railway passes between two rocky eminences. There is a sudden raggedness and a feeling of brooding history. The clifted pedestal to the left lifts a dark fortress against the sky. According to some, Iain Bacach, the fifth Chief of the MacDougalls, was imprisoned during the last months of his life there on Dumbarton's Rock.†

---

* The stations along the West Highland Line now bear their Gaelic names as well as English. Queen Street Station's sign reads "Sraid na Banrighinn."
† Some accounts claim that Iain Bacach died in Dumbarton's dungeon; however, in others he appears at a later date in Galloway, where he is befriended by Dougald Macdowall. In these stories, he makes a pilgrimage to Galloway and dies not long after. Dougald Macdowall was his executor.

Beyond Dumbarton, the long-reaching light of the lowering sun illuminates with glowing colors the old manuscripts of the hills. The first mass of mountains appears, the blue peaks of Cowal rising across Gare Loch. Then the hills close in on the railway line, followed by the mountains—the Black Ardgartan and the Cobbler—which rise abruptly from the shores of Loch Long. Below the Cobbler's jagged profile, a deep valley winds westward into the mist. I am spellbound! These mountains are Prussian blue and magenta, silhouetted against a bank of cumulus—buff, gray-tufted, and backlit by the hidden sun. The railway runs high above Loch Long. Each curve of the track brings a new view of the water far below and the upsweep of mountain across the loch. Each successive panorama grows more grand.

Across the aisle, a girl of perhaps eighteen stretches out a long leg neatly fitted in denim and ending in a high-heeled pump. She smiles over the top of a romance magazine. In the next seat, two elderly women are unwrapping their supper, one course at a time. They tell me that the yellow-blossomed bush so magnificent on the hillsides is called "broom." One lady remembers that her mother used to say, "As long as the broom blooms, kissing will be in fashion."

At the head of Loch Long, the railway swings eastward to reach the shore of Loch Lomond. The elderly ladies inform me that there is a grand view of Ben Lomond ahead and advise me to move to the opposite side of the coach. I take an empty seat across the isle. My camera has had little rest. The conductor warns, "Yer goin' t' wear it out, Laddie."

The lass with the smile leaves us at Tarbet Station. Her seat is taken by a young fellow who is on his way to play football in Oban. He looks up at the click of my camera's shutter, grins, and returns to his paperback, which sports a gun-slinging cowboy on its cover. Later he tells me "Westerns are all right." He is from the outer islands, but living in Glasgow where he can find work. His manners are fine and genuine, his knuckles freshly scarred, perhaps from the rigors of a recent game. He returns again to his book. I suppose he has seen the beauty sliding past these windows many times. Ah, we often grow complacent with a horrible rapidity.

We have been traveling in the shadow, but as we enter the wild upland moor of Glen Falloch a flood of light falls upon the sides of a great U-shaped valley—plowed by a glacier in ages past, rock-strewn, and in places newly planted to softwoods. Greens and yellows rise up the flanks to fade into the pinks of rock faces. Beyond, a cobalt dome (Sron Gharbh) rises above the nearer hills. With a sudden hollow rush, the train crosses a trestle. Far below, white water churns between a tumble of boulders.

Chapter 1

My map tells me that Crianlarich is our next stop. It is an important point on the West Highland Line, surrounded by mountains and significantly situated at the meeting of Strath Fillan and Glen Dochart—old routes for Highland armies and cattle drives. Here the railway divides into two lines. One runs westward down Strath Fillan to Tyndrum, Dalmally, and Oban's waiting harbor. The other climbs northward to finally reach Mallaig and the ferry west to Skye and the Outer Hebrides.

Just beyond Crianlarich, there comes on our right a momentary look down the depth of a glen—magnificent, earth and atmosphere meeting in mist, with a hundred shades of blue and lavender. This is immense, dramatic country!

My excitement builds. Mountains are all around us now, with Ben More towering to three thousand and eight hundred feet. In Strath Fillan, the river runs gleaming and peaty brown between the banks it has cut in the moor. On the right, somewhere beside the river as its flows over a gravel bar, MacDougall clansmen fought and won the Battle of Dalrigh.

We are descending into the village of Tyndrum. Coach wheels click over the rail joints with increasing rapidity. Ahead and beyond the village, the mass of a mountain (Beinn Bhreac-laith) rises into a blue-gray, nearly purple world of a storm poised on the brink of cataclysm. Just to the west, the great shape of Cruachan has taken on cosmic dimensions as it rises to merge with the embattled cloud.

We leave the storm behind and the evening is bright again. Yet as the train swings beyond the massive shoulders of Cruachan, a feeling of threat rises within me—an overshadowing. This is the Pass of Brander, the defile in which our Clan experienced its darkest hour![15] As the ledges press the track to the brink of River Awe, I sense this as a place to get through and leave behind—the same impression that takes hold of some who travel through Glencoe.

Then we are through the pass, with no down-rush of an enemy with Douglas at their head. Instead an angler, knee-deep in Awe's current, has a salmon on his line. His rod bends and, in a silver flash, the salmon jumps.

The blessing of an uncrowded coach allows me to switch sides once more, this time to view Loch Etive reaching northward into its mountain wilderness. Now Oban's crescent harbor and Dunollie are but a few miles away. The photographs, the long-studied maps, and the delightful images from Black's description of Oban[*] are assuming the reality of

---

[*] J.W.N. Black, *MacDonald's Guide to Oban*. Long out of print. A delightful traveler's guide for Oban and the surrounding area from an earlier era. In 1981, Oban was not so changed from the descriptions in this charming guide.

earth, sky, and sea. They are taking form, as might the fulfillment of a prophesy come true. There comes a brief view of heather moor threaded by a narrow road, before the train rumbles through rock cuts and hurries down Glen Cruitten. A cottage with roses at its door flashes by; the green of a golf course drops away toward the rooftops of Oban, cupped between the surrounding heights. Suddenly there is a glimpse over a tall pointed spire of brown and the roofs of gray stone buildings to a square-towered cathedral facing a bay. The scarred summits and broad-shouldered mountains of Mull and Morvern rise as a backdrop in the sun-filled west.

We cross the brook that comes tumbling down from Glen Seileach, pass through a deep rock cut whose walls are like stone portals opening on Oban and the sea, and come to a stop under the station canopy.[*]

With suitcase, pack, and briefcase, I head confidently up Albert Street to find the Heatherfield Private Hotel—up, then back. A redheaded constable, who must be the pride of the force, shakes his head. He does not remember such a place. As I stand perplexed beside my impedimenta, a man calls from across the street to ask if I am lost. He quickly solves the mystery. The Heatherfield is on Albert *Road*, not Albert *Street*. Mr. Young—I shall not forget his name—gets his car out, drives me to the front door of the Heatherfield, and helps carry my duffel into the hallway. What a fine introduction to the people of Oban!

Settled in, I take a walk along the Esplanade—along the curve of harbor whose waters dance with the zigzags of a hundred reflecting lights. Dunollie was as yet unseen, and I stop my walk before it comes in sight. I want to see this castle of the Clan in the fresh of morning, for by now my capacity to absorb is exhausted. My soul seems full like a brimming spring threatening to overflow, as did the witch's spring on Cruachan in the legend about how Loch Awe was formed.[71] I lean against the stone wall that runs along the seaward side of the Esplanade. The quiet colors of late evening wrap the Island of Kerrera and the far mountains of Mull. Below the wall, an inward-riding ripple catches the sky's hue and spreads it among the pebbles of the beach.[†]

---

[*] In 1981 the old wooden station was still in use. It was painted blue and white, sported a bit of Victorian decoration, and had a canopy roof over the platforms. The new station is an efficient comedown. The railroad (along with steamboats, which came as early as 1816) transformed Oban when it arrived in 1880.

[†] Also see Chapter 24.

Chapter 2
Dunollie

Along the Esplanade

An unexpected boon—a white-hulled brigantine with stay sails set, coming through the thoroughfare between the Maiden Island[*] and the clifted spine of Kerrera's Rubha a' Bhearnaig. She slides past Oban's upper waterfront of church towers and hotel fronts to join the boats riding at anchor and the island ferries moored to their pier.

I am walking up the Esplanade toward Dunollie. Saint Michael's Craig, which rises at the foot of the cliff upon which Dunollie stands, is now in view and, before it, a small round tower and high stone wall fronts the curving road.[44] One more step and I shall see the castle!

A MacDougall is bound to be moved, but it was Sir Walter Scott who wrote, "Nothing can be more wildly beautiful than the situation of Dunollie." Mendelssohn and the great landscapist Turner were equally impressed.[†] There rises the square tower, atop that mass of volcanic rock thrust up in ages past and formed as if intended for fortification.

For centuries a place of strength has stood atop that headland rampart, commanding the inner waterways of the ancient Kingdom of Dalriada. At least four times, smoke and flame wreathed those heights during the seventh and eighth centuries, when Dun Ollaigh was razed only to be rebuilt by its destroyers. Then, sometime in the thirteenth century, the MacDougall Lords of Lorn built this stronghold with its thick-walled keep.[42‡]

Transfixed by Dunollie, I find I have passed the gateway to the drive leading to Dunollie House.[87] The choice now is either to retrace my steps or climb the retaining wall that curbs the Shore Road as it dips down to round Port Mor at the foot of the castle's promontory. The latter seems more exciting. I find myself on the turfed-over slope of an ancient sea beach and at the foot of Clach na Choin, the "Dog Stone"—that pillar of conglomerate stone whose base was once scoured by the ocean before the present shoreline rose. Legend has another genesis for the scalloped base of this massive rock—it was the chain of Fingal's restless hound, Bran, that wore away the stone whenever the epic hero hitched his dog

---

[*] The origin of this island's name appears lost. It is said that a light appears on this island warning of death within the the family of the MacDougalls of Dunollie. The light was seen when Captain Alexander was killed storming Ciudad Rodrigo in Spain.
[†] See Chapter 25.
[‡] Simpson, *Dunollie, Oban, Argyll*, p. 60 ff.

here.[68] I climb another fence with only small damage to the seat of my pants and stand upon the drive to Dunollie.

The drive is arched as magnificently as a cathedral aisle by trees splendidly tall. As it was not the hour set for my visit with the Chief of Clan MacDougall, yet having nearly reached Dunollie House, I sit under a tree whose branches spread a roof and make a shadowed wall around me. A white curtain of shower has filled the Sound of Kerrera and, lighted by a misty sun, it slowly spreads its folds across Oban Harbor. From the steep side of Conc Carnach, which rises to the east, comes the bleat of sheep—a plaintive cry half swept away by the sound of the passing wind. Strange to hear that wind like the flowing of a burn,* for around me the air is nearly still. To my left the drive takes a sharp turn as it approaches the Chief's home. That turn is called the "windy corner," for often the wind comes seeping inland there, funneled between the ledge-faced ridge that flanks the drive to the east and Dunollie's promontory to the west. So this is why Dunollie House is tucked where it is—sheltered from the torrents of the storm but deprived of a long view down the green pasture to the Sound of Kerrera.

In the days when William Wordsworth visited, no one would have reached the "windy corner" without being announced by the cry of the disabled eagle kept on the heights of Dunollie.[66] Today I am unheralded except for the songbirds that twitter amidst the rhododendrons and in a flaming red azalea at the base of Dunollie's rock. And now, that approaching shower moves in among the trees along the drive. The air is filled with the vapors of the sea.

Despite the shower, Dunollie House gleams white with a new coat of paint.[44] As I approach the front door, two speckled hens escorted by a rooster are pecking in the gravel drive. For a moment I am surprised by such a bucolic sight, and then am immensely pleased. This is the home of a Highland chief, not Versailles. I pause at the entryway, turning to look back and upwards. The old castle stands high above the trees—a tower of dark stone against the gray sky.

On turning back to the entranceway, a most unusual object catches my eye. By the doorway rests a lichen-covered rock bearing the incised shape of a foot. What a solid reminder of the position of the person I am about to visit! It was the ancient Celtic custom to consecrate a chief

---

* A brook.

while this new leader of the people placed a foot in just such an incised print, symbolizing a following in the footsteps of duty and authority.[23, 51*]

At the House

The Chief, Coline Helen Elizabeth MacDougall of MacDougall, wearing a skirt of MacDougall tartan, receives me in the sitting room, which was remodeled and enlarged by Leslie Grahame MacDougall, the Chief's husband and a member of the Royal Society of Architects. Coffee and shortbread are brought in, and we sit and talk of Clan Society activities and of a diabolical plan championed by "outsiders" to connect the island of Kerrera to the mainland by building a causeway.

The keepsakes of Dunollie House chronicle the lives of the later MacDougall Chiefs—years at Dunollie and years away in the navy, army, and medical service. Here is a model of a Chinese junk and one of an American birchbark canoe, the flag flown by Admiral John MacDougall (twenty-fifth Chief) and the ensign flown by his great-granddaughter, our present chief, as an officer in World War II.[†]

By the proxy of an oil painting, I meet Admiral John MacDougall, who gave Dunollie House its present dimensions. Going to sea at the age of thirteen, the Admiral spent many years far from this house below the castle. As a young First Lieutenant, he was aboard the H.M.S. Leander when decks were cleared for action against the U.S.S. Constitution. Much to John's disappointment, wind and a thick fog prevented the splintering carnage that might have followed.[‡] Actually, and as those on board the Leander were soon to learn, the War of 1812 was already over.

Appropriately, in the women's parlor hangs the portrait of the Admiral's beautiful wife, Elizabeth Sophia Timins. The Admiral met her quite by chance. Intent on remodeling Dunollie House, John went to view the renovations Elizabeth's father was making on their home. After the visit, John could remember only the lovely Elizabeth Sophia. In the painting, she wears a bonnet adorned with a full wing of feathers. On a chair back, close by the painting with its lovely face, hangs the bonnet itself—a touch that binds past to present. That touch is everywhere in this parlor. Elizabeth Sophia's daughter was married in this room, and

---

[*] This stone was found at Soroba on the southern outskirts of Oban. It was brought by cart at the direction of Colina MacDougall, the wife of our twenty-ninth Chief and daughter of Alexander MacDougall of Soroba.
[†] This refers to Coline Helen Elizabeth MacDougall, 30th Chief, who passed away in 1990. Due to their father's military postings, the 30th Chief was born in England, her sister Jean in Ceylon, and her sister Hope in Ireland.
[‡] Jean MacDougall, *The Highland Postbag*, p. 186.

here is her wedding dress of homemade lace. Sadly, she did not live long after her marriage. Here also is also a silk dress of MacDougall tartan that probably belonged to this same young lady. Nearby, the male fashion is represented in a pair of tartan trews cut from one piece of material, to include feet.

The portrait of Coline MacDougall of MacDougall's mother, Colina, who was herself an accomplished portrait painter, also graces the wall. She was quite deaf when the painting was made, and as the artist liked to keep his subject in conversation while he worked, Colina MacDougall kept up her own monologue. The lovely white-haired lady who looks so kindly from the canvas talked, with a Miss Marple touch, about the past and local murders.

A large woodcarving of the arms of the MacDougall Chiefs, in color and bold relief, occupies the hearth of an unused fireplace.[59,60] These arms bear the heraldry of two royal lines, but the position of this representation seems a symbol of something closer to the heart. It is another Celtic tradition that the chief is the keeper of the central hearth from which radiates the well-being of the entire clan family. In this concept lies the strength of our Highland heritage, which always keeps in touch with the earth and the communal pride of belonging. This tie persists, even though the clan is dispersed around the globe. Few realize the number of clanspeople who come to Dunollie from across the sea, nor do we often appreciate the hours that Madam MacDougall of MacDougall takes from her busy day to make them welcome. Our tour of Dunollie House ends appropriately in the oldest part of the Chief's dwelling, upon the flagstone floor of the original kitchen and below the bright copper orbs of hanging jam kettles.[*]

The Castle

The path to the castle ruins leads up from the gravel drive in front of Dunollie House to the portal in the outer curtain wall.[†] One passes through this gateway to stand in the castle's grassy courtyard. Beyond a fragment of what was the eastern wall enclosing the yard,[‡] there spreads an unsurpassed view of sea, of islands, and of the mountains of Mull and Morvern. Closer, just across the narrow opening to Oban Harbor, lies the

---

[*] The old kitchen is part of a small thatched house called Laich Biggen, which stood below the castle while still occupied by the Chief of the Clan.
[†] A public path to the castle leaves from Ganavan Road.
[‡] This may be a portion of the old chapel.

rocky ramparts of Kerrera.* One is level with the gulls turning on the wind that sweeps upwards from the water one hundred feet below. "Massive" is the word for the walls of the keep that rise above the courtyard. The walls are thick enough to contain the stairway and still be defensively strong. Over the stairs, great stone slabs carry the ponderous weight of the walls above.[42]

DUNOLLIE

The stairs of Dunollie Castle turn upwards from darkness to light—from the purple-gray of shadow to the yellow-green of stones tapestried with lichen. I mount the worn treads half-wishing that I might meet one of the claymore-wielding Lords of Lorn, and I enter the hall above half-expecting to see Mary of Sleat with her skirts spread upon a window seat and in her hand a letter from her husband, Iain Ciar, written from his place of exile and hiding.[62] The hall is empty. Its timbered ceiling is gone and the walls rise upward like a great chimney to the sky. Where once *clarsach*† music filled the hall, there is now only the cry of gulls and the rote of the sea upon the sands of Port Mor and the rocks of Camus Ban.

---

* The channel here is narrow, especially at low tide. I once saw a fishing boat aground in the narrow passage below the castle, waiting for high tide to be pulled free. In the old days of cattle drives, the animals were swum to the mainland at a point just below the castle.
† Celtic harp.

A steady chill wind, wet from the ocean, comes through the west window. There are two climates here in Dunollie's castle hall—one in the wind and the other out. I sit in the recess of what was once a north window before it was blocked up (perhaps to keep out the winter's blast) and eat my lunch. The sun's disk, a round white orb through the ever-passing cloud, casts a mist-filtered warmth into my den. I listen to the gulls and the sea, and think on the centuries of living these walls have housed—the laughter round the torch-lit board, the quiet weeping of yet another widow, and the first cry of Mary MacDougall born in 1741, the last birth within this ancient place.

Across the hall, the rocks of the fireplace are still blackened. There, above the corbels that once supported the third floor, is the recessed chamber in the east wall where chiefs of Clan MacDougall slept under an arch of stone. On the opposite side is the vestibule, lit by a window slit where the stairs reached the third floor and turned to climb to the parapet.[*]

Were I a poet, I would compose a poem about the ruins of Dunollie. But not being so endowed, I finish my last plum and, with a boy's lively fancy, begin to tour the defenses upon this rock above the sea.

"Keep no less than twelve men to hold the house" was Chief Iain Ciar's admonition to his wife, who was left to defend Dunollie when her husband slipped away from under the Campbells' noses to join the Earl of Mar and the Rising of 1715. Certainly, this number was not just a proverbial dozen, but rather a proven minimum and a rule passed down from father to son.

Seated by the fireplace in Dunollie's hall, the glow of the burning peat upon his upturned face, the boy Iain Ciar would have heard often the story of how Dunollie had stood, the only remaining stronghold of the Royal cause along the coast of Lorn. It was not an old story then, for it belonged to his father's generation. It was a tale from an unholy time that wore the garb of religious fanaticism. With the battle cry of "For Jesus and no quarter," the troops of the Covenanters massacred the MacDougall clansmen at Dunaverty.[13] Soon after, a column of smoke rose from the Island of Kerrera proclaiming that Gylen Castle was lost. Still Dunollie held.[†]

---

[*] A visitor to Dunollie's hall will note that the floor slopes upward toward the north and seems to be composed of small beach corbels imbedded in earth. This appears to be an addition made after the castle was in ruins. The corbels once outlined the form of a eagle. See Chapter 42.

[†] Simpson, *Dunollie, Oban, Argyll*, pp. 82–83, has information on Dunollie's occupation during this era.

Chapter 2

One quickly understands the advantageous placement of this stronghold. North and east there is scarce room for an enemy to place his feet below the walls of the keep, and to the west and south the curtain walls are a continuation of the vertical cliffs. As long as supplies and the will held, so might Dunollie—supplies, will, and water. Here is a mystery. Where and what was the water supply for Dunollie? No well or cistern has been found. The mystery may have been solved in 1959 when N. Robert Ballantyne, a professional water diviner, detected a deep source of water inside the keep itself.

A ferry passes below the castle heights outward bound for Mull and for the islands that lie beyond that great island and the tall mountains of Morvern. The passing ship reminds me that I have a schedule to keep. Time enough to pay my respects to the Celtic cross by the postern wall, erected to the memory of Colonel Alexander MacDougall, twenty-ninth Chief of the Clan, and then I shall be off to Ganavan.

Chapter 3
Ganavan

I take the seaside road from Dunollie to Ganavan, the place of "white sands" where Miss Hope MacDougall of MacDougall lives. I am well aware of Miss MacDougall's scholarship from reading her book, *The Island of Kerrera, Mirror of History*. I am about to discover that the daily life of our Highland ancestors lives again through the displays that fill her home.*

The sea rises and falls in undulations of purple and green. Seaweed gives the blush of purple to the water, so Miss MacDougall tells me as we sit upon her window seat. Beyond the Maiden Island rise Mull's blue mountains of the showers, and northeast, across the Firth of Lorn, the green island of Lismore lies below the sacred heights of Morvern. Inside Miss MacDougall's sitting room, a bright wood fire burns upon the hearth, heating water in a black iron kettle. Before us are spread a number of notebooks. Every page gives evidence of Miss MacDougall's skill with pen and camera as well as of labors expended in a meticulous collection of facts.†

I have come filled with questions. Where is the cave of Iain Ciar? Where exactly did the Battle of Dalrigh take place? How lies the "Arrow Rock" in relation to where the MacDougalls and the Campbells fought at Allt Dearg? I am left to watch the fire—not without some anxiety, considering the twigs and branches piled for fuel on the hearth—while more notebooks and additional maps are brought forth.

The records spread before me, the anecdotes told, and the insights given are a historian's priceless treasure, but all around us in this house at Ganavan is a chronicle in artifacts arranged to speak eloquently to even the casual observer. The story told is one of endurance and ingenuity—a testimony to the spirit of a people and of a native appreciation for design and beauty despite a daily life upon a hard land and an indifferent sea.

By the fireplace is a wicker pack-creel filled with dark blocks of peat, while close by a peat spade reminds one that, for those who cut and piled this fuel, the peat warmed at least twice.

---

* Hope MacDougall of MacDougall was the sister of Coline, the 30th Chief. She passed away on December 23, 1998, and bequeathed her displays to following generations as *The MacDougall Collection*.
† Miss MacDougall's writing efforts began at the age of six. Her subject was birds, and she made a camouflage garb of green crepe paper to wear in her researches.

A loom, built solid like a New England timbered barn, occupies more than a corner of another room. A warp of MacDougall sett awaits the shuttle. Miss MacDougall is wearing a tartan skirt made from material she has woven on this old loom.

Nearby, coals of reflecting orange paper gleam below a hanging pan, frying equally realistic-appearing eggs and bacon. Around this hearth are placed the utensils of cottage cooking implements and tableware. In the hallway and mounted on a sturdy stand is a hand gristmill. Its two stones of gneiss are more than two feet across. The handle for turning the upper stone is in place, and a cloth skirting about the lower stone is ready to catch the sifting flour. Miss MacDougall pours a cup of roasted grain through the central hole in the upper stone. I watch her set the stone to rumbling over kernels and then take my own turn to quickly appreciate the skill demonstrated—the whole body must be in harmonic motion with the turning stone and not just one's arms. Later we have hot bread baked from the flour ground between these stones.

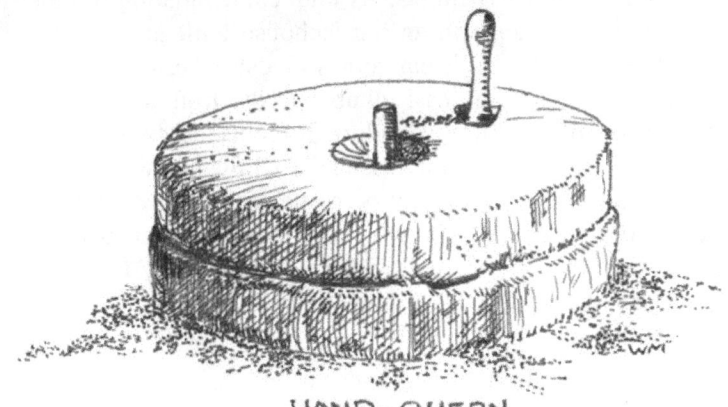

HAND-QUERN

It is obvious from the collection of assorted accouterments how much the Highlander loved snuff. Most prized was the highly refined powder such as Chief Iain Ciar obtained from a MacDougall tobacco spinner who resided in Oban—for this, Iain Ciar bartered the then experimental potato.[74] One wonders if the attempt to subdue the "wild Highlanders" might have been better accomplished by cutting off the supply of snuff rather than by hauling cannon and canister northward.

A stair banister substitutes for a horse in displaying a set of harnesses. A closet has become a creamery, exhibiting the development of butter churns and the folk art of butter molds. Overhead, a large collection of bells hangs like an elaborate chandelier. One gentle tug on an old bell pull saved from a local church, and there sounds a carillon.

The afternoon has passed all too quickly. Miss MacDougall has a meeting to attend this evening. I am to learn how involved she is in charitable acts. She is a worker and a leader in the cause of the shut-in, the aging, and the sick. There is time to see the beautiful shag rug made from wool that the lady of Ganavan has dyed using natural dyes. At the rug's center is a cross of pastel lavender—a color derived from lichens gathered on Iona. With a smile, I am told that the only color that has faded came from bog myrtle, the Campbell's plant badge.

As I was admiring the rug, Miss MacDougall pointed to a border hand-lettered on the top of the four walls of the room. The words are from Isaiah and from Psalms and began with "For you shall go out in Joy/ And be led forth in peace/ The mountains and the hills before you/ Shall break forth into singing/ And the trees of the field shall clap their hands."

Declining the kind offer of a ride back to Oban, I set out along the shore-side road under a heavy sky, which has brought an early evening to this land of long summer twilights. As I am contemplating whether there is light enough to photograph an old icehouse built into a cave below Ganavan,[3] Miss MacDougall's car comes to a stop beside me. She hands me a bag of shortbread, and as I climb into the front seat after all, she gives me another gift—a bit of Clan lore. It seems that two hundred years ago, the old sea caves in Saint Michael's Craig below Dunollie were much larger than they are now. It was in one of these caves that Iain Ciar secreted the Blacksmith of Taynuilt after stealing that artificer away despite the Campbells' vigilance. There in the cave, the blacksmith repaired the arms soon to be used in the Rising of 1715.

Chapter 4
Kirk, Glenmore, Pulpit Hill, and McCaig's Tower

Kirk

A Scottish breakfast is intended to launch one (cholesterol and all!) upon the day.

When the brass gong that hangs in the lower hall of the Heatherfield Private Hotel sounds, there is no hesitation among the holiday guests. They take their places at the white-clothed tables and Archie Campbell—young, straight-backed, and with a gentleman's manners—brings tea, porridge, toast (which, while awaiting marmalade, stands in its rack like books on display), eggs, and bacon all in proper order. An easy congeniality pervades the room. One is greeted by a pleasant "good morning" from each table and a "where are we off to this morning?"

The friendliness must be genuine, for there is nothing in the weather this Sabbath morning to inspire congeniality. The rain during the night has continued—not the fine descending mist to which one becomes accustomed, but a steady downpour. Mrs. Campbell's shy and pretty daughter finds me an umbrella and I start off for Christ Church, Dunollie.

The Presbyterian congregation has moved its place of worship several times since it was organized in 1834. The brownstone church it occupied for nearly ninety years stands at the head of George Street and has now been converted into "Dunollie Hall," a meeting place for all denominations. The new white church upon the Esplanade is rather overshadowed by the size of the Cathedral of the Roman Catholic Diocese of Argyll and the Isles,[*] but the church takes no second place in beauty. It was designed by the gifted architect, Leslie Grahame MacDougall.[†]

Passing Dunollie Hall, I step out into the openness of Corran Park and into the full sweep of wind-driven rain. Another umbrella just ahead tilts against the pelting drops. Under this black canopy, a little lady trudges over the shining pavement. One hesitates joining another umbrella carrier for fear of adding one's own dripping eaves to the other's deluge. I keep a respectful distance while inquiring if, by chance, the lady is on her way to church. She is on her way to the Cathedral, I am

---

[*] The Roman Catholic Cathedral was built in 1886. The framework and interior were constructed from prefabricated sections of corrugated iron. One should take time to view the interior. See Charles Hunter, *Oban—Past and Present*, pp. 46 and 50.

[†] Husband of the 30th Chief of Clan MacDougall.

informed. This subject being terminated, I next venture the observation that the harbor is beautiful even in the rain. It is lovely in a gray, driven way, and across the harbor a grain field makes a square of yellow below Kerrera's umber cliffs. A low laugh from which all the humor is surprisingly dehydrated issues from under the neighboring umbrella.

"Perhaps for you," the lady said, "you being as you are from away."

Well, I think to myself, so God in his grace sends the stranger among us. The little lady continues, under her umbrella, while I join those drip-drying in the entryway of Christ Church, Dunollie.

In the pulpit this morning is a young guest minister of the Kirk, nervously performing before a candidate committee sent by the Parish of Lismore and Appin. Perhaps he finds some comfort in the prayer for the day, which begins, "Oh Lord, whose way is perfect, help us, we pray thee, always to trust in thy goodness." Apparently God is helpful, for I later heard that the young man was called to minister to the faithful in Lismore and Appin.

After the service, Jean MacDougall Hadfield, the middle daughter of our late twenty-ninth Chief, takes me up and behind the pulpit to view the tall window given in memory of the church's architect. In vibrant colors, the window portrays the events in Christ's earthly mission: the last supper, the crucifixion, and the resurrection. Surmounting all is Christ seated in glory. Even in the subdued light of this rainy day, the story glows in reds and blues of particular richness.

Glenmore

The sun has its turn in the afternoon. My itinerary calls for a leisurely walk through Glenmore on the old road that leads from Oban to Kerrera Ferry. This is the way people and cattle traveled before the present Shore Road was built. It leaves the present paved Oban street—also named Glenmore Road—and is plainly marked "Public Footpath to Kerrera Ferry."[*]

The old track is deeply worn and largely grassed over. The bank on the left rises sharply and provides a sprig of bell heather for my bonnet. Thus far, this is a one-sided glen falling away to the west, so that one looks over rooftops to the high wall of Kerrera. The outskirts of Oban are quickly left behind. The track runs pleasantly downward under overhanging hazel bushes.

A heron, rowing the air with its long wings, lands in a marshy area to my right. A little burn comes down the steep banks to my left. Looking behind, there is a glimpse of Oban's curving waterfront. The ground

---

[*] See Map 3, p. 274

rises. Again looking backwards, there is a spill of houses into the hills and, beyond, bits of Oban Bay. Above the blue water is Dunollie; to the west, the green heights of Kerrera.

Now the track is running through a shallow valley, with rock and cliffs exposed in the greenery on both sides. At the top of the rise there is a series of gates, a series of pens, and a sheep dip. To the west the ground drops to the "Skating Pond."* Two swans are sedately patrolling the blue and green surface.

Beside the track as it slopes southward, a ewe is nursing its lamb under the protection of a rowan tree. When those clusters of berries are red and the heather purples, Glenmore must be at its best. It is lovely now—peaceful and seemingly far removed from busy Oban. Looking ahead, one sees the back side of the steep cliffs that wall the Sound of Kerrera at the ferry.

Underfoot has become boggy. A small brook is using the track, leaving for toll a black muck and a garden of yellow flag. Below this deposit and the carpet of moss, one's feet feel the stones of the old track, which is now a pathway and descending more steeply. A view of the Sound of Kerrera opens. Across the white-capped surface of the sound nestles the ferryman's cottage—a small white block below dark arching trees.

Just ahead a small burn ripples over the track, and then the old road follows a green curving descent, formed like a ramp, steeply downwards to the ferry. On both sides rise the ramparts and towers of the Ardbhan Craigs.

Pulpit Hill

To fully appreciate Oban, that important harbor for the Highland world of sea and mountain, one must see it from Pulpit Hill. Set aside as a public park, Pulpit Hill provides one of the finest vantage points in the area. What is more, it is accessible by car as well as on foot.

What a text this pulpit has to offer on this Sunday afternoon! By means of arrows and names incised on a pedestal placed on the brow of this outlook, one can identify the mountains that rim the horizon: east, the peaks of Cruachan; north, the massed giants of Appin and Glencoe; northwest, the corried heights of Morvern rising above the green island of Lismore; westward still and beyond Kerrera, Mull's mountains rise sunshaft-lit and shower-crossed. Above this world of mountains and the

---

* Madam Coline MacDougall of MacDougall and her sisters used to skate on this pond when girls. Nancy MacDougall Black told the author that skating on this pond was forbidden after a child was drowned.

sea, cumulus sweep landward while, higher up, the sky is feathered with fans of cirrus.

All afternoon a regatta of sailboats has been filling the bay with color and life. The boats with their bright striped spinnakers bellied full make the long reach across the harbor and turn once again toward the dark green shore of Kerrera.

One looks down from Pulpit Hill upon the slate roofs of Oban. The many gabled houses range downward from the high moor to the harbor's crescent and the line of harborside hotels. The burgh is a study in gleaming white and warm sand brown, accented by the orange roof tiles of the old steamship office and the red stack of a cruise ship moored to its pier. Here is lovely, tree-bowered Oban terraced above the sea—"the gateway to the Highlands and the Western Isles."

Across the bay, Dunollie sits like a watchdog whose haunches are the promontory rock.*

McCaig's Tower

If a Highland breakfast launches one upon the day, a roast beef dinner at the Heatherfield revitalizes the body for the evening. Then I set out for McCaig's "Coliseum," whose arches form a stone crown above the burgh.[76]

The structure has been dubbed "McCaig's Folly," but not by many of the residents. A gift to Oban, it has become a place of cloistered quiet and of flowers, and a vantage point from which to view the sunsets and far-flung magnificence.†

The narrow and twisting streets leading to the tower climb as steeply as a stairway, but one can find excuse for resting by turning to look at the widening view—a foretaste of the arch-framed vistas that await.

The sun is free of cloud for the moment. Its level rays flood Glen Seileach, south of Oban. The farther slopes of the glen are golden above the shadowed green of the valley floor. High up the glen's glowing sides, the hunting lodge of Soroba (once a MacDougall estate) gleams white among a copse of fir trees.[51]

---

* See Chapter 27.
† The morning view can be equally magnificent, especially on one of those pristine mornings when everything seems to be holding its breath for a new beginning. Below, the harbor's reflections make two worlds, while the sun behind one sends out its long, golden light to touch the tops of Kerrera's green hills and on to awake the mist-topped mountains of Mull.

Chapter 4

Oban spreads below, its slate roofs a shade darker than the gray water beyond. The fishing boats lie closely packed. Nearby shine the riding lights of the larger vessels.

A procession of somber clouds, from out the western sky, planes flat the tops of Mull's purple heights, making tabletops for giants. The lowering sun is lost behind the dark bank of cloud, and then reappears in a starburst of light upon the molten edges of cumulus. An avenue of splendor gleams upon the Firth of Lorn. Then the sun is gone, only to make its hidden presence known in a light-filled veil of pink-gold that illuminates the far reaches of the ocean. Now the evening begins, cool and fresh, with shadowed grays and a lemon yellow in the western windows of the mist.

With the chill, fires are lit. The smoke drifts upward from the chimney pots below, and with the smoke comes the sound of pipes. From whence it comes I am not sure, for the notes have permeated and blended with the evening. It is past ten o'clock; how far past, again, I do not know, nor will I look to my watch and thus deface this timeless moment.

Chapter 5
Lismore

The small island ferries are a practical lot and built for their trade rather than with an eye for elegance. One of these ramp-prowed vessels lies moored to Oban's railway pier, its diesel engine vibrating the steel deck as if impatient to be untethered for the run to Lismore. There seems no hurry to collect the fare. Later a crew member comes around with a cigar box of change to take care of this detail. The "lounge" is a small cabin aft of the well deck, and there I pull on a heavy turtleneck sweater and a slicker over that, for the rain is fast advancing landward, swept by a rising wind.

Having sheltered my camera in a plastic bag, I join the only other passenger. He stands beside a car that has seen its best years and is being taken out to end its days on the island. The owner tells me he intends to do the same, now that he has retired from his position in Glasgow.

We stand leaning on the bulwark as the lines are cast free. The ferry takes the inside course between Dunollie's headland and the Maiden Island and plows out into a choppy sea skudded with white wave crests. Below Dunollie, the sea breaks upon a lichen-dusted ledge. Saint Michael's Craig below the high cliffs is masked under a canopy of greenery. Here and there appears a shadowy recess between the high-reaching tree trunks. I fancy that should the ferry's engine cease its throb we might hear the Blacksmith of Taynuilt busy at his secretive labors within the crag's hidden cave.[*]

Dunollie's ivy-covered tower stands proud despite its ruin. It is still a storm-facing fortress, rising dark against the low-draped sky. This is high-seated Dunollie as seen from the sea. Its parapet is now crenulated with vegetation, but once, from that vantage point, the guard watched the MacDougall galleys fill their sails to plow the Firth of Lorn. Then, like as not, there would have been the flutter of a handkerchief from the arched window of the castle's hall and a whispered "*Beannachd.*"

But we will have to do with imagination, for today even the seals are absent from the rocks of the Maiden Island. There are two sheep who watch us pass without excitement.

The hills of Benderloch lie northward, spread with a veil of softly illuminated mist. To the west, the sky is dark with advancing rain, and through this rain the ferry heads into the corbelled slip of Lismore's Achnacroish. My friend by correspondence, Alistair Livingstone, Baron of Bachuil, is waiting in the rain with his ample white hair thatched

---

[*] Also see end of Chapter 3.

sideways under the brim of a "Sherlock Holmes" hat. We make haste to his van and head south upon a narrow dirt road to view the island.

I open and close a succession of gates while Alistair blows the car horn at the cows, which oblige by moving half a cow's length to one side. One black heifer chooses to run before the car. Three of its mates join in the scramble down the road until the game proves more effort than fun. I shall always remember this part of Lismore as shrouded not in rain but in the blowing waters of the sea, as if the passing of time has taken substance in the form of silver curtains moving along the remains of habitation. We pass a ruined mill and then the tumbling wall of a barn with a tree growing in its center, spreading its branches in place of roof and thatch. Here is another house with its equally roofless outbuildings and, beyond, a maze of stone walls shoulder-high and stretching over the hillocks and out of sight—hundreds of feet of prodigious labor.

There on the hillsides are the contoured remains of old lazybeds[77] once laboriously turned by a hand-and-foot wielded *cas chrom*.[84] These are the grassy remains of the gardens for which limestone-rich Lismore was famous. Now the countryside is dotted with sheep, which find shelter in the stone shells of the houses. Alistair tells me that the present human population is no more than one hundred and fifty. Ten times that number used to live here.

We are heading toward the southern end of Lismore and Achadun Castle,[27] but the blowing wet is too discouraging. We return northward, passing the old school. Pupils no longer straggle through the doorway or rush out under the fine granite lintel. The island's young go to the mainland for their education. A bit farther along the road, Alistair stops to pick up the mail at Lismore's only store. There is a good supply of Wellington rubber boots among the other essentials with which the store is hung, shelved, and stacked. I should have bought a pair!

It appears to be "drying up," to use a local phrase. We drive on to the old cathedral church of Saint Moluag ("cathedral" for its historical importance and "church" for its present size).[53] It stands, with rain-glistened roof slates among the gravestones, upon the ecclesiastical ashes left by the fires of Vikings and the Reformation. Only the choir remains of the cathedral built in part by Bishop Martin, a MacDougall of Dunollie. In its day, it was the seat of the Catholic Church established upon the near and far islands of the Hebrides.

Two fellow saints, Columba with his white doves and Moluag with his staff,[72] stand side by side in the twin windows of the church's eastern facade. They are robed in white and wear mantles of translucent blue—like a watercolor wash—as if the first pure light of Christianity were shining through. It is especially to the memory of Saint Moluag that this place is dedicated. Legend says that he lies buried somewhere near this cathedral church. In the window representation, Moluag stands with his crosier held in his right hand and, in his left, an open book with the words "Thine is the Kingdom." Behind him, in contrasting dark glass, is a high proud galley, a symbol of this man's fearless travels to bring that Kingdom to earth among the warring Scots and Picts.

Reformation zeal plastered the interior walls of what was left of the Cathedral. Now part of this plaster has been removed, exposing the old archways, the carved moldings, and the marks of the masons who labored here.

Lismore, like Iona, has a sacred history and a special presence. Miracles still happen there. Valerie, the Baron of Bachuil's lovely wife, tells us of such an incident. A recent gale blew down a neighbor's tree. The job of clearing away the remains was begun, but the neighbor, only having a handsaw, postponed the task until he could get better equipment. During the night, the tree righted itself. Valerie pointed, and I saw the tree itself—a bit over-pruned at the top, but upright and thriving.

Alastair's ancestral home lies between the cathedral church and the Fire Knoll—that ancient, manmade mound that holds its significance secret.[*]

Lismore holds the bones of sacrifices to Celtic gods as well as the bones of Christian missionaries. Here, in the place of ancient and not-so-ancient relics, the Livingstones,[26] as Barons of Bachuil, have been the keepers of the blessed and blessing staff of Saint Moluag for centuries.

As we dry before a fire in the Livingstone's spacious sitting room,[†] Alastair brings forth the remarkably preserved remains of Moluag's sacred crosier. Local people no longer bring a bucket of water to be stirred by this staff and then carried back to ailing cattle, yet it is miracle enough that the pastoral staff of the Saint still exists. Alastair next produces the charter drawn up in 1544 that renewed the commission to the Livingstones of Lismore. The charter was granted by the Earl of Argyll and is witnessed by the Chief of Clan MacDougall and the head of the MacDougall Cadet of Raera as representatives of the ancient Lords of Lorn.[‡]

For a century and a half, Lismore was part of the principality ruled by the MacDougall Lords of Lorn. On the west shore of the island near

---

[*] See Chapter 27.
[†] This room was once a chapel where Alastair's grandfather preached the Gospel with all the religious conviction of the early saints.
[‡] In 1990, the Baron of Bachuil acquired the original charter chest, which was made from one piece of wood.

the site of a still older Norse fortification stands the ruin of Coeffin Castle,[37] once a MacDougall stronghold guarding the Lynn of Morvern.* Standing in his backyard, Alastair points the direction to take, and I set out to visit this castle.

The way leads up a great swell of pastureland. I arrive at the top of this expanse to witness that atmospheric marvel of the western Highlands—the lifting of the mist and clouds and the coming of the sun as on the first day of creation.

The pasture that folds down toward the sea is brilliantly green, like a rich tempera over gold. It is flecked with yellow iris and meadow buttercup. Above the waters of the Lynn, the mist lifts one floating tress after another, revealing the blue mountains of Mull and the peaks of Morvern. Overhead, the firmament is filled with gleaming cumulus while the clear sky is an ethereal cerulean blue. On Morvern's shore, the shafts of sunlight sweep swatches of glowing green across the cobalt mountain's shoulders. A tint of lavender plays upon the more distant crags and lingers in the far glens. The Lynn glints with silver below that fairy-haunted steep.

This is my first experience in walking the Highland hills in a kilt. It proves a garment that dries even as it is getting wet and that moves freely with every stride. I make my way over a tall stone fence and, between the clusters of sheep, descend toward the sea. The lambs of spring are still young enough to romp, bunt each other, and kick up their hind legs. I am whistling and cannot name the tune. Then the words come back:

> Sing me a song of skies that are blue,
> Days of delight when summer was new,
> Then in my heart I'm dreaming of you,
> Dreaming of you, Lismore.

I come to the edge of the pastureland where the land drops precipitously down to the sea. A lone stunted pine has branches that reach out only on one side, as if swept constantly by a gale. Beside this wind-combed pine, I look down upon Coeffin's tumbled pile as it stands alone on a sea-washed finger of ledge. No wonder that the haunting voice of the Viking princess, Boethail the lovely, has been heard about this castle for years.[71]

---

* See Map 4, p.275.

CASTLE COEFFIN

Scions of Somerled, the kingdom builder; children of Dougal, his eldest son; what men of sinew first built these walls upon this passageway of grandeur! What women graced this hall! Surely, such a place as this nurtured a poet race!

Alastair had mentioned that a narrow but deep burn must be crossed when going to and coming from Coeffin. I must have traveled the hill above the brook's source on my way out, but on returning I discover a tributary quite suddenly, hidden in a lush patch of yellow iris. It was my first experience of dropping into a Highland brook. Dressed in a kilt, one becomes aware of bare legs a considerable way up.

A quiche and strawberries with cream are waiting when I return, and after lunch the Baron of Bachuil cuts me a walking stick from a patch of blackthorn—the same tough wood from which the crosier of Saint Moluag was fashioned. His wife shows me a flower garden with stunning roses and the tallest delphiniums I have ever seen. The Bonny Prince could not have been treated more kindly than was I by this gentleman keeper of the Bachuil Mor and his wife.

It is not the fangs of the "sea wolves" (as our ancestors called the gales that tear at the west Highland coast) that attack the ferry as we clear the protection of Lismore, yet there is wind enough to drive the returning rain across the crested sea. With spray breaking over the well deck and flooding the scuppers, we pitch and roll back to Oban. It is grand to taste the salt sea in the air and feel something of the wildness our forefathers braved in their long galleys. I also learn that there is no decent way to descend a ship's ladder in such weather when clad in a blowing kilt.

Chapter 6
On the Shore Road to Gallanach

The Sound of Kerrera is in one of its somber moods. A fine but very efficient rain sweeps down its gray length and across a verdant and dripping land. A sloop, dragging its tender and sailing before the wet wind, is making into Oban. Beyond its triangular sail, the hills of Kerrera rise dark and thrust upwards by ledge.

I am on the Shore Road, trudging toward Gallanach and walking where once the prehistoric sea beat upon the base of the Ardbhan Craigs.[*]

Beginning with the Swallow Rock, once scoured and scalloped by the pounding waves, the crags rise to tower two hundred feet above the Sound—a wall of rock with scarce root-hold for even the cliff-brave spleanwort. What I first mistook for intrusions of quartz interlacing the rock face proves to be whitish lichen. This encrustation may be responsible for the crags' name: *Àrd Bhàn*, the "White or Fair Heights." The entire mass of rock appears to be conglomerate, a common component of this rugged coastline. It is composed of cemented corbels well-rounded by some ancient sea intermixed with angular pieces of quartzite, some nearly translucent and tinted with lavender and pink.[67]

There is no protection from the wind and rain as I round the curve of the crags. One could make a fortune in this country by manufacturing miniature windshield wipers for eyeglasses.

Rain or no rain—or perhaps even more, in the rain—this is a romantic coast in the sense in which Scott or Stevenson would have seen it. In the imagination's eye, the yachting sloop becomes a smuggler's boat. One senses that the crags are filled with cave-like crevices that might shelter watching eyes[68]—perhaps the eyes of desperate men who, as the misty night comes on, light misguiding lanterns upon the rocks as was done on Cutter Island father down the Sound, that stormy night when the revenue boat was lured and wrecked. This is a coast with a storybook past—and with an adventurous present, from the stories of smuggling that one hears.

I find no other occupant in the deep crevice where I take shelter to change camera film. From the "cave" I can look back along the high curve of cliff to see Dunollie upon its distant headland. North and south

---

[*] Nancy MacDougall Black informs the author that these cliffs are called the Ardbhan *Rocks* by the natives of Oban. See Lore of Lorn, Note 68, for remarks on the change in sea level.

before me run the deep waters of the Sound, walled from the Firth of Lorn by Kerrera.[*]

These were the home waters for the galleys of Lorn and the channel through which passed so much Scottish history. Here were moored the ships of King Alexander and, later, the fleet of the Norwegian King Haakon. Both kings sought the allegiance of Ewan de Ergadia, third Chief of Clan MacDougall and Lord of Lorn.[†]

Cattle swam or were transported across the Sound in the days when they were brought from the islands to mainland markets.[‡]

The Sound was the last ferry passage for produce traveling from Mull and the islands beyond and, in reverse, the first ferry for supplies moving to the islands. In more recent times and before the coming of the steamboat, mail was a part of this traffic. Passing across the Sound, it was carried by postal runner over the hills of Kerrera and by boat once more to Mull. The Kerrera ferry was maintained by the Chiefs of Clan MacDougall and manned by their tacksmen for centuries.

At the ferry landing, the roadway is filled with sheep. They follow a black-eared and black-nosed leader who seems to know where the rest are bound. They are fat with wool and this load widely overhangs their slender legs, which appear unequal to the task, but this cannot be the case. Ahead and high above the road, two sheep have climbed to a precarious perch on the edge of a rock outcropping. They are gazing across the Sound at the emerald green fields encircling Kerrera's Horseshoe Bay.

Public domain upon the Shore Road ends at the high iron grill and the gatekeeper's cottage.[19] The sign upon the gate reads "No Entry." Considering that the entire Shore Road was built largely through the instigation of the MacDougalls of Gallanach, it seems a just prerogative that they should have kept to themselves that part which is their own. The sign poses a problem all the same, for it is my purpose to get a picture of Gallanach House. I rationalize that the sign pertains to motorists. As no one is at home in the gatekeeper's cottage and there is no lock upon the gate, I let myself in.[§]

---

[*] The Kerrera ferryman told me that the Sound is about sixty feet deep.
[†] See Lore of Lorn, Note 70, "Horseshoe Bay."
[‡] One customary place for swimming cattle across to the mainland was from Aird an T'naimh, the "Point of the Swimming," on Kerrera to the shore just below Dunollie.
[§] As I trudged on in the rain I did not realize that Gallanach is still in the hands of a principal cadet of Clan MacDougall. Lacking that information cost me the chance of meeting Major James Williamson MacDougall of Gallanach. Happily,

Chapter 6

The drive leads through a park of fine tall trees and around the base of Dun Ormidal, the high seat for the largest of the Iron Age forts in Lorn.[5]

Legend says that a spectral goat haunts those steeps, whose cries are the harbinger of impending death within the family of Gallanach. One tends to discount such tales, but as I was soon to experience, there lies in this country, just beyond the fingers of modern civilization, a remote world of heath and crag where one does not feel inclined to voice his or her doubts concerning the ancient unknown.

Passing through a narrow notch between high rock walls, the drive emerges once again at the seaside. The waves roll in upon the corbel strands. Gallanach House stands well back from the shore in its own green park and cupped in an amphitheater of steep and silent heights. The road ends in the graveled drive before the mansion. Between the sea and the magnificent cliffs that rise to the south of Gallanach, there seems no place for its continuation even if there were a need. Southward, as far as one can see, the Atlantic breaks white upon the rocky coast below the talus slopes of Creach Bheinn.

GALLANACH

---

the author later had the opportunity to meet the Major and to visit Gallanach. See Chapter 29.

From where I stand upon the road, at a trespasser's respectful distance, Gallanach House is framed between tree trunks and overhanging leaves. It sits steadfast upon a lawn that radiates a golden green despite the gray sky overhead. This massive house replaced a two-storied "laird's box" of whitewashed stone. In style it is the product of the nineteenth century "baronial revival" in which crenellated towers keep company with wide, tall windows designed to let in light with no fear of attacker's missiles.[*]

Gallanach House is a balanced delight.

Having taken the photograph for which I had come, I shoulder my pack and retrace my steps beside the hill of ancient men and of wild cries in the haunted night.

---

[*] Such windows did present a liability, however, in the form of house taxes, which were at least partly based on the number of windows. Consequently one often sees where windows were later removed to save taxes.

Chapter 7
The Old Track to Kilbride

Midway down the Shore Road that runs from Oban to Gallanach lies Port nan Cuilc, the "Port of Reeds." Despite its lackluster name, this place has seen days of some importance. Today it is a place of caravans and holidaymakers. The remains of an old pier, the remnant of busier days and a place where once boats were built, is now cluttered with second-hand gear. I make my way through this collection until I find a man who looks like a native; I ask if he can point out the beginning of the old track that runs eastward, climbing the high hills to reach Kilbride.

He cannot. Perhaps he does not know that once Port nan Cuilc was the beginning of an important drove road eastward through Kilbride and Kilmore, and then on over the many miles to trysts at Crieff or Falkirk. I am left to consult the topographical map.

After a false start, I find a road that leaves the Shore Road between a high cliff[*] and a substantial white house named "The Anchorage" that advertises itself as a B&B (bed and breakfast). This promising road climbs and crosses the head of Glen Seileach (which runs southward from Oban and behind the wall of the Ardbhan Craigs). From the head of the glen, the way of the track to Kilbride seems clear. An old road, worn deeply into the great hillside to the east, runs diagonally upward until it disappears around a protruding shoulder of broken moor.

The way to this track leads through a gate at the rear of a farm. It seemed proper to get permission to go on and only prudent to make sure that this was indeed the old track to Kilbride.[†]

My knock brings to the door a formidable woman who leaves no doubt that Queen Boddicea could have struck fear in the hearts of a Roman legion. The track up the hill does lead to Kilbride, I am told, but it passes through land owned by Major MacDougall of Gallanach, who allows no one to pass and who keeps all the gates locked. That this land is still possessed by a MacDougall is information of high interest, but I already know that the bit about locked gates is an untruth. There is nothing for me to do, so advises this Amazon, but go down to Gallanach and get permission.

---

[*] This cliff ends the wall of the Ardbhan Craigs and is the site of another Iron Age fort, Dun Uabairtich.
[†] I later learned this was Gallanach Beg, "Little Gallanach," and a part of the Gallanach estate. Some time after my visit, the farm house was renovated and occupied by Charles Williamson MacDougall of Gallanach until the death of his father, Major James Williamson MacDougall, in 1999.

I am not about to hike back to Gallanach. I might tell this woman that I already have a blister on each heel, but I doubt if she would care a fig for that fact! With the sagacity of my forebears—who have tended either to the pulpit or the bench—I announce that I have just been at Gallanach, taking pictures of the mansion.

"Well, if that's the case, you might as well be off up the track," the woman replies.

I assure her that I will carry nothing off, to which she replies that I could carry the whole place away for all she cares. With that blessing, such as it was, I let myself through the unlocked gate and begin the climb toward the gray cover of the clouds. The track's two ruts are a peaty mire, as if one of those old droves of black cattle had recently passed. The way grows steeper with each step, and as if in way of a reward for the climb, an expanding view down Glen Seileach is seen over the crimson stalks of foxglove (*miaran na sithe*, "thimbles of the fairy women"). Down the glen's full length and in a white veil of rain are the outskirts of Oban, while appearing on the rises and disappearing in the hollows is the Glen Seileach Road—one of the old routes to the Sound of Kerrera and the Inner Hebrides.*

The track leads upwards now, following the musical burn, which I have already crossed at the farm. I have one last view of the Sound spread out below—Port nan Cuilc, green Kerrera, and the gray-blue Mountains of Mull—before entering a pass held between up-sweeping moors. This pass seems a funnel for a "hang on to your bonnet" wind blowing fresh, strong, and rain-laden. I find myself bending more and more against the blast and, thus, watching the dark mud work its way in and out of my shoes. To sense the character of this country, one cannot always travel in comfort. Professor Blackie,[75] who loved and tramped these hills wrote:

> I'd have him whipped back to the reeking town,
> Lord of some breezeless garret in the mews,
> Who ducks for shelter when the rain comes down
> And picks his dainty path with shining shoes.

There comes to me, as I go on, an appreciation of that depth of faith that spirited the families of Kerrera when they went this way each Sabbath to Kilbride or miles more to Kilmore when it was that congregation's turn to serve communion.[58]

In my imagination, I see the womenfolk with their plaids tented over their heads and the men with their Sunday boots tied about their necks.

---

* By 1989, the uglier face of Oban had crept out into Glen Seileach in the form of what appeared to be large warehouses or garages. It still is a lovely glen.

Chapter 7

And so, I cross the height of land and look out on the gray-blue waters of Loch Gleann a' Bhearraidh.*

This long, narrow loch is Oban's reservoir. It is difficult to believe that Oban can be so near. I have seen no human being upon this track, and except for a wire fence, the way leads through a world that might have belonged to centuries past—a realm of hollows and blue-green heights up-thrust, abrupt, and all covered with a filter of finest rain and misty light.

The track becomes a pathway worn into a steep hillside running down to the water. The path parallels the loch and leads through a garden of fern, foxglove, yellow buttercup, and spearwort. Rounding the head of the loch, I disturb the long-legged stance of a heron. It spreads its slate-gray wings in a slow, majestic flight just above the surface of the water.[66]

My way has been easily traced until I reach the head of the loch. There now seem to be many paths through the bracken. The map shows the track as passing between two lochs, but here in this solitude one of the lochs has vanished. Perhaps the water level was raised and joined the two lochs to form a larger reservoir?†

Pondering, I turn to get a better bearing, and as I do so, a most amazing event takes place. A great wreath of mist comes pouring like a white vortex through a high notch in the seaward hills.‡

It descends as if the sky had given way. Spreading outward as it comes, it blankets the loch and all the land over which I have traveled. There now seems no option but to take the most likely route eastward.

My choice must be a sheep path, for it takes me around the high corner of a peaked hill and out above the valley through which the old track must have followed. I stand upon the high moor, looking down

---

* Older maps call this "Loch na Gleann na Bheathrach."
† This mystery was solved several years later by a note from Major James Williamson MacDougall in which he wrote: "*Loch na Gleann na Bheathrach* means 'loch at the head of the glen' and is on the old drove road from the Sound of Kerrera to Kilbride, Kilmore, and on through Glen Lonan to the markets at Falkirk and Crieff. The loch was made into a reservoir in 1880 when the bridge across it was improved. [Author's note: The 1976 Ordinance Map I used shows what appears to be a land bridge dividing the loch in two.] In 1943, the Water Board took over more land and erected a fence around the loch and later enlarged it by pumping up water from Loch Nell. The bridge has now disappeared from view and the remains are rarely visible. The water is very deep at the dam end. An old employee who used to take me fishing there before the war liked to recount wonderful tales of the mysterious objects which he had seen flashing out of the heavens to plunge into the dark depths."
‡ See Chapter 30.

upon the scene of mounds and declivities verdant with fern and spotted with umbers and purples. Beyond the valley a massive hill rises, sweeping upward to a crown of ledges whose color is that of a brown glaze laid over red. From whence does this intensity of light come that bathes this rugged landscape stretching onward under sodden skies? Where originates this ethereal light that creates such saturated color and causes one's heart to cry out with joy?

It is surprising how wet these steep hillsides are. The thick carpet of moss is like a sponge. The rushes growing in the hollows speak of more, still more, soggy footing.

Descending into the valley, the thought comes that here are the hues of our clan's tartan when it is woven from wool colored with the "ancient" natural dyes. Here are the rich greens and the large patches of moss turned an orange-red. In this carpet grows the purple-blossomed bog heather. Here too one finds the white oval petals of the mossy saxifrage. The only hue needed to complete the MacDougall sett is blue. This deficit is soon rectified. Beside one of the many brooklets that thread the hillside, there nods the delicate and true bluebell.[63]

The small burns that flow unseen but not unheard in their deep furrows join with a larger stream, and along one bank run two parallel fences enclosing what must be the old track winding down to Kilbride.

The only living things I have seen since the heron took its flight over Loch Gleann a' Bhearraidh have been large black snails without shells, misting themselves upon the moss. I mistake them for leeches until I touch one with a rush stem and it puts forth two knobbed prongs. Now there are sheep on the hillside. Ahead is a very civilized-looking tree and, just beyond, two Highland cattle stand red-brown and belly-deep in dark green fern. They stare at me with eyes half-hidden under long bangs of curly hair.

The track passes a large pen fashioned from massive rock slabs set on end and looking as ancient as the stones of Dunadd. Below is an inn and what appears to be a line of holiday cabins. Beyond the inn and nearly hidden in a group of trees is Kilbride where, beginning with Iain Ciar, lie the Chiefs of Clan MacDougall along with a great many of their kin. Often have these hills echoed with sorrowing lament. They have heard the repeated practicing of the pibroch, for here at Kilbride was once a MacDougall school of piping.[24]

Somewhere on the rise of ground southeast of the roofless chapel and burying ground is the place where Iain Ciar was born in the home of his mother's parents.

It is long past lunchtime. Under the dripping shelter of a tree in a walled corner of the old burying ground, I cut two thick slices of raisin bread, spread a plastic bag upon a wet and lichen-covered rock, and sit.

This is a place of lichens and a place thickly planted with standing and leaning gravestones.[56] The church where the faithful sang psalms is in ruins. Ivy has covered the coat of arms of the MacDougall Chiefs that crowns the doorway to the tree-covered enclosure where Iain Ciar and his Mary of Sleat lie buried, sharing in final devotion the arms of the MacDougalls and of the MacDonalds of Sleat.[*]

Contrary to impressions given, there is nothing of great antiquity left standing here at Kilbride; however, the present roofless church stands upon the foundations of a chapel first recorded in 1249.[†] At the west of the grave, a contoured yard is proof that this was early a sacred resting place. There, lying flat and half-buried in the sod, are several slabs bearing much-weathered Celtic braid and that ubiquitous symbol of our ancient forebears, the great two-handed claymore.

Behind and to the side of the walls enclosing the graves of Iain and Mary are the rows of stone—several formed in the old Celtic style of the

---

[*] The arms pictured on the flat slab are weathered; however, with diligence one can still make out a lion in the upper left quadrant, a castle in the upper right, a galley in the lower left, and a hand in the lower right. See Lore of Lorn, "Chiefs of the Clan and Their Coats of Arms."

[†] In 1643, the Synod of Argyll closed the churches at Kilbride and Kilmore in favor of having one church located at Oban.

wheel cross—that mark the burials of successive heads of Clan MacDougall.*

I stand reverently beside these memorials, and having done this simple act of respect for which I have come, I wring the water from my stockings, take the road up from Kilbride past the high and slender Lairgs Cross, and once more cross the treeless moor. The road, like a narrow ribbon, runs westward over the heath.

Whether walking or driving, one should pause and listen. Here are small sounds nearly lost in a grand quiet: the bleat of sheep on the distant hillside, the twitter of a bird rising above the heath, and the music of running water. Two lines from Scott come to mind:

> And silence settled wide and still
> On the lone wood and the mighty hill.

As I reach the main road to Oban,† the rain, which had ceased during my stay at Kilbride, returns. Crystal-bright drops collect upon the crimson glory of the bell heather[63] that covers the roadside bank before the once-MacDougall house of Soroba.[51]

The clouds are level with the top of Creag a' Chait (Crag of the Wild Cat)[66] which crowds Oban on the southeast. Glen Cruitten lies filled with mist. To the left of the road and rushing through its chasm, the Black Lynn carries the waters of Glen Seileach to the sea.‡

A short distance more and my tramp will have completed its circuit—a circumambulation from today to today, across the high moors where the past merges with the present and where time takes flight on the wings of the heron. There is a sprig of bell heather in my bonnet, larger blisters on my heels, a feeling of a dream fulfilled, and from my stomach a vote in favor of a hot dinner at the Heatherfield.

---

* Madam Coline MacDougall of MacDougall, thirtieth Chief of the Clan, is buried along with her husband, Leslie Grahame MacDougall, in an adjacent enclosure. Their graves are marked by a lovely stone cross with Celtic designs. Now Jean MacDougall Hadfield, Hope MacDougall of MacDougall, and Major James Williamson MacDougall also rest with their ancestors at Kilbride.

† Route A816 from Kilniver to Oban.

‡ This same burn, as it flows through Oban, once connected a shallow tidal pond, Loch a' Mhuilinn, with the sea. The loch has now been filled, providing the flat industrial and market area crossed by Lochavulin Road in the southern section of the burgh. In the early 1700s, the burn powered a mill owned by the MacDougalls of Dunollie. See Charles Hunter, *Oban–Past and Present*, p. 11.

Chapter 8
The Islands and the Sea

This is an extraordinary day, both in terms of weather and experience—we sail from Oban aboard the *Columba* on a passage around the island of Mull and back by way of the Sound of Kerrera.[*]

The morning brings a grand solitude of over-arching cloud above the Firth of Lorn. The waters of Oban Harbor are unruffled. The dark green hills of Kerrera reflect their verdant image upon the silvered sea. We collect an escort of arch-winged gulls, and the *Columba* lays its glinting wake out past Dunollie.

Great kingdoms of cloud rest upon Benderloch and Morvern. They rise like the *Dun na Feadhreadh*, the "fairy castles," that humans have seen on the rim of the western sea. The reflections of their misty world shimmer upon the waters of the Firth. Passing between the gleaming column of the lighthouse off Lismore[79] and Duart Castle on Mull,[40] we enter a universe of islands, firmament, and the living waters of the sea.

The mountains of Mull are at first obscured by mist, but as we proceed up the Sound of Mull the curtain slowly rises in a dramatic and magnificent atmospheric spectacle, allowing the green shores of Morvern, cut by ravines and strewn with pink rock, to materialize. Far ahead the gray sea is swept with watery fields of blue, telling of the sun's emerging victory. Behind the *Columba*, the blue mountains of Mull appear swirled in tatters of rising vapors and floating upward from a radiant fog bank that still lies about their bases. Steep after steep makes its majesty known in dark shadow or touched by a brush of light to glow in tints of green and yellow. In my dreams of the Highlands, never had I imagined such a vast, powerful unity. The ship's wake curves backwards upon the surface of the Sound, its line carried on in a sweep of white mist rising upon the mountains to merge with the clouds above.

Then we come to the land of sun. Mull's shore-side pastures are brilliant in greens and golds below the shadowed heights before which float the gray fragments of mist touched with buff and lavender. Upwards these rifts of cloud rise, to dissolve in the liquid blue of the sky—a Hebridian blue, I would name it, a blue purged of any stain by three thousand miles of ocean.

We overtake a yacht outward bound with a red and yellow striped spinnaker filled with the rising breeze and seen against the dark green and purple-scarred shores of Morvern. The steeps of Morvern wear their ancientness upon their brows. They are a wilderness of up-thrust and

---

[*] On later visits to Oban, this voyage around Mull was not regularly available.

broken crags upon which the lingering tufts of cloud cling and waft. We pass beneath their solitude of treeless moor cleaved with secret glens. Legend tells that Somerled, the kingdom builder, came from hiding in a cave somewhere in Morvern to launch his galleys upon the riptide of Scottish history.*

We emerge from the Sound of Mull and meet a gentle ocean swell, which bears past the hull the submerged orbs of jellyfish. The horizon now reaches away northward to peaks rising from the sea; speculation arises among the ardent photographers who line the rail as to whether we are looking at the Cuillins, those amazing peaks of Skye, or the nearer mountains of Rhum. In a rolling brogue one passenger announces that we are looking at Ben Nevis and its neighbors. A passing ship's officer is asked if this is the case. He answers that he hopes to God it is not.

Low-lying Coll is in front, of that there is no doubt, while on the port side ranges the old lava escarpments of Mull. We are now in the midst of the Inner Hebrides. I stifle an impulse to shout with a spirit set free! What an expanse of islands and rolling sea—an immensity, yet self-contained as if there were no need of a world beyond.

On our course up the Sound of Mull, I try but fail to see the ruins of Aros Castle.[32†] Once, the castle was a vital link in the MacDougall's ring of power and one of the transmitters of warnings through the means of beacon fires.‡ Such a signal would eventually reach the island of Cairn na Burgh,[36] the outpost of the Lords of Lorn that guarded the ocean edge of their realm.

We come as close to Cairn na Burgh and its neighbors of the Treshnish archipelago as treacherous reefs allow. It is a green tabletop raised upon red-brown columns of basalt. Ruins that may be part of the old stronghold stand alone and exposed upon this high and treeless pedestal. In the teeth of an Atlantic gale, Cairn na Burgh must be a wild and buffeted place. One wonders if the descendants of Somerled drew lots to decide whose turn it was to man this garrison.

With engines stilled, we drift past Staffa. Many writers have likened the closely packed columns of basalt that gird this island to great ranks of

---

* For a scholarly account of Somerled and his rise to power on the west coast of Scotland, see R. Andrew McDonald, *The Kingdom of the Isles*.
† See Chapter 31.
‡ The sending of beacon signals from Aros to Dunollie on the mainland would have to have been via Ardtornish Point on the Morvern side of the Sound.

organ pipes. Certainly the surf must fill Fingal's Cave with the throb of diapasons.*

No giant emerges to fling boulders at our passing ship, which is good evidence that there is no giant in residence. The name of our ship painted boldly upon the prow would certainly have provoked Fingal had he been at home, for after all, it was Columba and his associates who labored so effectively to exchange the mythical heroes with the apostles and to replace Tir nan Og, the "Land of the Forever Young," with the Christian's hope of Heaven.

"You must see Iona. It is a place of color magic," Madam MacDougall had advised me. The white sands that floor the sea between Mull and Iona are responsible for the crystal greens, while the beds of wine-colored kelp create the purples. The combination transcends the explanation. One imagines the boats moving shoreward through the rainbow waters, bringing the holy men to this island that was to become the center of a spreading faith. One sees these men step ashore as if from a page of illuminated manuscript, with a labyrinth of Celtic design weaving the mystery of earth, sea, and sky into the intimate sacrament of worship and the marvel of their Christ.†

Here on Iona wonder and religion are wrapped in a homespun cassock. It is a holy place in which one senses a spirit so nearly pagan yet so simply and fully Christian. And those who feel that presence enjoy the hope that it will go with them.

Today a large crowd disembarks from the *Columba*. Many hurry on toward the towered Abbey Church, and I find myself almost alone in the Nunnery.‡

The walls are a delightful mosaic of colors. Pink granite predominates, but black slate has been used for the pinnings and there is a sufficient assortment of other rock for variety. As a festive touch, a plant with lovely lavender flowers fills the spaces between the rocks. A succession of three round arches spring from solid columns and, roofing an alcove, there remains intact a mason's delight—a cross (groin) vault. The last prioress may lie buried below. The first prioress was Bethag the sister of Ranald, who reestablished Iona as a sacred community

---

* A Gaelic name for this cave is *Uaimh Bhinn*, the "Cave of Melodies." In 1829, Mendelssohn wrote that a "hissing sea" lifted his boat towards an "immense organ, black and resounding." See Chapter 25 and Chapter 33.
† Dr. Curtis MacDougall, the renowned teacher of journalism, told the author that his ancestors came from Iona, where they had the hereditary duty of tending old Druid ruins once situated near the present ferry landing.
‡ The Nunnery is the first ecclesiastical site encountered after leaving the ferry.

(c. 1200).* On the sheltered sides of column capitals, one can still discover the remains of carvings, a lingering bit of leaf work and net work still persisting. Over a small window facing the road there is incorporated into the arch work a *sheila na gig*, an ancient figurine of a fertility goddess. It seems a strange ornament for a nunnery, unless it was thought to represent some primitive anticipation of Mary.

I join the people visiting Saint Oran's Chapel. The doorway with its rounded arch and large toothed moldings seems made for shorter people. A few tourists have entered the Reilig Odhrain, the old yard beside the chapel where one walks upon the graves of Scotland's first kings, their stones long since weathered to a faceless silence. Walking there one may recall from school years the lines from Shakespeare's MacBeth:

> Where is Duncan's body?
> Carried to Colme's Kill†
> The sacred storehouse of his predecessors
> And guardian of their bones.

In the Abbey Church, no one is speaking as we stand in the nave between its high stone walls of pastel mosaic. A meditative silence commands the spirit as one approaches the chancel. By the wall, a MacKinnon Bishop sleeps in effigy with his miter upon his head. The cool shadows of the ambulatory call one to "pace one's thoughts" in a world set aside from pressing errands and anguish. It was this world the Viking raiders violated, rending the holy hush with what must have seemed an outpouring of hell itself.

I find myself alone in the museum, which is located behind the Abbey. I say alone, yet one cannot be so, for there is a presence—a row of warriors whose forms are carved upon the displayed grave slabs. They stand shoulder to shoulder, dressed and ready for battle in their padded surcoats and conical helmets. The craftsmen whose chisels fashioned these figures gave them rubber arms, that they might remain within the confines of stone and still hold their great swords point down and before them. For all the stylization, one perceives in these figures a stance of resolution, ambition, and pride as well as a communication of mortality. I find myself turning back to these figures as I leave, saying, "*Beannachd leibh*, God's grace upon you."

Walking behind the priory, I come upon a woman making the most of the sunshine by hanging out her washing. Her relatives are all in the

---

* Ranald was the brother of Dougald, the first Chief of Clan MacDougall, and thus uncle to Duncan, the second Chief of the Clan, who was at about the same time establishing the Priory at Archattan on Loch Etive.
† "Columba's Church," i.e., Iona.

States, she tells me as she pins up a red bandanna against the backdrop of Mull's cobalt hills. They have all done very well in America and have come back to Iona for a holiday. She asks me if I agree that it is an existence on the rush, a life of urban pressures and even danger, to live in the States. The woman looks surprised when I explain that I do not live in a city.

Our return voyage takes us around the southern coast of Mull. That coast begins in low, scattered fragments. Readers of *Kidnapped* will remember that Stevenson's hero, David Balfore, found himself shipwrecked in this desolation. The kelp rises and falls between the great rocks in a wasteland inhabited by seabirds and seals. Eastward, the coast changes. It rises until it towers in the red granite walls of Aoineadh Mor, the "Great Steeps," whose tops are seven hundred feet above the sea.[67]

The afternoon sun shines upon the ramparts and sets them aglow. Frozen in their plunges by distance, the waterfalls gleam like braided lines of whitest chalk upon the sheer faces of the cliffs.

High upon the wall of stone protrudes a basaltic sill with columnar jointing reminiscent of Staffa. Such evidence of Mull's volcano of the Tertiary Era (which may have risen to a height of 15,000 feet) radiates outward to both the islands that ring Mull and to the mainland as well. In those far-distant times, in an era of titanic upheavals, the volcano must have predominated the entire area.[67]

To the south of our homeward course rise the suggestive Paps of Jura and to the southwest the Garvellachs, "Holy Islands," placed like stepping stones leading to the dark hills of Luing and Seil and to the headlands of the Highland coast.

We enter the blue-roughed waters of Kerrera Sound with the light from the lowering sun flooding the arching heights that wall the mainland. On Kerrera's southern shore, Gylen Castle is a tiny tower amidst the immensity of sea crag, up-thrust knobs, and deeply furrowed glens.

Crossing to the starboard rail, I scan the mainland heights with camera ready for a glimpse of Iain Ciar's cave—that hiding place for an exile high up in the cliffs above the talus slopes. In this cave, a fugitive in his own land looked down upon Kerrera, and in the dark of night crossed the Sound to be with his wife.[70*]

There are the two ravines that were in the photograph Miss Hope MacDougall of MacDougall shared with me. The cave should be just to the left, and there it is—a dark, round swallow's hole high up in the face of the cliff.

---

* See Chapter 29.

Ahead, Oban's waterfront gleams like a town of gold in the evening sunlight, while northward rise the Highland peaks of Etive and Glencoe—massed, mighty, and a distant blue.

Chapter 9
Evening Atop Cnoc Carnach

A half moon rides high in the south's pale sky. The great dome of the heavens is crystal clear. The only clouds are those caught upon Ben Cruachan's peaks. I am standing on top of the hill behind Dunollie, Cnoc Carnach,[*] four hundred feet and more above Oban's bay. Before me and in a full circle spreads a far-flung panorama of Highland mountains, islands, and the sea—certainly one of Scotland's grandest views.

Here is a place intimately connected with every change of weather. On the climb up, I passed a stunted tree perpetually bent by the winds. Here also is a lookout associated with the human history of Argyll. Signal beacons have been lit upon this hilltop on a hundred dark nights, and from this height the sparks of jubilation have erected a fiery column.[80] From this vantage point the MacDougall Chiefs could view both Dunollie and Dunstaffnage, and the water routes to the ramparts of their Lorn. Here too, long before, must have come those people whose bones have been found hidden in cists discovered along the road from Oban to Dunollie.[1] Perhaps from this very spot those early people sent fire wheels rolling down this hill, in conjured imitation of the sun's life-giving passage.

Turning *deiseil* (clockwise) in sacred tradition,[†] this soul-stirring view is rimmed by a circle of mountain-piled horizon. Below, the tower of Dunollie is silhouetted against the sea, which spreads westward—an expanse of pale blue washed over with a golden pink. Across the dark fingers of Kerrera's shore, the mountains of Mull rise, lit by the same colors that tint the sea. West and northwest, over the Firth of Lorn and the island of Lismore, the mountains of Morvern wall Loch Linnhe. Clockwise still, there rise that wilderness of peaks that stretches northward from Benderloch to Etive, and beyond to the great domes of

---

[*] According to Dwelly's *Illustrated Gaelic-English Dictionary*, carnach can mean "heathen priest" or "stony ground." In recent times this prominence has been called "Battleship Hill." Charles Hunter writes in *Oban—Past and Present* that this name came about during the World War I when Cnoc Carnach provided a sweeping view of the Grand Fleet anchored outside the bay. During World War II, an Observer Post upon this hill kept watch over the busy harbor, the assembling fleets, and the constant coming and going of the flying boats from their base at Ardantrive on Kerrera. It was a plane from this sea base that spotted the Bismarck during the famous search for this German battleship.

[†] Such a clockwise circumlocution seems common in ancient sacred ceremonies. Thus, who would be so rash as to turn otherwise when standing so exposed under the eyes of the old gods?

Glencoe. To the eastward, one looks over the valley that holds in long shadows Oban's expansive cemetery,[*] Dunollie Farm, and Lochan Dubh. In the distance towers the mass of Cruachan. Its deep corries are blue; its flanks glowing pink; and its peaks, now free of cloud, are sharp as a claymore's edge against the eastern sky.

Southward, one looks down upon Oban and its bay.[†] Terrace upon tree-dense terrace, the brownstone houses and white gabled cottages gleam in the mellow light of the lowering sun, while above the burgh rolls the green moor and, higher still, the fantastic hills, eroded into a tapestry of shadowed creases and sun-burnished promontories. Southward again, past Pulpit Hill and beside the Ardbhan Craigs, the Sound of Kerrera leads to distant islands and the outstretched headlands of Nether Lorn.

So often comes to mind lines from Scott—this time the following, remembered but never before so memorable:

> The western wave of ebbing day
> Rolled over the glen their level way;
> Each purple peak, each flinty spire
> Was bathed in floods of living fire.

I have brought a lunch—fish and chips, done up in butcher's paper and again wrapped in the pages of the Oban Times. The feast is still warm. As I begin to eat, a lass appears, as if the charm of the evening had collected itself into human form.

"What brings you here?" she asks.

"I'm a MacDougall," I respond as if that were answer enough. It seems to be sufficient.

"I'm a MacDougall, too," she says.

Actually, it is her husband who is the MacDougall, and she is Miriam, a fair maid of Appin. Her husband, who follows her up the steep slope, is Angus. They live in Oban, and he works on a nearby dairy farm. Their two young children and a playmate politely join in eating the abundant chips.

Angus loves this land that spreads before and around us. As he talks, a sensitivity and an appreciation of beauty appears, which take natural wings upon his excellent vocabulary. He takes his clanship for granted. This is his countryside and his earth upon which he stands—though he is

---

[*] The cemetery occupies land donated by Dunollie.
[†] Gaelic *an t-oban* means the "small bay," which seems a bit strange now, when Oban is the principal port for the western Highlands. It is also interesting that the name appears to have a Norse origin.

well aware that the title belongs to Madam MacDougall of MacDougall, of whom he speaks with great respect.

Angus points to peak after peak calling them by name. Patiently he corrects my pronunciation of "Cruachan," until he says that I have it "near enough." The view from that mountain, he tells me, is grand beyond belief, but its rugged pile is no place for a person without respect for the wilderness. Several unfortunate climbers lost their lives last year and more shall do the same this summer, Angus predicts.

We stand upon Cnoc Carnach and upon the edge of the evening. The golden sun descends on the purple mountains of Morvern. There will be no grand sunset, for the heavens have been blown clear of cloud, yet the western sky glows with the red passing of the sun. Above us arches the quiet grandeur filled, as Emerson once described, "with light and deity," and in this immensity, the white half-orb of the moon shines upon the Sound of Kerrera.

Chapter 10
Ardchattan, Brander, and Dalrigh

Ardchatten Priory   From MacDougall Stone

An American driving a rented car upon what seems to him the wrong side of the road is bound to be a hazard both to himself and to others, but to make the most of rapidly passing hours, there is no better option. The car awaiting me at Oban Motors was a black Morris of considerable vintage that kept its major defects to itself for nearly a day.

On a July morning and under a high, dry canopy of stratocumulus—gray-bearded and interlaced with white—the Morris and I headed north to Ganavan House. In the cause of Clan history, Miss Hope MacDougall of MacDougall has courageously donated her time to be my guide and mentor for the day. She was ready and waiting among her bags packed with lunch, maps, and reference books. Her smile was brave. As we drove along hugging the left side of the road, I repeated the axiom given me by a car renter in Galloway: "Remember to keep the passenger side to the hedge."

"Yes," Miss MacDougall replied, "but not *in* it."

Thus began an exceptional day for which I shall always be most grateful.

Ardchattan

> Still in the waterlily's shade
> Her wonted nest the wild swan made.
> Ben Cruachan stands as fast as ever;
> Still downward foams the Awe's fierce river.
> ~ Sir Walter Scott

We cross the bridge that spans the Falls of Lora[*] where the tides churn in and out of Loch Etive. According to legend, it was this tidal race that, storm-aroused, kept the funeral cortège from bearing Chief Iain Ciar's body to Ardchattan.[62, 81]

Today the Falls of Lora are in a placid mood. Hope MacDougall remarks that her mother, when a little girl, was told that the foam of the falls was known, by those who understand such things, to be the suds of fairy washings.

Loch Etive is a mirror of silver and black on whose surface, framed in bright cloud, is reflected Ben Cruachan's dark image. In the shore's green shadow floats a pair of swans, like two white and stately galleys with high, graceful prows.[66]

We follow the winding road along Etive's quiet waters to Ardchattan, that holy place founded by Duncan, second Chief of Clan MacDougall, and burial place of his successors for nearly five hundred years.[81]

One might leave Ardchattan unimpressed and perhaps confused unless one has done one's homework or is in the company of an expert guide, as is my good fortune.[†]

The old priory was built with nave, transepts, and choir; but the nave has been swallowed up within the walls of a much later and secular mansion. So only the ruins of the choir and a portion of the transeptal chapels are open to the public. A greater portion of the choir dates from a fifteenth century reconstruction, but part of the massive transept arch (actually two arches superimposed) and the south transept, itself, are the remains of Duncan's original thirteenth century priory. The older portions can be identified by the greenish sandstone, probably quarried from the Island of Mull.[52]

---

[*] The turbulence of these falls is produced by the discharge of Loch Etive meeting the tide. The bridge was built as a railroad bridge in 1903. For a time its single lane was used for both trains and cars, which (Madam MacDougall of MacDougall informed the author) could lead to excitement.

[†] Since this account was written, much work has been done at Ardchattan. Historical and cultural displays now provide information to the visitor.

To fully enjoy Ardchattan one must enter into an architectural treasure hunt. Under the low arches of what was probably the sedilia is the piscina where the holy vessels were washed. There are fragments of multiple roll-and-hollow moldings, and around the opening of a pointed arched window in the north transept one finds a casement with dog-toothed decoration typical of the medieval mason's work in Lorn.[7]

The priory was first occupied by the Valliscaulian Order,[*] and in a niche of the choir's north wall there is a fragment of stone with a carved leaf design that may represent the order's emblem, the cabbage plant.[7]

The choir's floor is now a close-mowed lawn, and its checkerboard of grave slabs are wiped clean of any identification by centuries of weather. There is no indication of where Duncan and the early Chiefs of the Clan lie, but standing in the center of the choir is a MacDougall memorial of special interest. Once the base of a freestanding, disk-headed cross, this stone bears the inscription:

> Sir Eugenius, son of Somerled MacDougall, conventual prior of Ardchattan, caused this cross to be erected by John O'Brolchan at Ardcattan in the year of the Lord 1500.

A passing gull had scored a direct hit upon the face of this stone. Miss MacDougall endeavored to remove the result while I prepared to photograph what may well be the earliest record of the Galley of Lorn placed in conjunction with the royal Lion for the armorial achievement of the MacDougall Chiefs. Another heraldic beast is also represented, which appears to be feeding a heart to the rampart lion. Is it a wolf? If so, it is significant that the word "Lorn" is said to be derived from a word meaning "wolf."[†]

Not far from this stone, covered against the elements by a large box set against the north wall of the choir, is another treasure. It is the cover to a tomb chest magnificently carved in the manner of the Iona School.[9] Here, according to the inscription, lies Somerled MacDougall,[‡] his

---

[*] The name of the order is derived from *Val des Choux* or the "Valley of Cabbages."

[†] In August of 1998 the author revisited Ardchattan to find that this base of the wheel cross was missing. Other stones have been cleaned and set up for display, including several stones that have incised figures with their hands held as in the act of prayer. Equally interesting is a tapered grave slab of reddish sandstone displaying the classic claymore and symbolic animals. Illustrative placards have been added, which are very helpful.

[‡] Not to be confused with Somerled, the progenitor of Clan MacDougall and Clan Donald.

mother, his brother Alan, and his two sons Duncan and Dougall. The latter two were also priors of Ardchattan.*

All five, along with a cadaverous personage symbolizing mortality, are represented upon the carved surface of the slab. Duncan and Dougall stand in the habits of a prior, Somerled MacDougall in a long padded coat and conical helmet, Alan in what may be a shorter shirt of mail, and between them, their mother dressed in late medieval fashions including a wimple framing her face. They are as near a family portrait from the early fifteen hundreds as is possible to see.

Cairns

It is not much over three miles, as the raven flies, from Ardchattan Priory to the Pass of Brander, where "downward flows the Awe's fierce river." The motorist, however, must take a longer route—back across the spans of the Connel Bridge, down the south shore of Etive, and through the edge of Fearnoch Forest—to reach the village of Taynuilt.

Just before the present Bridge of Awe, we turn down a private road, which leads past several farms until it reaches the banks of a fair-sized brook. Here we leave the Morris, cross the brook on stepping stones, and continue along the high west bank of the river until we reach a field of bracken, strewn with the Cairns of Brander.

An image, terrible and momentary, arises in my imagination as I stand amongst these cairns. I saw the dead of Brander lying in groups just where the cairns were placed—lying as they had fallen in clusters on the day of our Clan's defeat. The rain was washing the blood from their bodies. Then reality returns. It is not raining and only the tall spikes of the foxglove are red.

"How many do you count?" Hope MacDougall calls.

"Ten cairns," I answer.

Routed from their own trap laid for Bruce in the dark pass somewhere near the Falls of Brander on the east side of the river, the forces of John Bacach, fifth Chief of the Clan, retreated and crossed the Awe close to the field where we are standing. Here, hard pressed, the rear guard of the MacDougall clansmen made their final stand.[15†]

We eat our lunch overlooking the river as it cascades from one brown pool to the next. Before us and across the river rises the base of Cruachan, which walls the pass to the east. Miss MacDougall had brought tea enough for two and an extra egg for which I exchange half an

---

* The MacDougall Chiefs held the right to appoint the priors of Ardchattan.
† See Chapter 34.

orange. As the river pours toward Loch Etive and the sea, we talk of MacDougalls past and present, of old events, and of issues immortal.

Lochan nan Arm

Retracing our way, we regain the Morris, cross the river on the new Bridge of Awe, and drive through the Pass to glimpse Castle Fraoch Eilean,[46] which is situated on an island at the head of Loch Awe. It was by this old tower house that John Bacach, sick in body and harried in spirit, moored his galley during the battle within the Pass of Brander. The top of the roofless tower appears above the island's trees.

The road to Dalrigh runs eastward through Glen Lochy, surrounded by the Grampian summits and dominated by views of Ben Lui. At times, those great up-sweeping sides of blue are lit by a white light that makes plain the waterfalls and brings to life the greens and russets of the high moors. Along the road-banks, mile upon mile, a natural flower garden welcomes us into Strath Fillan. The bell heather is at its best in this high country. Its red-purple is accented by yellow buttercup. We stop to photograph and find mixed with this display of color the delicate blue speedwell along with small white daisies.

Just south of Tyndrum, one comes to "the meeting of the waters," a place where several streams join with River Fillan. This meeting place lies in what geologists aptly term "knob and kettle" topography. Through this strange landscape the river twists its way, cutting through the black moor turf, washing away the gravels left by the glacier, and falling over the corbel shoals. The streams converge as did the glacier ice that cut and scoured the surrounding glens of Cononish, Falloch, Dochart, and the Strath itself.

We park beside the highway just before it crosses over the river and, taking a dirt track just beyond the bridge, walk westward into the land of "knobs and kettles" in search of Lochan nan Arm.* The lochan lies hidden in its hollow.

It is Hope MacDougall who finds the lochan. Responding to her call, I find her leaning forward and looking into the water.

"Do you see any arms?" I ask. It is a poor joke, as "arm" refers to armies and not to weapons.

"No, but I see the Campbell's badge." She points at the bog mertyl growing half-submerged in the dark tarn.

We climb to the top of a nearby hillock and sit surveying this spot where Chief John Bacach nearly settled his score with Robert Bruce for

---

* See Map 5, p. 275. The main road (A82) has been slightly relocated since this description was written.

the murder of John's cousin, the Red Comyn, before the altar of Dumfries' church. Miss MacDougall reads from Barbour's epic written to immortalize his hero, Robert the Bruce, and I recall what I can of Barrow's classic work on this man so determined to gain the throne of Scotland. Together we speculate as to what took place over six hundred years ago when the battle cry of the MacDougalls and their allies broke the stillness of this mountain-girded place.

The Battle and the Brooch

Surprised and beaten at the Battle of Methven during June of 1306, Bruce retreated into the mountains above Loch Tay. With his decimated cavalry and a few infantry along with his wife, daughter, and a number of ladies, Bruce worked his way eastward, probably shadowed by the MacNabs,[2] who may have alerted the MacDougalls to the enemy's progress toward Strath Fillan.

Bruce's objective may have been far-off Dunaverty on the tip of Kintyre, which he had provisioned for just such an exigency.

One can imagine the rearing of horses, reined up short when the men of Lorn emerged with a shout from their hiding place among the hillocks to block the advance of Bruce. Supposedly, Bruce planted his standard on a knoll that lies above the level ground to the east of the river and is still known as Tom na Bratach, the "Hillock of the Banner." Bruce must have realized almost immediately that whatever advantage he had in cavalry was minimized by terrain and was being depleted each minute by the swift work of the MacDougall lochaber axes slicing the hamstrings of the horses. The ladies were hurried back along the route they had come, to the Chapel of Saint Fillan.[72]

How long Bruce continued to fight is not known, but in the end he fled on horseback westward across the corbelled shoals of the river. Mounting a very steep bank, he saw ahead of him an oak forest rising up the sides of Beinn Dubhchraig.[*]

There was hope of hiding in that wilderness could he but cross the intervening knobs and hollows.

Had we been present that day seated where we are, we would have seen what took place. As it is, we can only retell the old story and use our imaginations. Three of John Bacach's men, two of whom were brothers of one called Indosser, are breathing fast and running hard to intercept Bruce by the shore of the lochan. One grasps the bridle, one grabs Bruce's leg, while the third leaps astride the horse and grapples with the

---

[*] Perhaps a remnant of that forest survives in the scattered trees that can still be seen and in what the Ordnance Map labels a woods called Coille Coire Chuilc.

man who would be king. It is a desperate attack against a man in armor whose reputation as a horseman is well known and whose battle ax is a flashing arc of death. Two clansmen go down, but the attacker on Bruce's back hangs on. Again Bruce strikes, and in his dying grasp the third kinsman holds fast to the knight's mantle. Did the garment give way or did the horseman slip it free? Bruce is away to the sheltering oaks, and there on the banks of the lochan lie three men. In the locked fingers of one kinsman shines Bruce's silver brooch.[73]

The afternoon is passing, and we must hasten back to Oban where I have a much-anticipated appointment to take Madam MacDougall of MacDougall out to dinner. On returning to the car, I discover that I have left a camera on the knoll beside Lochan nan Arm, and so again, there is a MacDougall panting across the sedges and mossy tufts between the hillocks of Dalrigh. All the knolls look alike, and the lochan must be rediscovered.

I return, holding the camera aloft in sign of rare victory for the absentminded. Miss MacDougall stands beside the Morris with a smile, holding out a cup with the last of the tea.

Chapter 11
Dinner With the Chief

Madam Coline MacDougall of MacDougall is carrying a fur-piece over her arm with tasteful elegance. As she steps up to the waiting Morris, I open the car's front door, stand gallantly aside, and instantly see my mistake. This is the driver's side of the automobile. How fragilely floats our pomp upon the circumstantial. Here I stand like Charlie Chaplin in an old movie, but the Chief's charm comes quickly to my rescue. She protests that she really will feel quite confident if I drive.

We do not have to travel far. Our destination is the Lancaster Hotel, one of those ocean-facing hotels that stand gable to gable along the upper arc of Oban's waterfront. I had called to make a reservation, and we are met at the hotel entrance by the proprietress, who leads us to a corner table in the dining room.

No piper with kilt a-swing precedes us. Such fanfare is not necessary. Madam MacDougall has a *presence*. From birth to marriage, she was the Maid of Lorn, a title which alone belongs to the eldest daughter of the Chief of Clan MacDougall. On her father's death in 1953, his daughter Coline MacDougall of MacDougall became the thirtieth Chief of the Clan and representative of the senior line from Somerled,[61] in which converge the royal houses of Norway and of Scottish Kings of that ancient kingdom called Dalriada. The fearless determination of the old Lords of Lorn lights Madam MacDougall's hazel-gray eyes. One senses the inner sinew of command cohabiting with a heart of Highland sensitivity.

The menu placed before us features the best of Highland fare—salmon and venison. We order venison.

Our conversation turns to mutual friends bound by that kinship that unites the generations in a closely woven cloak of belonging. Across the Atlantic, clanspeople will be meeting when this day's twilight spreads over Linville, that gathering place of the MacDougall Clan Society in the blue mountains of North Carolina. And in Nova Scotia, MacDougalls will be gathering to dedicate a new cairn erected to the memory of their ancestors who cut clearings in the dark forests of new Scotland and there lit their lamps.

Our dinner finished, we fill our coffee cups at the large urn set up in the middle of the lounge, where there lingers an aging odor of cigars, and take our coffee to the porch, where large windows give an unobstructed view of the harbor and of Kerrera beyond. The flashing jewels of the channel markers blink red and green through the soft twilight while the lights along the curving shore make shimmering paths across the water. There is, in this evening, an invocation to memories and story-telling.

The blinking navigational lights remind the Chief of an incident during the war. It happened early on, before she joined the service. The war touched everything and everyone. In her idle moments, the Maid of Lorn knitted a scarf and donated it to the cause. It was the custom to put one's name and address on a card and tuck it into items sent; in time, there came an answer from a thankful sailor and an enclosed picture of his ship. Coline MacDougall framed the picture under glass and hung it in her bedroom. One night she saw a series of reflected flashes in the glass of the photo. The flashes seemed to be coming from out to sea. They came again; it was certainly code. The authorities were alerted and, as a result, a spy was captured.

When the Chief entered the service, she had hope of being a driver. Driving is something she truly enjoyed, but she was assigned instead to setting up target ranges for practice bombing runs. There was, she remembered, one bombing incident very near to Oban. In those days, the Firth of Lorn was busy with convoys making-up for the sea. A lone bomber suddenly appeared and dropped his load, sending to the bottom a ship loaded with fine horses supposedly being sent to safety. A woman at Dunstaffnage received a medal for swimming out and saving one of those animals.

The twilight dims to evening, the pathways of light upon the harbor surface shine more brightly. Madam MacDougall speaks of her mother, Colina, who was also a MacDougall of a line long absent from the Highlands. Colina was just a baby when her folks brought her to Soroba House just south of Oban.[51] The weather turned cold during that visit, and the little girl's clothes, hung out to dry, froze to the line.

"Ah, you see," spoke up her nanny, "the wee lass has come to stay."

The prophesy came true, and Colina became the wife of Colonel Alexander MacDougall, twenty-ninth Chief of Clan MacDougall. Outward appearances gave the impression of two contrasting personalities. Colina was a person of warmth and social graces; the Chief seemed grave and reserved. To his friends, however, and to those with a genuine interest in Clan history, Alexander MacDougall showed a genuine congeniality. He did have little patience with the superficial. On one occasion when a young visitor twitted, "Oh, Colonel MacDougall, you simply *must* show us your castle; it's just too *terribly* romantic," the Chief disappeared until the guests had left.

Attached to the Army Medical Corps, Colonel Alexander spent many years away from Dunollie, as did many of his forebears in the days of empire in service on either the sea or the land.

Chapter 11

Madam MacDougall has always been interested in the Orient. Some of her best memories are the trips she and her husband took by steamboat. A relative was a captain on a steamer that carried, along with cargo destined for faraway places, twelve passengers. They were always welcome on the bridge.

But then, the Chief observes, nearly every Highland family lives in a network of far-flung relationships and interests. There are relatives around the world. Upon the seas of existence through years of new hopes and old wars, of social revolutions and economic change, these people have traveled and taken a bit of Scotland with them. And the fortunate come back.*

We drive back to Dunollie through an evening in which peace, like a warm mantle, lies upon the sea and the land. There are troops encamped upon the castle grounds—Boy Scouts had spread their tents, welcomed by Madam MacDougall as they had been for years by her father.

---

* For fascinating information on MacDougall families spread around the world, see the final chapters in William L. MacDougall's *Kings in the West Beyond the Sea*.

Chapter 12
Glen Etive

Glen Etive

Northeast of Oban lies a land of mountains. It is a wilderness largely uninhabited and, except for its deep and secluded glens, uninhabitable. It is an awesome country of up-thrust grandeur, forever emerging from the primordial mist amidst the voices of wind and falling water. Through this land of mountains, Etive's sea loch reaches north toward the guardians of Glencoe.

An excursion boat runs up this loch, but does not put ashore. If one wishes to explore Glen Etive, one must travel by car either by way of Dalmally, Black Mount, and the Moor of Rannoch* or via Appin, Ballachulish, and Glencoe. Both routes are equally and necessarily roundabout, for there are no highways through the mountain fastness that walls Loch Etive on both the east and west.

One can, of course, go by one of the above routes and return to Oban by the other and, in making this circuit, see the grandest of Highland scenery. Incidentally, in doing so, one would traverse, roughly, the northern boundary of the old realm of Lorn once held by the MacDougall Lords. The road from Oban to Ballachulish rounds the head of Loch Creran and crosses the Strath of Appin where the MacDougalls were embroiled on both sides of one of the last clan battles to redden the heath in these western Highlands.[16]

---

* See Chapter 36.

Chapter 12

Having crossed the Strath, the road runs along Loch Linnhe, that great inland-reaching arm of the sea which extends northward into the Great Glen.

This morning the steeps of Morvern, which rise across the great expanse of Loch Linnhe, ascend literally to the sky. The tops of Beinn na Cille, Meall nan Each, and Creach Bheinn are planed flat by a level ceiling of cloud. I stop at a small cottage store in Keil to buy tobacco. On a high staff beside the shore, the golden and royal standard of Scotland with its red rampant lion folded and unfurled against the blue background of Morvern's heights.

> O! Caldonia! stern and wild
> Meet nurse for the poetic child
> Land of brown heath and shaggy wood
> Land of mountains and the flood
> Land of my sires!
> ~ Sir Walter Scott

If there is *any* hope for an individual, such a sight as this will lift his soul from out the crabbed confines of the self.

The mountains to the right become more grand in height and peculiar in shape. The pinnacles and old volcanic bastions all but force Ballachulish into the sea. On this morning, the tallest peaks are cloaked in drifting rifts of cloud and, as women dressed in a veil, are all the more lovely and mysterious.

Glencoe

Glencoe, above which hangs the mist-swept crags, is at its gloomy best. This is the "valley of tears," which (long before that morning of horror when the sun rose above the corried walls to light the snow, red with MacDonald blood) was held by the MacDougall Lords of Lorn—even until the last of those Lords, Black John of the Spears, who stoutly defended his possession.[62] Here in this glen was born Allen MacDougall—Ailean Dall, "Blind Allen"—one of the most gifted of the Clan's poetic children.[25]

Glencoe is at its somber best, but I cannot say that my passage through the glen is enjoyable.* The old track has been replaced by a highway to the Isles (A82). This well-paved surface entices the holiday-bound to drive as if pursued by all the Bean Nighe who ever washed bloody garments in the chasmed streams of this place. I come upon a fresh accident.

---

* See Chapter 35 for a far more enthusiastic view.

A car is overturned upon its crumpled top and perched upon an outcropping of ledge beside the road. I cannot guess how the car landed where it did, unless kicked there by some disgruntled warrior of Fionn's band, nor do I intend to find out. I have it very much in mind to stay alive and not to hit any of the multitude who wander about the glen.

Thus, I fail to experience the wild, dark wonder of Glencoe; though in all fairness, no amount of traffic and no crowd can dispel the feeling of awe engendered by the bulk of Buachaille Mor, with its high cliffs mounting into the clouds. It was on such mountain tops, the summit worlds of the whirlwind and the thunder, that man first heard the voice of God, and it is no wonder that the warriors of Fionn are said to sleep within the hidden caves of Glencoe's heights and there, beside their dogs and arms, to slumber through this less heroic age.*

Etive

At the head of Glencoe and just before one enters into the rock-strewn wastes of Rannoch Moor, a single-lane road turns off to the right to twist its way down between the mountains and into Glen Etive. The road follows River Etive, a stream whose bed lies deep in the solid rock and whose water is as clear as liquid air. The stream falls from pool to pool and sparkles over the granite corbels. In a sky-blue sweep between dark ledges festooned with broom, it plunges whisky-colored into a froth of white. To one side of the falls, the waters find a less dramatic descent in lacework over the face of a rock. And so the river reaches a sandy estuary through which it wanders to Loch Etive.

In my attempts to describe one place of beauty after another, I am reminded of a farmer in my home state of Maine who, when showing a neighbor his herd, exclaimed, "There is the best damn cow in this whole country—and there's a better one." If Glen Etive is not the most splendid and serene place in all Scotland, then there can be few places in this land that surpass it.

Not a soul is in sight. The clouds are rising, and there is a hint of sunshine away off where Loch Etive must lie hidden between the blue-green steeps. I park the car on the high road above Lochan Craig na Cailleach—that lochan of azalea shores and small islands castled with pine and black spruce. Pulling on my Wellingtons (which I finally had the good sense to buy) I set off down the declivitous moor to the lochan's edge.

---

* See Lore of Lorn, Note 71, "Fingal or Fionn." Ossian's Cave appears as a great elongated keyhole in the richly weathered face of cliff on the south wall of the glen.

Whenever I shall recall those lines quoted by both Scott and Burns:

> My heart's in the Highlands,
> My heart is not here
> My heart's in the Highlands
> A-chasing the deer

then my thoughts shall return to Glen Etive.

Northward rise Buachaille Etive Mor and Buachaille Etive Beag, the "Big and Little Shepherds or Watchmen" of Etive. They are massive cones of purple-blue ledge and crag powdered with green. Between them sweeps down, and then upwards, a glacial valley through which runs the old high pass to Glencoe. Down the precipitous ramparts of what must be the western extension of Bidean nam Bian drops a white thread of waterfall in three great plunges from the mist-lit corrie above to the floor of the glen below.

Glen Etive
From a full-color oil painting by Walter M. Macdougall

Magnificence encircles the glen and beauty carpets its floor. Here there are large patches of red-orange sundew spiked with green rush and interspersed with the yellow bog asphodel and the crimson-pink of bog heather.[63]

Only here and there remains a bloom upon the hedge of tall rhododendron—the queen of all the heaths—which rounds the lochan and which must, in early summer, be a spectacle of delight. I have to hunt for a place to penetrate this enclosure before I can reach the water's edge. The essence of the Highlands, distilled from the mountain mists, has gathered in this lochan, where silver ripples dance upon the reflections of Buachaille Mor and Beag.

Just above the cottage of Druimachoish, I park the Morris close by another lochan, which is nearly hidden in a dark circle of conifers. Almost the entire surface of this little loch is covered with the image of Meall nan Gobhar's clifted eminence, and upon the lochan's still surface of intense blue-green, float flotillas of white water lilies.

One might suspect that a coven of witches are meeting beside this cauldron of color, for against the roadside fence lean a number of large brooms—long-handled and tied at the ends with bundles of heather bush—but these are not the parked conveyances of convening hags. The brooms are the property of the Forest Commission and positioned here in case fire should threaten the newly planted Glen Etive Forest—rather crude protection, but then one would guess that fire danger is not often high.

Climbing a Granite Steep

Slats nailed to a post provide a ladder for crossing the fence, and the traces of a trail appear between the boulders. The path leads up a steep fire lane between the dense plantings of larch and spruce.

At the head of the fire lane, the mountainside rises abruptly. Crawling upwards, I learn how handy are the stoutly rooted ling (heather bushes) when one needs a firm hold. The crevices between the rocks are deep and filled with a black, peaty muck. Much of the ground cover is moss thinly spread upon the ledge beneath. This moss has a proclivity to slip free under one's foot, leaving the wet stone exposed. Suddenly I remember that I am quite alone, and take added care to watch my footing.

Near the top and just before the final rise of granite cliffs are older trees, native Scots pine, which at one point have been strewn like fallen jackstraws by a whirlwind. There are fresh deer droppings aplenty.[66]

I look expectantly to the top of the ledges hoping to see a stag standing against the sky. In that hope I am to be disappointed. All other

Chapter 12

anticipations, however, are fulfilled when, with legs that feel lead-weighted, I reach a vantage point from which one can look down Loch Etive's shining way flanked on both sides by *beinn*, *stob*, and *meall*.

Highland Gaelic has grown among the mountains and is rich in descriptive terms for their shapes: *meall* indicates a great, shapeless hill, *stob* a pointed peak or sometimes a stump-like shape, *sron* is nose-like, and *beinn* a small, peaked mountain.

The loch approaches out of the haze of a far world. It is an avenue between blue ramparts—an avenue upon whose surface the mountain breezes trace rippled patterns across the reflecting calm. This is the ancient waterway of Loch Etive, reaching into the northern wilderness of Lorn and a habitat of peace.

Over the loch the sky has cleared to reveal an arch of blue under which float the island-clouds of cumulus. The sunshine is warm upon my back. I pack away my sweater and rummage for a second lunch.

Below this perch, a golden eagle[66] turns above its verdant hunting ground. It wheels far out over the glen and across the River Etive, whose meandering way is outlined by trees and a yellow ribbon of sandy bank. Beyond the river, Beinn Chaorach sweeps upwards, and to the right, high against the sky, rises the sharp peak of Glas Bheinn Mhor. Down this mountain's valleys, a fan of streamlets converge to join in Allt Mheuran. The sound of their united tumble reaches this spot across a mile or more of atmosphere. The whole glen is filled with the distant and constant music of their waterfalls.[81]

No wonder the love story of Deirdre has lingered here in Glen Etive.[71] Well might this princess of youth and beauty, along with her young warrior, have built a hidden bower in this glen and here known an azalea and heather-scented bliss.* Lured back by trickery to civilization, this princess became Deirdre of the sorrows.

Nearby my aerie and rooted in a niche grows bell heather mixed with fern. From where I am sitting, the spray of crimson is seen against the dark storm clouds that still fill Glencoe's sky beyond the Guardians of Etive. The bell heather burns and yet is not consumed. Beside it, as if by an added miracle, blossoms the only white heather I have seen in the wild. After climbing Buachaille Mor, Professor Blackie[75] wrote:

> Thou lofty shepard of dark Etive's glen
> Tall Titan of Grim Glencoe,
> I clomb thy starward peak not long ago
> And call thee mine, and love thee much since then.

---

* The bower is said to have been at the falls on River Etive near Dalness Farm.

This granite steep I have climbed is but a high hill compared with Buachaille Mor. Yet in the years to come, I shall find the contours of this mount upon the map and remember the distant sound of waterfalls, the turning gyre of the eagle, the bell heather's crimson seen against the dark cloud, and the far-reaching of Loch Etive between its Highland peaks.

The road extends perhaps another mile and a half to reach the head of Loch Etive. Behind, the two great shepherds of Etive rise, framed in rhododendron and white blossomed rowan trees. Rounding a curve, a red deer stands for a moment in the road, its large ears alert. The road ends at an old pier and a dilapidated building whose metal roof has rusted a reddish brown. Across the loch, a wall of crag-scarred mountain sweeps upward, olive in the swaths of late sunlight and blue in the shadow of the clouds. These shadows gain a life of their own as they silently stalk the contours of the mountains.

A grand and solemn seclusion reigns, interrupted only by the wavelets washing around the blackened pilings of the broken pier.*

An independent soul is a self-concept many cherish, but except for the unenvied hermit in his cell, it is a figment. We crave a friend with whom to share the day's adventure, and this craving is all the more acute when we are far from family and home.

I shall always be warmly grateful for the generosity and friendliness of Jean MacDougall of MacDougall and her husband, Dr. Stephen Hadfield.

The Hadfields know a song about Bangor, Maine, which is only forty-five miles from my home. Strangely, I have never heard this song before this evening, when we sit before the picture window in the Hadfield's sitting room. As we engage in delightful conversation, one of the island ferries passes on the far side of the Maiden Island. Only its stack and masthead light shows, moving like a giant hooded monk with a lantern striding along the backbone of that rocky protrusion from the sea.

Dr. Hadfield possesses an encyclopedic mental storehouse of fascinating facts. And his wife's kindness is matched only by her insight.

Later, in the quiet of twilight, we walk upon the point before their home. The distant lighthouse off Lismore blinks in the gloaming, while between the sea and the grass the sheep rest upon the warm sands.

---

* See Chapter 36 for a description of the route taken on the return to Oban.

Chapter 13
The String of Lorn

Southwest of Oban is another area that, like the wilderness of Loch Etive, is largely uninhabited. It never was densely populated, though the remains of old cottages, roughly outlined in tumbled stones, can be found where now the buzzard[66] circles above the sheep. This is the Highlands of Nether Lorn. It is not mountainous as is Etive, though Beinn Chapull rises to a rugged respectability of nearly two thousand feet. It presents a jumble of high hills deeply cut by streams and eroded into a varied pattern of declivities, protuberances, and rocky escarpments.

Across this rough countryside stretches the demarcation long known as Sreang Lathurnach, the "String of Lorn,"[83] a bridle path used for centuries that threads its way over the wild upland moor and follows the watershed between Awe and the several lochs to the north. Among these lochs is Scammadale, which lies long and narrow between steep hills. It is toward this loch that I drive on a cloud-hung Sunday morning.

By the shores of Loch Scammadale, so the legend tells, someone in the MacDougall force dropped the Clan's crystal talisman.* A more

---

* Until fairly recently, two such crystal spheres were kept at Dunollie. It is true that one of these, which was about the size of a baseball, was cracked. There has

fanciful version declares that the crystal sphere leapt from the holder's hand and flew into the loch. The year was probably 1294, and the Chief of the MacDougalls, as Lord of Lorn and High Sheriff of Argyll, was out to settle a dispute with a rising and ambitious clan[2]—a brave and cunning people whose aggressiveness, in years to come, was to give rise to the plea:

> From the powers of darkness and from the avarice of the Campbells, dear Lord, deliver us.

The nature of the dispute that brought forth the forces of Lorn and set them marching along the shores of Scammadale is not known, nor are details clear of the battle that was to take place before the sun went down.

It is one of those watercolor mornings, still wet and flowing, and I am on my way to view the place where the ring of striking claymores, the anguished cry, and the sound of war pipes set the clifted heights along the String of Lorn ajar and where the blood of both MacDougalls and Campbells intermingled in the waters of Allt Dearg—the "Red Stream."*

At the head of Loch Scammadale, I park the Morris in the yard of Bragleenmore Farm. The woman of the house is busily vacuuming—thus breaking the Sabbath, as was I, according to strict Scottish rule. The car will not be in the way and, yes, the farm lane to the right of the bridge (which leads into the farmyard) is part of the old track to Allt Dearg.

This track twists up a pasture upon which Ayrshires share the green grass with a minority representation of Highland cattle. Climbing still, the way leads through the pass, keeping high above Allt Bragleenmore flowing deep within its chasm and filling the glen with the sound of its descent. Across the valley, another stream plunges downward in white braids between the cliffs, adding its harmony to the water voices.

The track crosses a lovely stone-walled burn above Eas an Fhitheach, "Waterfalls of the Raven." I am beguiled by the beauty about me. Then across the path appear the remains of a sheep—a skeleton wrapped in a torn coat of fleece, no flesh upon its rib cage, and no eyes in the empty skull. I walk on toward Allt Dearg mindful that violent death had once awaited ahead for many of our kinsmen.

---

been some speculation that these spheres were brought back from one of the crusades.

* The author of the *West Highland Series, Booklet #5*, p. 11, states that Allt Dearg is named for a battle in 719 fought between elements of the Kingdom of Dalriada.

Chapter 13

There is a great adventure—close I should think to the thrill of discovery—in reaching a place of which one has heard much but whose actual appearance is a complete surprise. Allt Dearg drops into a miniature grotto and then spills forth in twin falls, which cast their foam across a pool. The stream ripples over a bed of pink and gray stone, and then dashes headlong down a canyon to Allt Bragleenmore, far below.

It was here, according to the story, that the MacDougalls met the Campbells, who had boldly crossed the String of Lorn and thus had come beyond the border agreed upon by parley. In this lovely place of falling water, the fierce fight began that was to end in the death of Cailein Mor, the name-giver to all the Campbell Chiefs to come.

From the Red Stream, the track mounts a steep bank and continues over and around the rolling hummocks to the head of the pass and the String of Lorn. The weather has not cleared, but rather, as the natives say, it has "dried." A dome of high arched stratocumulus spans the immensity of moor, which rises to rim the sky in rocky heights, then falls away into the twisting valleys of the streams.

The lower portion of the track to Allt Dearg leads up through a glen filled with the sound of cataracts and the plaintive call of sheep, but beyond the stream one is aware of the quiet. The stillness literally hangs over the heath, as tangible a presence as the gray and white quilting of the clouds. One hears the wind as it passes the ears. A raven[66] speaks from a newly planted woods across the valley. One comes to the cairn piled to the memory of Cailein Mor in a world which seems silently to await God's next command in the process of creation.

Across the valley to the west of the cairn and high upon the opposing hillside perches the "Arrow Rock" from which, supposedly, the shaft was winged that killed the Campbell's Chief. While it is true that the long bow is capable of deadly accuracy up to three hundred yards, the clansman who gave flight to this arrow must have repeated a potent charm, for by rough measurement upon the topographical map, the flight of that fatal arrow would have been near three hundred and fifty yards!

Somewhere close to the spot on which I stand, Colin of the Campbells fell as did many men that day, and lying here among these stones they left their tale to the story-makers.

It is said that the battle march of the MacDougalls (*Brosnachadh-Catha Chlann Dughaill*, "Clan Dougall's Incitement to Battle") was first played here above Allt Dearg amidst the strife.[24*] Now in the quiet below the clouds, one might chance to hear the echo of those pipes, faint, yet reverberating through the years. I listen, but only wind whispers past my

---

* Dugald Gordon MacDougall, *Bràiste Lathurna*, p. 81.

ears, lisping ancient incantations and bearing the clean, herbal aromas of the moor.

<hr />

The Morris is developing a malady that can only be described as a severe case of ambient-gear-shift. One must hunt for reverse and will succeed only through perseverance and good fortune. On roads where the passing of two cars often necessitates backing to a "run-around," my travel has become a serious undertaking.

As I drive out of the farmyard at the head of Loch Scammadale, I meet the farmer himself, seated upon a tractor pulling a load of hay. It is clearly my place to back up, but luck fails and reverse cannot be found.

The farmer looks like a mechanical sort, so I get out of the car, acknowledge that I should retreat, and offer him the chance to try his hand upon the wandering gear lever. He tries.

"My God," he exclaims, "this thing is a threat."[*]

---

[*] Rented cars upon subsequent trips have been very satisfactory. However, it is getting more difficult to rent cars in the Oban area due to high insurance and the risks posed by "foreign" drivers.

Chapter 14
Loch Awe, Melfort, and Degnish

Degnish Farm

Leaving Loch Scammadale squeezed between its long mountains and regaining A816, I turn south. The weather is deteriorating, with lowering gray clouds and a chill in the air—suitable weather, perhaps, for traveling through Glen Gallain. The old stories say that here was the home of a witch. People used to sing while trudging through this valley, and some would kneel and pray before entering the glen and then throw their hats into the air. The aim of the latter action is not recorded, but it must have raised spirits. On second thought, that might not be what one would wish to accomplish.

At the head of Glen Gallain, the broad valley of the Braes of Lorn opens eastward cradling Loch Tralaig. Once this was the home of the MacDougalls of Corrielorne.[23] The farm buildings seen in the distance are dwarfed by a great sweep of hillside that is scarred by a stream hidden in the deep crevice of its own making. The hillside is topped by a crown of cliffs.

Passing the entrance to the Braes of Lorn, Route A816 follows the River Oude down the Pass of Melfort and skirts the east shore of Loch nan Druimnean, where the MacDougalls and Campbells fought for keeps over a dead woman and some stolen cattle.[14]

Just below Kilmelford[*] where the highway joins the seaside, a narrow road branches to the right. It follows Loch Melfort's northern shore—winding, dropping, and climbing through a woods of handsome hardwoods to reach Degnish Point, once the home of the MacDougalls of Degnish. In 1647, their leader Iain MacDougall and many of his kinsmen and supporters fell at Dunaverty.[13, 18]

At the end of the paved portion of this road and shortly before reaching Degnish farm, I meet the present owner of Degnish farm and his wife. He styles himself as a retired academic. His blue bonnet bears a clan badge that I do not recognize. I explain my MacDougall interest in Degnish and my hope to look across Seil Sound to the islands of Torsa, Luing, and Seil.[†]

---

[*] See Map 6, p. 276.
[†] See Chapter 16.

Enthusiastically, I produce a copy of "Walking in South Lorn"[*]—a guide with an intriguing map showing the route for a day-long tramp from Ardmaddy to Degnish and return.[†]

I point out that the view from the top of Dun Fadaidh[‡] across the Sound of Seil to the islands and the sea is especially recommended. I am quickly informed that while there is an old public track from where we are standing, north to the road leading to Ardmaddy,[§] there is not and never was a public path through Degnish lands. (I now know what the guide's author means by "trackless.") According to the owner of Degnish farm, it is a shame the booklet was ever printed. During the lambing season or when the shepherds are moving the sheep, as they are today, the last thing one needs is some bothering hikers.

It has begun to rain—a condensing of the murk that besmudges the afternoon. Both husband and wife doubt that I would see much, yet both seem to appreciate my earnest interest in Degnish and my eagerness to look out over the Sound. With their directions, I follow a fence down through a swale, where recent hard labor has grubbed ditches in the black muck to increase drainage. Ahead, rough and desolate, rises Dun Crutagain. It appears to have pulled a cloak of rocky moor about its bony shoulders.

On such a chill, wet day one realizes that this land was not created to be comfortable, nor is it a land upon which to make one's fortune. It is not that this land is hostile; it is just a hard place to make a living—thin soil, abundant rock, acid peat, and today, wet as a sponge.

They are driving the newly sheared sheep up to the high land—up from the gates of Degnish farm to a place where the sheep will feel no better than the place at which they are presently located. There is a great deal of shouting and the waving of shirts on the part of the shepherds; not at all the orderly whistling to wise and obedient dogs that one sees in demonstrations. Watching this process, I doubted if these shepherds would spend much time looking for the one lost lamb out of ninety-nine.

---

[*] From the *West Highland Series*, #5.
[†] "Things to see" mentioned in the guide include the "wishing tree" and the ruins of corn-drying kilns. The tree is an ancient hawthorn gnarled, so it is said, by coins inserted in its bark and left as votive offerings. The kilns may have been where the MacDougalls of Degnish dried the grain for the bread carried by the men leaving to fight for the Royalist cause.
[‡] Gaelic place names are fascinating and enigmatic. Is this the "torched fort" or does it refer to the "beacon"? The owner of Degnish told me there is no remaining evidence of a fort on the top of this vantage point.
[§] See Chapter 16.

Chapter 14

The mist drapes across the tops of the high hills like a cold, soggy blanket over a world of stone, bracken, rush, and ling. As predicted, the far view, which must be grand from the top of Dun Fadaidh's rounded cone, is lost in mist and rain. There is to the west over the nearer islands just a suggestion of the southern cliffs of Mull. But all is not lost! There is Torsa, olive green in a gray sea. In this light, features do not stand out, yet I fancy I can see the pile of the castle ruins. Beyond Torsa is the silver path of Cuan Sound, which separates Seil from Luing. North, up the Sound, is Clachan Bridge with a loophole of light showing the opening below its arch. For all the wet grayness, this too is the Land of Lorn—the place one's heart remembers.

Loch Avich

At the inn in Kilmelford, a road leaves A816 and climbs abruptly eastward toward Loch Avich. A far-spreading view opens to one's back, and one should stop and look. Loch Melfort reaches out into the world of island and shimmering sea—Degnish Point, Luing, Lunga, the holy Garvellachs, and a little north of west, the mountains of Mull. Further north, in diverse light and shadow, are the deeply sculptured hills that embrace the Pass of Melfort. Here by the road, a burn splashes white between deep banks of crimson bell heather.

The narrow road twisting eastward into the Highlands of Lorn is a challenge. It runs through open range for sheep, steeply climbing around sharp corners and blindly descending through a countryside of lochs and a complex of knobs and valleys. It is a land with a wild loveliness all its own—shadow-crossed, rumpled and wrinkled, and colored with a hundred shades of greens and blues, but as the road precariously negotiates along the steep shores of Loch an Losgainn Mor, a driver will be too preoccupied to appreciate the fine and momentary views.

Approaching the head of Loch Avich, the road enters a dense coniferous forest. This area north of the loch was the home of the MacDougalls of Narracan.[23]*

Two miles down the north shore of the Loch, a dirt track leads northward to Loch na Sreinge and Allt Dearg.† This track climbs, with a dense planting of trees on the left and open moor on the right. I keep to this track for perhaps a mile and then scramble up to the top of an eroded

---

* The trees make it difficult to identify much or to see the island ruins of Caisteal na Nighinn Ruaidhe (see Lore of Lorn, Note 35). There are descendants of the MacDougalls of Narracan living in the United States. Hopefully they will be able to discover more information.

† See Chapter 13.

hillside to look down on Loch na Sreinge. Ahead is the pass to Scammadale, a blue defile in the green mountains that, now here and now there, yellows in the patchwork of sunlight. The Arrow Rock is a small but prominent dot, high on the mountainside above the cairn erected to Cailein Mor.

At the foot of Loch Avich sits Drissaig House. Katherine Lindsay-MacDougall told me that this house has a stained-glass window depicting the differentiated arms of the MacDougall Chiefs. My ring at the door is answered by one of the present tenants, a young lady—attractive and patient. As I try to explain my reason for calling, I suddenly realize that the frosted glass of the door depicted the Clan MacDougall crest with the motto in Latin.

"That's very interesting," the young woman responded, "We have been wondering what that emblem stood for."

The road rounds the end of Avich, which lies shining between dark forested hills, and joins the road that parallels the north shore of long and lovely Loch Awe. Turning left, a short distance brings one to Kilmun—another house with MacDougall connections.[23]

The house is now occupied by a couple who are raising prize-winning Red Setters. The couple is enthusiastic about history. The house sits back from the road; however, the original drove road once ran past its front door. The low attached ell is of considerable age. Between the house and the present road can be seen low mounds, the remains of a rectangular enclosure of considerable size. Nearby is an old cemetery that supposedly contains the mass grave of people who died of the black death. The story is probably true.

Ardbrechnish

Running up the south side of Loch Awe is Route B840, which leaves A816 back in the Pass of Kintraw. Keeping close to the loch, this road often passes through park-like stretches overhung with trees—including flowering chestnuts and red-wine-leafed beeches—and opening on water-bright vistas. Like so many secondary roads, this one is narrow, with lay-bys marked with black and white striped poles.

About ten miles down the loch's southern shore is Innis Chonnel Castle.[49*] The first thing that impresses one is its size. It rises solidly from its island foundation, which is perhaps ninety feet from the shore of the loch. The reflection of its fifty-foot walls darkens the waters as one stands on the pebble beach and wishes for a boat. The second impression

---

[*] It is easy to miss this castle, as the steep bank from the road down to the loch is wooded at this point.

is that one has been transported back in time and is about to be challenged at any moment from the massive square corner tower. One has to pause and remember that inside, the floors are gone and much of the interior is in ruins.

Two miles before this road joins A819, one comes to Ardbrechnish, an azalea-surrounded estate now turned into a hotel. Its many ells and chimneys are clues to past remodeling. The situation is beautiful, with a grand view over Loch Awe to the heights of Cruachan. If in looking at the front of the house one senses a resemblance to Lunga House in Craignish, then one is not mistaken. James Thorp, who expanded Ardbrechnish, married Anne MacDougall of Lunga, who insisted that her new home resemble her childhood home.

But Ardbrechnish was a MacDougall house before all this. One is not surprised to find that it came into the possession of Campbells through marriage. The house at that time consisted of a tower block—still the oldest structure—and the southwest corner of the house.[*]

The owner answers my ring and confirms without any hesitation that this is indeed the house where the MacDougall hounds materialized out of the hearth. Would I like to see the very place?

As I follow this gracious man into the oldest part of the house, I review the story in my mind. It was after Ardbrecknish fell into Campbell hands. Two women were washing in the sink when, from behind them and in the direction of the fireplace, there came a growl. Turning, they saw two great hounds materializing and rising out of the hearthstone. The hounds stretched and disappeared through a closed window. The sight left the women white-faced and without voice until one whispered, "The MacDougall Hounds; flesh will be torn."

The kitchen into which I am led is a small room. The proximity of the sink to the fireplace gives real drama to the tale. One would be within twelve feet or less of the apparition as one turned from the sink. The fireplace is of interest. It is recessed into the thickness of the wall and has one great stone as its lintel, which the present owner feels might have originally been a grave slab. As one stands at the sink, the window through which the hounds passed is on one's left. On the day of my visit, it was open, letting in the breeze.

Standing at a table, a woman is helping a young girl with her hair. The owner introduces this woman as Mrs. Campbell.

"I want no trouble between you," he says. "I just painted that window sill, and I want no hounds to make a mess."

---

[*] This original portion of Ardbrechnish is easily distinguished. It is a narrow, three-storied block, white with crow-stepped gable.

The view grows more uplifting as one descends the loch. Just before the road drops down through a series of curves to join B819, a view simply demands that one stop. To the left rises the massive form of Cruachan, while in front is a great valley receding into blueness. Ben Lui peers above that glen's mountained walls. Today this whole mountain kingdom is seen through a misty vale. Upon the braes, the broom and whin glow yellow. The high mountainsides are turned pink in the long light, and the corries and valleys are washed with a pale blue.

Ahead, the road rounds an arm of Loch Awe, reaches Kilchurn Castle, that stronghold of the Campbells, and heads toward the Pass of Brander.

Chapter 15
Craignish and Lunga

Craignish

Route A816 winds through the hills and skirts the seacoast of a land whose human history reaches back to the beginnings of human habitation along the fringes of the west Highland coast and forward to the relatively late appearance of the "clans." This is the road to Dunadd, a principal seat of the old Kingdom of Dalriada. There Fergus, the brother of Lorn, was king and began the long succession of the Scottish throne.

Passing through Kilmelfort, the highway rounds Loch Melfort and passes the Arduaine Gardens. One of the joys of this country is its gardens—delightful enclaves away from the traffic, and places filled with bird song. Their walks wander between plantings of native and exotic shrubs and flowers. At Arduaine, the banks of azalea keep company with a cedar of Lebanon, and people take each other's pictures standing under a plant whose umbrella-like leaves make them look like the "little folk" from a fairy hill.

Just beyond the gardens are the sands of Asknish Bay. On this particular day, several families are taking turns holding down the cloths on the picnic tables against a breeze fresh from the island and the sea.

From the sandy shore of Asknish Bay to Loch Craignish, the highway takes a climbing and twisting way, as if following the path of the man who first kept company with "the fiend whose lantern lights the mead." Having made a series of sharp turns above the valley of Staing Mhor, A816 runs pleasantly downward for a short distance through woods to where a road branches to the right, leading to the sea-surrounded world of Craignish peninsula.

This turn I take, for I am bound for Ardfern, that lochside hamlet where the white-hulled yachts turn upon the mirror of the tide. Each of these boats rides upon its twin while their masts shine varnished-yellow against the green bastions and blue-shadowed glens of Loch Craignish's far shore. Behind the anchored yachts, the gulls and terns engage in a raucous clan squabble over a low-lying island called Eilean Mhic Chrion.

Loch Craignish is filled with islands from its head to its opening upon the Sound of Jura. These islands are forged from upthrust layers, resulting in jagged profiles, and like the rocky shores of the loch, display the volcanic dikes of more violent times. Now, in these geologically peaceful times, the islands are feathered with birds. Black-headed seagulls nestle in the sea pinks and stand upon the yellow-lichened rocks, while all around fly and paddle their equally noisy neighbors: eider ducks, megansers, red-beaked oystercatchers, and that aeronautical marvel, the tern.

Between the tip of the peninsula's pointing finger and the island of Garbh Reisa lies the current plowed thoroughfare of Dorus Mor—the great southern door to the Inner Hebrides.

I suspect that many people of Craignish have a prayer something like this: "Let our sporrans jingle with the money left by visitors, but send not the despoiling crowd to trample this garden Thou hast planted east of the islands and the sea."

Craignish is a garden—a green, wild flower garden, despite the stone erupting through the heath and sod. I have read that there are remaining enclaves of the old Caledonian Forest here in Craignish.[64] Certainly there are fine woods with Scots pine and the spreading branches of massive hardwoods.

My destination is Innisaig, a dignified stone house whose tall windows face the anchorage of Ardfern and whose yard is surrounded by a dense hedge of rhododendron. The hedge is penetrated by a gate that is only inches wider than a car. This is the old Dower House for the MacDougall estate of Lunga, now owned by Katherine Lindsay-MacDougall of Lunga. Katherine, who is an archivist with an Oxford degree, is inspecting her roses as I thread the needle gateway and manage to get the Morris into an appropriate gear for driving up to the front door.

Lunga House

We drive from Ardfern across the high back of Craignish peninsula to Lunga House[50] where we are to have tea with the present laird, Colin Lindsay-MacDougall.[20]

The high and solid walls of Lunga House appear above the trees as one rounds a curve in the drive. The present mansion consists of additions to a sixteenth century L-shaped keep. Here in high gables and expanded ells stands a residence befitting the laird of an estate literally stretching from sea to sea across the peninsula and containing some three thousand acres.*

Such a crenelated edifice is a grand bequest and a great burden as well. Colin describes the constant need for repairs upon the mansion house and the war he has waged and won against dry rot—though one might think this an exotic malady in the west Highland climate. The Laird of Lunga is doing much of the necessary work himself. One can only admire his determination to hold the stealthy besiegers at bay. In

---

* See Chapter 37 for a description of the setting of Lunga House.

Chapter 15

this age, the house must pay something for its keep, and Colin is turning many rooms into flats for rent.

We have tea sitting about a wood fire crackling in a great fireplace, and with that most agreeable ritual completed, Colin takes us on a tour of those parts of the house not occupied by paying guests.

The hall is an impressive room. Four tall and stone-framed windows fill the gable wall. Their light falls upon a raised dais. The lofty ceiling is divided into deep bays by the crossing of massive beams. The walls below gleam with raised cedar paneling newly refinished by the Laird and his helpers. From these same walls, the portraits of the MacDougalls of Lunga and their wives look down as if expecting the candles to be lit while musicians gather to tune their instruments. The portraits include Colin's grandfather. He was said to be the most handsome man in the Guards. He was riding a white horse up and down the line when he was killed.

Dark paneling surrounds the long table in the dining room, enclosing a space meant for shining silver and crystal laid on a field of white linen.

The paneling is light again in a special sitting room with large roof windows. It seems that the Head of the House of Lunga who built this addition was an aid to the Prince Regent during the "Exposition," and this special paneling was a fringe benefit. An unusual painting of a piper hangs in this room. His pipe has only two drones and he has obviously removed his bonnet out of respect, for the artist has faithfully painted the line where the tan stops.

There are stories everywhere in this house. The sitting room is spoken of as Mr. Spencer's room. Colin explains that while out on a drive, the ladies of a previous generation found a stranger who was obviously in need of help. He said that his name was Spencer. Taking him home, they left him in the sitting room while they went to see what could be done. On returning, they found him dead. No one could ever learn more about this poor fellow.

Standing on the broad stair landing, Colin draws back folding doors to expose a window in which the shield and crest of the MacDougalls glow in yellows, blues, and ruby red. In the center of the quartered MacDougall shield are the arms of the wife of John MacDougall of Lunga, Willelmina Liddell, whose dowry brought added means for enlarging Lunga House.

The MacDougalls of Lunga have their own variation of the Clan Tartan. It is a sett identical with the official pattern but with the red exchanged for a deep heather purple. The result is a beautiful, dark tartan. There are two stories concerning the origin of the "Lunga purple," and both may well be true. The Lunga MacDougalls were redheads, and

Colin's grandfather thought this tartan was a better color complement—a touch of vanity that is truly Highland. The second story says that this tartan was designed as a subdued "hunting sett."

Colin has a fine collection of tartan material from the past. I had not realized how compact and stiff the old, "hard-woven" material was. No soft saxony or pliable worsted made up the old belted plaid, but rather a material so closely woven that it was nearly impervious to rain. Katherine remembers being told that such tartan when wet would slice the back of a man's legs.

Colin brings out a pitcher decorated with the MacDougall Arms. This gold work was done by itinerant artists. They laid the metal leaf using honey as an adhesive and baked the finished work in the kitchen oven.

That evening as we all sit at dinner before the large windows of Melfort House (a hotel overlooking the length of Loch Melfort), the Laird of Lunga proves to be as gifted a storyteller as he is an informative guide. To the west, the evening mist draws its curtains about the islands as we crack the shells of a bounty gathered from near their shores.

Lunga Cross

I awake with the light of a clear morning flooding the guest room windows of the Dower House in Ardfern. The yachts have turned about to face the incoming tide, and the terns and gulls have resumed their dispute.

Katherine has planned an itinerary that will make the best of the day. We drive in her car—she has seen quite enough of the Morris and its wandering gearshift—down the peninsula of Craignish to visit the ancient chapel at Corranmore. This little chapel is beautifully situated. Seen through the two round arch windows in the east wall, the loch lies as majestically somber as the clouds above. All seems holding still, but a magic light on the far hills accentuates the olive greens and the apricot tints. I have heard such views described as "noble." That term seems appropriate; if not noble, then call it holy.

Here lie buried the more recent generations of the MacDougalls of Lunga. Their grave slabs are carved with the Arms and at their head rises a wheel cross erected to the memory of John MacDougall of Lunga, who died in 1871.[20*]

---

[*] Katherine Lindsay-MacDougall has erected a memorial to her mother, Helen Margaret Lindsay. One of Helen's sisters married a Sir Walter Maxwell-Scott of Abbotsford while another married Lord Francis Hill, 6th Marquis of Downshire.

Chapter 15

There are far more ancient stones at Corranmore—stones that bear medieval claymores and Celtic labyrinths. These stones have been removed from the turf in which they had long lain neglected to the protection of a canopy within the walls of the old chapel. Katherine has been active in the preservation program that has saved these stones for generations to come.

Just outside the chapel walls, there is a large rectangular slab inscribed with radiating lines and slotted with a square hole near one end. This is the base for a cross, now lost, whose foot once fitted into the square socket and whose shadow, falling across the incised lines, signaled the hours of labor and prayer. We do not need the hour cross today to tell us that the sun is fast climbing its morning path.

Tam, Katherine's black poodle, has disappeared, and we drive on to see if he has gone calling on a friend down the road, as he likes to do. There is no sign of the gregarious Tam. We continue on to the southwest shore of Craignish's long finger where lie, before Craignish Castle and out to sea, the high mount of Scarba and the northern end of Jura. Between these two islands is Corryvreckan, the great tidal whirlpool. Its noise often reverberates across this seaside world when the Celtic storm goddess, Cailleach Bheithir, calls forth the waterspouts upon the vortex. Today the sea lies untroubled. A grand serenity presides upon this edge of the island sea.

We return to Ardfern. Still no sight of Tam. There is a caravan converted into a teashop that overlooks the anchorage; there the proprietress tells us her problem as we drink coffee and devour her cakes. It seems that government regulations reach here—rules, in this case, concerning required but unnecessary plumbing without which the shop must be closed. The lady scrubbed away at an already spotless countertop. She suspects that someone with envy has set the regulators upon her. I suppose that no place, if populated, is immune from human meanness—not even such a favored place as Craignish.

Expressing our sympathy to the keeper of the teashop, we drive up the east shore of the loch to A816 and then north over the mainland end of the peninsula to again reach the sea. There we turn left onto a dirt road[*] that leads, finally, to Lunga House. We park by a stone cottage (one of many upon the Lunga estate) and walk down the road. Our purpose is to visit the memorial cross raised to the memory of Iain MacDougall, who was killed in action two weeks after war was declared

---

[*] This is now a paved road and plainly marked as the way to a new village of condominiums and a walled anchorage known as Crowhaven. This village sits close by the memorial cross.

in 1914, and to his father, Lt. Colonel Stewart MacDougall of Lunga, who fell leading the battalion of Gordon Highlanders he had raised and led into the terrible mire of the Western Front.*

One cannot escape the sense of tragedy when looking at one of the photographs taken at the last Oban Gathering before the "Great War." Many of those young and older men, straight of back and handsome in their kilts, would soon be dead, and many families would be left with shattered hopes.

The cross was fashioned in the "Iona style" by a MacDougall associated with the Oban monument company. It has been positioned here upon this coast to serve as a landmark for sailors. Such a service is most appropriate. The Lunga MacDougalls have long hoisted canvas upon this expanse of island-strewn ocean.

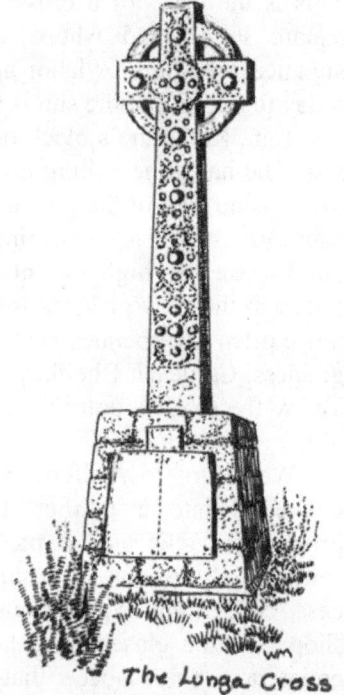

The Lunga Cross

We stand below the cross looking outward across the sea and the islands, toward the blue mountains of Mull. My guide is an enchantress. She enriches every view with those tales missing from history books. The island just off the shore was once a favorite hideaway for illicit whiskey-making. On the hill behind the cross, Mary Bheg ("Little Mary," who later was a nanny at Lunga House) kept watch for the revenue cutter. If seen, she was to wave her red pantaloons as a timely warning to her father and brother on the island. At a flap of red from the hill, the still would be secreted away and the menfolk gone before the officers could put ashore.

Mary Bheg knew the fairies' song but could never be cajoled into singing the melody. Once she had fallen asleep on a hillside and awoke to find the fairies' circle about her and the sound of their singing lilting in her inner ear.

---

* There is a memorial to First World War Veterans in front of the church in Ardfern. Inside is a brass plaque to Col. Stuart MacDougall of Lunga and his son Capt. Iain Lindsay-MacDougall.

Chapter 15

The fairyfolk—that tribe from the hollow hills—apparently have entered a time of hibernation, but the Highlander's touch with the world beyond is no more than lightly asleep. I doubt if there are many families in this land who do not have a story or two of events difficult to explain.

Katherine's brother, when a little boy, stayed late at play; and on his arrival home, his mother asked what had kept him. The explanation was given in all the genuineness of the young. He had been playing by the seashore when Grandfather had come walking along the sand. They had played and had a wonderful time. Mother chose not to explain once more that Grandfather was dead.

The sea shines as we walk back from the memorial cross. The hills are a patchwork of shifting colors as the sun's shafts and the cloud shadows pass across the sedges, the heath, and the prominences in a landscape similar to that which Scott described as

> Craigs, knolls, and mounds confusedly hurled,
> The fragments of an earlier world.

We drive south through the Bealach Mor, the "Great Pass," between the hills of Kintraw. It was in this pass that the horse bearing Katherine's great-grandfather refused to take another step. The storm was fierce and night was coming on. John of Lunga had to abandon getting home and turned back to find shelter. Next morning he discovered a landslide had come thundering down that would have crushed both horse and rider.

We stop in Kilmartin for lunch at a restaurant housed in a remodeled stable that retains its corbeled floors and large, pegged beams. There are exceptional gravestones[*] and at least two remarkable crosses at Kilmartin. Such crosses were often broken in reformation zeal; the arm of one of Kilmatin's crosses was discovered contributing to a rocked-up culvert. This cross bears the form of Jesus crucified, with a special poignancy in the turn of the head.

South of Kilmartin stretches the plain upon which so much went on and about which we know so little.[†] It was a sacred place, but one is left to wonder why a burial in a cist was heaped over with a great mound of white corbels. What forms of worship and ceremony transpired within these circles of stones and around many standing stones? Upon a rock that along with its neighbors forms the stone circle in Temple Woods, Katherine points out an incised spiral. Perhaps in that eloquently simple symbol we share the ubiquitous need to reach toward the eternal.

---

[*] Colin Lindsay-MacDougall informed the author that some of these stones were removed from Eilean Righ in Loch Craignish.
[†] Joan Pearson, *Kilmartin: The Stones of History*, and Graham Ritchie, *The Archaeology of Argyll*, Chapter 5.

From what was a salt marsh and before that a shallow sea rises the island rock of Dunadd,[*] once the royal center for the ancient Kingdom of Dalriada.[†] From a farmyard, one climbs the twisting path through several natural gateways that must have been incorporated in the fortifications. At the top, one hundred and thirty feet above the level plain, one discovers what is left of this acropolis of the Scots—and what remains is truly significant. One can trace the outline of a giant symbolic boar cut into the rock. Beside the boar is an inscription in that enigmatic writing now labeled Ogam. A cup has been hollowed in the ledge, perhaps to hold consecrating oil, for here the first Kings of Dalriada were invested and here they placed their foot in the incised footprint and promised to tread the pathway of royal responsibility. Standing by this footprint carved in the ledge, one sees the distant, blue peak of Cruachan. It was a small realm for so many mighty deeds.

Less than two miles south of Dunadd, Katherine draws attention to the mast of a yacht sedately passing behind a hedge row—the Crinan Canal. How pleased the old Vikings would have been. This water thoroughfare cuts across the narrow neck of Kintyre's long peninsula and connects Loch Fyne with the Sound of Jura.

While we have tea in a canal-side shop, several pleasure boats are let through the lock. Once this world was busy with the passing of working boats—the steam "puffers" of Para Handy's days.[‡] One of these steamboats is tied up in the crowded basin beside the lock—high wheelhouse, higher red stack with a black top, and a wide beam. At Lochgilphead, the eastern entrance to the canal, Katherine points out a pier—when she was a girl, a car would be waiting there for the Glasgow boat, to take them to Lunga.

We return to the Dower House in Ardfern to find Tam safely imprisoned in the entryway, his nose pressed against the glass. The wanderer had been brought home by a neighbor. Ardfern is a closely knit village.

---

[*] See *Argyll: The Enduring Heartland* by Marion Campbell for a delightful and accurate description.
[†] Archaeological evidence points to the location of Dunstaffnage as another locus for this ancient kingdom of the Scots.
[‡] See Neil Munro's classic, *Para Handy Tales*.

Chapter 16
Raera and Nether Lorn

Nether Lorn—the name has a magical whisper. There are no signs that read "Entering Nether Lorn." Quite appropriately, the exact boundaries appear vague. Lorn itself is described as running from Loch Leven southward to Knapdale. Eastward, the district includes Loch Awe and spreads to the present borders of Argyll.*

The southwest portion of this area—from Loch Feochan to Craignish and incorporating the islands from Seil to Scarba—constitutes the country of Nether Lorn.

The MacDougalls of Dunach once lived on the north shore of Loch Feochan.[41] It was their distinction and probably destruction to have participated in the Religious Wars of the mid-seventeenth century.[13, 23]

On the same side of the loch near its mouth lies the Quarry of Ardentallan, whose gray-green sandstone was used to build the churches of Kilbride and Kilmore, the Cathedral on Lismore, and the towers of Dunollie and Gylen Castles. Stone was still being quarried there in the 1840s when the Free High Church in Oban was constructed. At the mouth of the loch and above Minard Point rises Cnoc na Faire, the "Hill of the Watching." There is a hill of the same name on the southwest coast of Kerrera, and both these vantage points may have served as surveillance posts for our Highland ancestors.

Joining A816 at the head of Loch Feochan is the road that, following River Nell, winds through Glen Lonan to reach Taynuilt and the Pass of Brander. This way has been called the "Road of the Kings," for by this route the bodies of the Scottish Kings of old were carried in their last journey to the sacred island of Iona.

Returning to the head of Loch Feochan and taking the road past Loch Nell, a byway turns to the left, leading to Kilmore. "Kil" in a place name indicates the location of a church—in this case, a church dedicated to Saint Mary. This is a relatively late dedication, for the church was first erected in memory of Saint Bean—an eighth century missionary and churchman who may have followed Columba as Abbot of Iona. Records of this church go back to the fourteenth century, but the present remains are of a later date. The windows are of special interest, having pointed arches with the tops carved from a single stone. Several old grave slabs are in the surrounding yard. One of these bears the head of a cross composed of four circles, the hilt of a claymore, and the initials DMC,

---

*See the map in Michael Starforth's *An Official Short History of Clan MacDougall*, opposite page one.

added much later when someone, doubtless a MacDougall, saved the price of a gravestone. Kilmore, like Kilbride and Ardchattan, was an important religious center for the MacDougall kinspeople.

Returning to the south shore of Loch Feochan, perhaps a mile east of Kilninver at a place where one can look seaward to see the blue-green hills of Mull, one finds Creag nam Marbh, the "Rock of the Dead." Here, tradition says, the royal biers rested safe from the wolves[66] while awaiting the dipping of oars and the galley bound to the Holy Isle.

Beyond Creag nam Marbh and at the mouth of Loch Feochan lies Barnacarry Bay—the location of another quarry operation, which specialized in the manufacturing of millstones. Several of these stones can be seen half cut from the ledge. Westward still is the abandoned village of Tigh Cuil, above which rises the spiny cliffs and the ancient hill fort of Losgann Lathurnach, the "Toad of Lorn." South of this high landmark, between tiny Dubh Loch and Route B844 as it runs along Loch Seil, is a group of standing stones. Reportedly, Loch Seil contains the remains of a *crannog*—a manmade island that once served as a pedestal for an Iron Age "lake dwelling."[6*]

With so much of interest to see and visit, choices must be made. The late afternoon sun is finding loopholes in the clouds and shooting shafts that set the hillside glowing in emerald green and burnished bronze against the backdrop of blue-gray cloud. It is growing late. I choose to see Raera House, Ardmaddy Castle and, hopefully, something of Seil.

Just south of the junction of the road to Seil with A816 and close by River Euchar, one looks down from the highway upon Raera House. The house is surrounded by trees and seated at the foot of a high swell of hills. As a slate panel set in the wall of Raera House states, a Campbell built the house in 1743. If one is looking for the older residence of the MacDougalls of Raera, who have long been considered the senior Cadet of the Clan MacDougall,[21] one must be satisfied with a small earthwork situated a short distance northeast of Raera House and upon the steep bank of the river. By tradition, this is the site of Raera Castle. Here may have stood the seat of that distinguished family who once held sway in Nether Lorn. Later, this family established its principal residence at Ardmaddy.†

---

* The author has not visited the site of this ancient habitation. See Chapter 40.
† Colin Lindsay-MacDougall of Lunga relates that one of the MacDougalls of Ardmaddy played an important role in the history of the Michigan area in America. He founded a school for Indians on Mackinac Island. Using his tremendous influence as a leader of the Indians, he endeavored to play French against English and English against French to protect the Native American's

Chapter 16

Taking the road that leads to Seil (B8003) and then the narrow way southward over the hills of Kilbrandon and Kilchattan, I arrive at the gate of the Ardmaddy estate. There is smoke trailing from the chimney pots of the cottage close by the gate, and from inside the sound of children's voices. The occupants prove to be a family on holiday. The father is an ardent angler. As we chat, he tells me that he always carries a whistle by which he might guide searchers should he happen to break an ankle or a leg while out in the wilds. It seems an excellent idea, for in this land, once off the beaten path, one can travel all day cut off from the world of men by high hills, alone under an immensity of sky.

The gate is open, but I leave the Morris to conjure new evils and stride down the drive to Ardmaddy Castle.[31] The way is arched with trees and accompanied, for a distance, by the rapidly falling Allt Dallermaig cascading to the sea.

A beam of yellow spotlights the castle as it appears first through a wreath of sun-filled leaves. On a pasture below the drive, a mahogany colt races across the turf in pounding glee. It is a dramatic beginning for what proves to be a delightful visit.

ARDMADDY

---

interests and integrity. It is said that on his return to Ardmaddy he was killed when the horse he was riding went over a cliff.

Mr. Struthers, the present owner of Ardmaddy, is a young man, alive and full of interests. His wife I would describe as an English beauty, but as to her being English, I may be mistaken. She is busy making dinner as I arrive at their door. This is not the proper time to be knocking, but the Struthers not only allow me to photograph the exterior of Ardmaddy; they open the door and invite me into their home for a tour.

The old towerhouse of the MacDougalls of Raera provides the central foundation for augmentations made by generations of prosperous Campbells. The old tower walls are thick and carry circular stairs that once led to upper stories and that still turn downward to the vaulted cellar. There are two cellar chambers, each having a cannon-port. In another small room off the cellar passage, a long message scratched upon the pane of a barred window is dated 1745, that grim year for the Jacobite White Cockade. These lines, left by a prisoner of the Campbells, are filled with somber reflections upon the fate of men and princes.

The Struthers have been repairing the Castle, and in their labors have uncovered the date-stone that once surmounted the old tower's portal. Because of additions, the stone is now part of an inside wall. Mr. Struthers takes me into the sitting room to see this relic. It reads "I M C—1579". Undoubtedly, this is the stone mentioned in old histories of Raera. The initials are those of John (Iain) MacDougall, whose citadel this was.

Mr. Struthers points out a shortcut through the formal garden, abloom with roses and intermixed with well-tended vegetables.

"You'll find a fine chance for a photograph of the castle from the far end of the garden," he says as we shake hands.

The last level rays of sunshine are lighting the shore when I reach the high arch of grace that spans the narrows of Seil Sound and joins mainland to island. Clachan Bridge was designed by Robert Mylne, engineer to the Duke of Argyll, and was constructed by John Stevenson of Oban in 1791. The MacDougalls of Ardencaple shared in the cost. An arch bridge is a wonderful creation, and Clachan Bridge is especially fine. An indented rondel flanks each side of the arch, and for added decoration the bridge wears a rare Fairy Foxglove, which grows in the crevices and festoons the patterns of stone with delicate pink flowers. The bridge is proof that "a thing of beauty" may be practical as well as a joy for many generations.

One can see nothing but the hood of the car and the open sky beyond as one nears the top of Clachan's narrow and corbeled bow. There is a momentary act of faith as one passes over and down to the island of Seil. Just beyond the bridge stands the old inn, Tigh an Truish, the "House of the Trousers." Story has it that kilted islanders stopped at the inn during the years of proscription to put on pants before crossing to the mainland. To the side of the inn is a parking lot, and at the end of this lot a pathway marked "Public"—a rare notice in this country—that leads upward to a scenic outlook of grand proportion. I hurry upward, for already the lavender shadows of evening are spreading over the land.

There, on a narrow ridge, a vast view spreads westward. Below, the ragged coastline of Seil, creased with inlets and accented with escarpments, seems to have shattered into islands. Somewhere in this wild landscape is the one-time home of the MacDougalls of Ardencaple, and upon one of those rocky ridges are the remains of their ancient stronghold Ardfad Castle.[29*]

Across the pale blue sea, the mountains of Mull disappear behind a great curtain of showers—soft and gray in the hastened dusk. As I watch, the misty drape begins its journey toward the mainland. By the time I drive back to Oban, the rain has come in the darkness. The drops spatter against the window of my room in the Heatherfield. I lie listening, and as I listen, I hear within my mind a whisper repeating "Nether Lorn."

---

[*] See Chapter 39.

Chapter 17
Island of Kerrera

Kerrera Ferry

In this era of incomprehensibly complex and incredibly expensive modes of communication, the means of summoning the Kerrera ferry is refreshingly and remarkably simple. Under the sign that reads "Ferry Boat" is a large panel that is white on one side and black on the reverse. This panel pivots like a double-sided chalkboard. To call the ferry, one flips the panel from white to black.[*]

I turn the board and wait on the sloping stones of the jetty. From where I stand, the old track from this ferry on the Sound of Kerrera to Oban is plainly visible, leading at a steep angle up the hillside toward Glenmore.[†]

Samuel Johnson and his faithful Boswell took this road when they landed here on their tour of the Highlands. I have little time to conjure an image of Johnson's portly and puffing form bent low upon the upgrade, for presently a boat puts out from the opposing pier on Kerrera's shore. The ferryman proved to be a well-mannered boy, and his crew a younger lad. Both have honest smiles.

The ferry is an aluminum boat with an outboard motor, not one of the wooden crafts seen in old photographs with its tiller, broad beam, and bottom filled with a mat of brush laid to protect the hull from cattle hooves. Despite the contemporary appearance of the boat, I am about to cross the Sound in a passage from present to past. Miss Hope MacDougall of MacDougall has put the joy of a visit to Kerrera best in the title of her book: *Island of Kerrera: Mirror of History*.[70]

Our passage is curved by the tidal current, and our wake quickly lost in the gray chop. The high cliffs of the Ardbhan Craigs are left behind, diminishing in apparent height as the island's shore grows ever higher. Above the steep track that climbs from Port Kerrera's stone pier stands the ferryman's cottage, and higher still, the fine stone chapel-school built in 1872 by the MacDougalls of Dunollie for their tenants.

Walking the Track

With indifference to the old gods, I decide to walk the circuit around this MacDougall island counterclockwise and against the passage of the sun.[‡] Upon my impiety, the rain descends.

---

[*] On later trips, the author found the ferry operating only on stated times.
[†] See Chapter 4, p. 18, and also Map 3, p. 274.
[‡] See Map 2, p. 273281.

Chapter 17

The track leads westward across the stony pastureland high above Balliemore Farm. Amidst the rocks and the sheep, a young lass is petting a black-faced ewe.

"I see you have a friend," I call.

"Oh, I have many friends here," the girl answers, and with the wool-fat sheep at her heels, she goes skipping down the pasture through the silver rain.

Cloud by passing cloud, the gods relent. The rain ceases by the time I stand at the head of the lane that turns downward to the long, dormered cottage of Slaterach Farm[70] with its longer stone barn. Beyond the buildings lie Slaterach Bay and the island aptly named the "Shepherd's Hat." Outward from the bay, the sea spreads northwest in a grand expanse to the mountains of Morvern and west to the heights of Mull.

The gods relent and then forgive. Across the Firth lies Lismore, splashed with yellow-green as the sun shafts sweep across its shores. The lighthouse entrance of the Sound of Mull gleams white. There on Mull's shore, Duart Castle appears a brown speck in the rising mist. On the deck of the cruise ship outward bound from Oban, there must be joy over the clearing weather.

The way from Slaterach to Barnabuck (*Bar na Boc*, "Ridge of Roebucks") keeps high above the shore, and always on the open edge is a grand panorama. This view is seen over camel-back hillocks below—hillocks covered with bracken shining green after the rain. Ahead there is a clump of crimson foxglove backed by the blue mountains of Mull. I sit beside the track waiting to see if the approaching spotlight of sunshine will illuminate the foxglove.

To my back rises the high, inner moor of Kerrera. Above the corrugated contours of an old lazybed[77] and the heathered shoulder of a higher hill, the stratocumulus pass, trailing gray wisps toward the mainland. That intense Hebredian blue of open sky arches upon the pillars of the cloud. Away off to the west, the ocean is also blue where the sun shines upon the expanse. Nearer, the showers pass across the Firth of Lorn, spreading their white veils before the steeps of Mull. Upon these heights the pastel washes of the sun's brush appear and disappear. What enraptured lines must have risen in the mind of Keats when he traveled this same track across Kerrera!

Subsistence and not much more repaid the hands and feet that with *cas chrom*[84] turned the furrows of Kerrera's garden plots. A homespun shirt would have been upon the back that labored in carrying the seaweed up these slopes to keep the "soil in good heart." For all the labor of men, women, and children, even when the seasons were kind, there was need to scrape the porridge drawer and to measure with care the rent-paying grain. Yet for all the lack of physical abundance, hearts were filled with song. One cannot be surprised by either the spirit or the generosity of the people here—not while one sits beside the track to Barnabuck.

The sun's shaft misses the clump of foxglove, but another opportunity for the camera lies ahead as the track dips downward toward the old change house at the head of Barnabuck Bay. Several young calves are on the road—fawn-brown and white—while behind them lies the sea, pathed with the wandering avenues of the wind. As a backdrop for both the calves and the sea, rise the misty mountains of Mull. The calves stare at me with oversized eyes as the camera shutter clicks.

This portion of the track down the craggy hillside is known as Am Maolan, the "Wild Place," and so it must be when the storms sweep this open face of hill, but today a great calm presides. The road runs steeply down over the exposed rock of the island "chattered" by the years of passing carts and cattle. Cattle in droves and sheep in great number once arrived at Barnabuck from Mull to be driven across Kerrera on their way to market. When these droves put ashore, let the tacksmen protect their crops and the keeper of the change house get out the product of his still. The old pens at Barnabuck look like a ruined village of the trolls—low-linteled doorways and a maze of tumbled walls.

The road from Barnabuck, deeply worn by the passing of hooves, rounds Torthain Mor and runs southward leaving behind the Firth of Lorn, as turquoise blue as the Aegean. To the left the heather moor rises and then climbs steeply to a prominence of ledge. From somewhere up the heather slope, a bird carols that the day is lovely and passes blithely upon these undulating and up-thrust moors. Other birds attest that the song is true and then—silence, but for the sound of the passing wind.

By leaving the old drove road before it again reaches the shore, one can climb the flank of Cnoc na Faire until one stands on the edge of the island overlooking Kerrera's broken and turreted southern shore.[*]

On this particular day, the sound of the sea fills the air as it meets and re-meets the rocks below. To the east along the jagged coast, the ocean bursts white on red-brown ledge. Below the cliffs and to the left, the waves roll in on a long shingled point populated by sheep and geese. Just inland lies Ardmore Farm amidst its protecting screen of trees.

---

[*] Some caution needs to be taken in approaching the southwestern coast of the island. It was not until I rounded Kerrera by boat that I fully appreciated the height of the sea cliffs that face the Atlantic. Nancy MacDougall Black, who spent a great deal of her childhood on Kerrera, tells me that as children she and her sisters were not allowed to go to that edge of the island.

Chapter 17

The track eastward from Ardmore makes its ledgy way first along the coast and then inland. Gylen Castle is my goal, and the shortest route lies across the rising moor.*

Leaving the track through a gate in the roadside fence, I walk eastward high above the shore. The Atlantic swells that rush in and out of a sea cave below make the sound of a giant blowing across the mouth of his empty jug.

Gylen Castle

One sees Gylen on reaching the crest of the rising ground. It roosts upon a narrow promontory above the surging sea—"a gem of architectural design" mounted in a grandly rugged setting.[48†]

Gylen Castle

From a full-color oil painting by Walter M. Macdougall

---

* The normal approach to Gylen is to go through the gate at Upper Gylen Farm and follow the track that runs toward the sea. From this track one can follow a path that climbs up to the castle.

† Wallace-Hadrill, David and Janet Carolan, *Turner in Argyll in 1831*. Also see Chapter 25 for an account of the attention this artist paid to Gylen and its situation.

Here crumbles a treasure.* Doubtless much more of this tower house would have tumbled in or fallen down the precipitous cliffs were it not for restoration briefly begun, only to be terminated by the outbreak of World War I.†

Now the ceaseless weathering is again working its ravages. The checkered moldings disappear and the carved faces become featureless.‡

Back from the small bay on the west of Gylen's high perch and at the base of the steepest ascent, a finger of rock projects outward from a large outcrop. It must be the remains of a volcanic sill from which the softer conglomerate, top and bottom, has been weathered away. On this natural platform, perhaps a yard wide, the last MacDougall made his stand on the day that General Leslie's Covenanters burned Gylen and ravaged the island. Their battle cry was "For Jesus and no quarter." It was the grimmest of times for the people of Kerrera. I arrived at Gylen with that killing-time much in my thoughts.

Sheep have been up the curved stairs to the kitchen floor, and people with as little regard have been in the cellar. One stands by the great fireplace looking upward at the sky. Well, I did not come this far to be disconsolate, nor did I come unprepared. What remains is fascinating. The view from the open windows is grand.

To the south, the Firth of Lorn stretches to the Holy Islands.[69] Upon the horizon rise the mountains of Jura. Somewhere upon that steel-blue waste of sea, Somerled fought a great naval battle on the day of the Lord's Epiphany, which aided in establishing his power.[61]

From a window opening westward, one looks far downward to the ocean, swelling and breaking over jagged ledge. Beyond, sheep dot the green seaside pasture. The omnipresent mountains of Mull span the western horizon.

---

* The visit described in this chapter occurs well before the Gylen resoration project in the 1990s.
† This restoration was begun in 1915. Plans for this work were undertaken by John MacDougall, builder, Oban. His designs call for conical roofs on the round towers. Hope MacDougall of MacDougall noted that at this time a Scots fir beam was found fallen within the castle, and from this wood, this same John MacDougall fashioned an old-style three-branched candlestick similar to that carried by itinerate cobblers.
‡ By 2006 an extensive program of repair saved Gylen for future generations. The campaign began in 1994–1995. Principal contributors were the Ancient Monuments Department of Historic Scotland and the MacDougalls of Dunollie, with contributions from the Clan MacDougall Society of North America and other private donations. Repairs were completed in 2006, and on May 6 of that year a special celebration reopened Gylen to the public.

Chapter 17

Passing through the cellar chamber and out the arched doorway, I cross what was the inner bailey and stand gingerly on the outer edge of the precipice to photograph the south face of the castle. The slender stair tower rises three stories to the gable. Behind the tower is the rectangular block of the castle itself, with its large kitchen window and the arched window of the third story above.

The north portal door still retains its molding. It has an inlet for a heavy door, and the bar hole awaits a new bar. Stepping out through the portal and looking upwards, one senses the purpose of the openings in the floor of the projecting oriel window above. Even if one did not know the term "murder holes," one would realize the defensive intentions of these openings. Under the oriel window is a carved plaque. Even through a telephoto lens, I cannot make out the lettering, but the message is recorded in Hope MacDougall of MacDougall's *Island of Kerrera, Mirror of History*. The words were apparently adapted from Proverbs: "Trust unto God and not in men (me?), Thy son do well, and let them say."

※※※※※※※※※※※※※※

With many a backward look, I leave Gylen. Each time I turn, I find the carved faces high in the north wall watching my slow departure until I have gone too far to make them out, yet I am sure they still watch.

The track leads northward along Horseshoe Bay, where anchored the fleets of kings. Here is the field were King Alexander, the second of Scotland, dreamed a troubled dream and where he died of a fever in July of 1249.[70]

An old man sitting on a cottage step calls a greeting as I pass.

"Its been a fine day," he says.

"It has indeed," I answer.

"And did you not find peace in your walk?"

"Yes, and may it always be so on Kerrera."

"Aye," he nods, "may it ever be so."[*]

---

[*] Kerrera is a special place. Perhaps that is why I am more sensitive to the many changes I have seen there over the past eighteen years than to other places in Argyll. The reader will not miss some of the changes when comparing this chapter with Chapter 41.

Chapter 18
Dunstaffnage

On a fate-filled day in the summer of 1308, Alexander of Argyll, Lord of Lorn and the aged Chief of Clan MacDougall, awaited news from the Pass of Brander where the forces gathered by his son, Iain Bacach, faced Robert the Bruce. As the few survivors of that disastrous battle entered the portal of Dunstaffnage, there could have been no doubt in Alexander's mind. If the sun were not setting on MacDougall power in Argyll, then indeed, a dark cloud had passed across the shining disk. A fire of hatred for Bruce, the murderer of the Red Comyn, had filled the heart of Alexander's son, and its ashes had all but smothered the Galley of Lorn's proud beacon. Now the wolves with their greedy eyes would descend, and Bruce, himself, would be before the walls of Dunstaffnage, demanding the castle's inevitable surrender.

It was a time of irony. This Bruce who would soon be at the gate had managed to have himself crowned king upon the very stone that for years had been kept at Dunstaffnage.[45]

To a man with a Norman name, for all his connections with the Scottish royal line, Alexander would have to surrender the rock of his ancestors and a major citadel of the ancient Kingdom of Dalriada.

Alexander must have prayed that once again Dunstaffnage would be the duthus of the MacDougall Lords. This was to happen, but only briefly, when Alexander's grandson, Ewan of Lorn, married Joan, the daughter of Lady Matilda Bruce, and thus regained the castle.[62]

Ewan was to have but two daughters, however, and the title and Dunstaffnage would pass to the Stewarts of Innermeath and from them to the Campbells.

A visit to Dunstaffnage should be a major item on the itinerary of any visiting MacDougall or of any person interested in Highland history.

Dunstaffnage

The nest of fishing boats, moored gunwale to gunwale against Oban's railway pier, is resplendent with color in the momentary sunlight, and the waters around their hulls mix the colors of the sky with the reflected white, red, and green. The tour buses are loading in the square before the station. There is a bustle abroad, as if folks are hurrying to make the most of the good weather.

I board a regular run heading north and get off at Dunbeg. One looks across the rooftops of this village and sees Dunstaffnage standing upon the point, as it has for centuries, keeping watch upon the Lynn of Lorn and the entrance to Loch Etive. As one walks down through Dunbeg and around the bay, the castle is hidden and thus reappears dramatically, standing upon a gentle rise of green sward. For a moment, the morning seems transported to a day medieval. One expects to see a knight approaching, mounted upon a horse whose flowing mantle flashes the gold and azure of the MacDougalls.

Such an image is not as incongruous as it may seem. Duncan of Argyll, Lord of Lorn, was spoken of by a contemporary as a most comely knight. He or members of his family took part in the Crusades. The era of the Highland clans as so often romanticized was to come later. Duncan's grandson, Alexander of Argyll, was the principle power among a dozen barons who controlled the western Highlands and was the High Sheriff for the King of Scotland.[*]

Any description of the period from 1164 to the death of Alexander of Argyll in 1310 must account for the appearance of the great castles along the west Highland coast. C.J. Tabraham notes in his work, *Scottish Castles and Fortifications*, that at the time when such fortresses as Dunstaffnage, Duart, Innis Chonneaill (Innischonnell), and Ardtornish were being built, "Norman neighbors to the east were seemingly content, by and large, with castles of timber and clay." At the least, such stone edifices indicate increased prosperity, technical know-how, and civic stability. Michael Starforth, author of *An Official Short History of Clan*

---

[*] While such rules of office and charter indicate the influence of feudalism, the policy and social system in the Western Highlands also reflected the Celtic and Norse traditions.

MacDougall, feels that the introduction of sheep and improved agricultural methods may help explain the appearance of sufficient resources.*

It is known that the Norse practice of building stone strongholds was influential;† however, castles like Dunstaffnage show an understanding of the (then) latest designs. As R. Andrew McDonald put it, here is "evidence suggesting a sophisticated culture that was striving to be thoroughly contemporary."‡ Much is still to be learned about this period in west Highland history, when the MacDougalls rose to power.

Dunstaffnage is impressive.⁴⁵ It seems to have grown upwards out of the mass of conglomerate rock on which it stands. Rock and wall together rise sixty feet. Both the curtain wall and the towers that round the north, west, and east angles give the impression of great strength. They are massive. The walls are ten feet thick in many places.

Chapel

There is a place one should visit before taking a closer look at the castle. A path leads southwest from Dunstaffnage. Closely pressed by shrubbery, this way takes one to the chapel, hidden from the castle by a grove of trees. A bridal party walked this pathway on the afternoon of December 20, 1468. They walked from Dunstaffnage and into a scene overlooked by composers and librettists of tragic opera.

Sir John Stewart was on his way to marry the daughter of MacLaren of Ardveich and thus give their son, Dugald, a legitimate right to the Lordship of Lorn. Beside the bride and groom, the party included MacLaren and John MacDougall of Dunollie, eleventh Chief of the Clan, whose mother was John Stewart's sister. Stewart and MacDougall shared a common interest in this nuptial venture. Stewart's legitimate daughters were married to Campbells who, unless this wedding took place, would become the Lords of Lorn.

Hidden by the screen of woods, an ambush awaited led by Alan MacCoul (MacDougall)—a hotheaded and illegitimate kinsman of John MacDougall of Dunollie—who had risen against his own chief and in whom, apparently, the Campbell agents had found a willing assassin.¹⁶

Sir John Stewart was stabbed with more than one mortal wound and left for dead by the attackers, who were intent on phase two of their plan, the seizure of Dunstaffnage. The wedding party carried Stewart to the

---

* Suggestion made in conversation with the author.
† The similarity between Dunollie and Bergen Castle in Norway is often noted.
‡ R. Andrew McDonald, *The Kingdom of the Isles*, p. 250.

chapel, where he was married and a short time later left his bride a widow.

The chapel is fronted by a burial aisle built for and by the subsequent Campbells. Behind the aisle lies the small chancel and nave where the hurried wedding took place. The floor of the chapel is now a green carpet of closely mowed grass. The chancel is lighted by pairs of lancet windows deeply inset into the north and south walls, under arches of label and roll moldings. These windows are flanked by slender shafts with dog-toothed ornamentation. The chapel must have been a place of inspiration when the Chiefs of the Clan knelt before the altar and prayed to the King of Kings.[54]

I was surprised to find a bar hole in the doorway leading into the nave. There were more tangible threats to keep at bay in those days than that of the devil.

Castle

Dunstaffnage keeps up a good face consisting of the portal facade built in the sixteenth century and the present gatehouse, whose three dormer windows of the upper story peer over the parapet. (The upper stories of the gatehouse were rebuilt after a fire gutted the older structure in 1810.)

One enters the castle by way of a fore-stair, mounting to a plank platform that replaces the old drawbridge. As I pass the guardroom and step onto the slate tiles of the transe, a current of excitement passes through my body that seems to emanate from the stone walls close on either hand. Perhaps the musket slit positioned to cover the portal from an adjoining cellar has evoked this feeling, for such contrivances always do something to the pit of one's stomach. Otherwise, I am at a loss to explain the genesis of this sensation—it seems as if my passing suddenly activated a field of resonance—a resonance between these wails and something within myself too remote for memory. The feeling is transitory and passes as I step into the sunlight of the courtyard.

Dunstaffnage is larger than most Highland strongholds of its era. Dunollie, along with its outer-works, would very nearly fit within its courtyard. The living quarters, however, were never spacious. It is impossible to say how attractive they may have been. Certainly, fourteenth and fifteenth century living standards were not fastidious. One could make a study of the plumbing facilities enjoyed by the old Chiefs of the Clan by inspecting the drain chutes from garderobe latrines and slopsinks as they run through the wall of Dunstaffnage to empty down the outer curtain walls. There is a deluxe, double chute in the northwest wall that has been recently repaired by the Department of Environment, under whose authority national monuments are preserved.

This castle had its own internal water supply (a feature missing in some Scottish strongholds, which omission often brought about their downfall[13, 48]). Dunstaffnage's large square cistern is cut from the solid rock below the courtyard. Behind the well, in various stages of restoration and rubble, stands the kitchen with its walk-in fireplace. Above the kitchen are the remains of a later dwelling house whose lean-to roof slanted upwards to the curtain wall. The molded fireplace fronts of these quarters hang like big, empty picture frames upon the walls of the floorless second story.

A crew of men, employees of the Department of Environment, was "encamped" in the kitchen and working against the ravages of time. One workman was whistling an old Highland air—a lilting tune, grace notes and all—which echoed from the circling walls giving a welcome sense of occupancy.

The hall, once the center of activity within this fortress, occupied the east range between the gatehouse and the northeast tower.* It was originally lit by two sets of twin lancet windows, which were blocked up during later renovations. As is the case with many older features of this castle, the remains of these windows are best viewed from the outside, where the facing blocks can be plainly seen.

Parapets

The northeast tower, once four stories high, served as living quarters. The southwest tower rises over a prison whose entrance was a trapdoor in the tower's first floor. [Note: In 1981, the way to the parapets was closed due to restoration. The following description is taken from a visit to Dunstaffnage in 1990, when restorations had been completed.]

A new set of wooden stairs allows one to reach the parapet and look at the level of one of the arrow slits[8] into the southwest tower, with its inner stone platform and the original stairs turning within the thickness of the tower wall. The towers and curtain walls were all interconnected, so that when under attack the defenders could move and concentrate wherever needed. One can no longer walk around the castle within the

---

* A room has been opened to the public on the second floor of the gatehouse, in which several displays show an artist's perception of Dunstaffnage—galleys drawn up on the sands and a rendition of the hall when it was inhabited by the MacDougall Lords of Lorn. In another artist's rendition, the family of the MacDougall Chiefs are pictured dining under the timbered roof and below the high lancet windows.

wall, but thanks to the recent restoration, one can walk a major section of the parapet.

I have the chance to do this in the company of Donald MacDougall, whose illuminated manuscript history of Clan MacDougall is a labor of love and a treasure. It is a rare opportunity to walk the walls of the ancient seat of the Clan with a man who deserves the title of Seannachie.

At ground level, one tends to forget how strategically and beautifully situated Dunstaffnage is. One looks to the southwest across the Firth to the mountains of Mull, north and west up the Lynn of Lorn, and in front of the castle and over the estuary as far eastward as the Falls of Lora. Across the estuary is a fine panorama of the mountains of Benderloch, while southward is a clear view of the landward approach to the castle.

As Donald comments, Dunstaffnage was not built as an outpost of civilization but as a center of power within an active mixing of cultures, both old and emerging. There was constant traffic and communication with Ireland, with Norway, and increasingly, with the Kings of Scotland and (later) England.

Original stone slabs form the floor of the parapet. Each is lightly convex, and the meeting of their beveled margins makes a trough to carry the rain water to stone chutes projecting out over the walls. It is said that the parapets were remodeled for cannon and armed, in part, by guns recovered from a foundered ship of the Spanish Armada. More than the cannon, I would have liked to see the two-pronged beacon stand of iron that once stood mounted in a large stone upon the top of the east curtain wall.[*]

Imagination will have to do: There comes a call out of the night and a counter-challenge from the gatehouse. Below in the guardroom, the drowsing porter awakes, stands, and stretches. The drawbridge is lowered.[†] The Lord is aroused and enters the hall, his shadow leaping upwards upon the wall as the torch flares. In the hall a messenger is waiting. The courtyard echoes with hurried steps upon the stone treads leading to the parapet. A torch is raised to kindle the beacon, and fire leaps into the darkness. From hilltop, from headland, the signal fires burn. The head of the House of Dougall has summoned the Clan.

---

[*] This beacon is shown in a drawing of Dunstaffnage's east battlement in *Castellated and Domestic Architecture of Scotland*, Vol. I, by MacGibbon and Ross.

[†] The forestair arrangement at Dunstaffnage included a drawbridge from the top of the stairs to the portal doorway.

Chapter 19
Luncheon at Dunollie

I have an invitation to dine with the Chief at Dunollie. It is time to leave Dunstaffnage and head for the bus stop at Dunbeg. The tide is out and the crescent beach lies far exposed into Dunstaffnage Bay. Underfoot, the bladders of the seaweed snap. The sea worms have been busy tracing their own version of Celtic braids in the sand. By way of the beach and the village streets, I regain the highway above Dunbeg. A natural garden of fireweed[63] makes a pink-red foreground for the view across the water. On the far shore, the sun-struck hills of Benderloch rise steeply above the Moss of Achnacree.

There is time to enjoy the view, for the bus must be late. An older man passing by informs me that I will have a long wait indeed. The bus shown on the timetable has been discontinued.

I start to walk south and am rescued by a young fellow who is driving into Oban to buy parts for a fishing boat he is refurbishing. Making a rapid change to kilt and tie, I set off for Dunollie in great haste, like the rabbit in Alice in Wonderland who also was late for an important date. The way is becoming familiar, but there is always something new to catch the eye. The light and shadows are just right to make the flat-topped "Table of Lorn" stand out above the hills of Morvern across the Firth.

Madam MacDougall is concerned that lunch may have "dried out," but it is delicious and followed by a special dessert of black currant pudding with sauce and cream.

After lunch we visit the garden, with its pool surrounded by the dark steeples of yews. Close by rises an exotic sequoia, which was brought home by Admiral Sir John MacDougall. There is another tree of special importance—a Scots pine planted as a living memorial to Captain "Sandy" MacDougall, who would have been the twenty-fifth Chief but was killed at the age of twenty-seven storming Ciudad Rodrigo during the war against Napoleon. Family tradition relates that the Captain appeared to his mother standing by her bed, and on that same evening his sister saw him standing in front of her. The mysterious light warning of tragedy was seen that same night on the Maiden Island, just off Dunollie.*

The giant goldfish, actually more red than gold, wave their long tails below a green netting that protects them from the fishing of heron. (One arrived the very first day the pool was stocked.) Upon the pool's surface

---

* Jean MacDougall, *Highland Postbag*, p. 146.

float water lilies with large white petals tipped with pink. It was on a trip to China that the Chief became convinced her garden at Dunollie must have a goldfish pool. Goldfish bring serenity, she tells me. "They have been a perfect time-waster," she added.

There is much more to the grounds of Dunollie House than I realized. Hidden from the house by trees is the corbled quadrangle surrounded by the old carriage house and stables. In the eighteenth and early nineteenth century, the Chief's carriage bore his coat of arms on its varnished doors and, burdened with large wicker baskets, bore the family to England to visit relatives. The groom and men working on the estate slept in the loft over the stables. Beyond the low barn[*] that flanked the quadrangle to the west was the dog kennel, and beside it the ferret cage.[†] The center of the quadrangle is a square of grass with a pump.[‡]

Having toured the grounds, we carry out into the sunshine a stool and the Chief's beautiful Highland harp, given to her by a Clan Society in Glasgow on her twenty-first birthday. There, before the entrance to Dunollie House, Madam MacDougall sits with a tartan plaid folded over her lap and her fingers moving upon the strings. Buster, the Chief's dog, thinks the operation rather strange, but enters into the spirit of the occasion and even allows me to take his picture.

Another contingent of Boy Scouts arrives as I say goodbye to Madam Coline MacDougall of MacDougall.

---

[*] This barn has now been remodeled into an apartment.
[†] Ferrets were used to hunt rabbits. Miss Hope MacDougall of MacDougall told the author that once a ferret escaped and was found by the cook when she put her hand in the flour bin. Her screams brought Hope and her sister running. Past the kennel and across the roadway is another barn which has been made into a delightful cottage for the present caretaker.
[‡] Evidently this pump had not been used recently, for I was told that for a number of years it had been a nesting home for wrens.

Chapter 20
Weather

Window View

From this bedroom window in the Heatherfield, one looks over the slates and chimney pots of Oban's rooftops to the harbor, to Kerrera, and to the mountains of Mull. In a sense it is a restricted view—a framed slice of the wide splendor that surrounds one in the western Highlands—yet in this very limitation lies the advantage of focus. I shall sit here and record, as best I can, the ceaseless change of atmosphere, the varied manifestations of light that bathe this world, the nuances of hue, the procession of cloud forever sweeping westward, the advance of shower curtains, and the fanning of sun shafts through the casements of the mist.

The surface of the harbor is a silver-pink, roughed with gray. A cruise ship is returning, slicing the water with its black prow. Beyond the ship and beyond the gulls that wheel in the ship's wake and slide down the unseen banisters of the wind, lie the verdant hills of Kerrera, upheld on umber cliffs. The shore of this island is visible south to the white speck of the ferryman's cottage. Now as I watch, that white dot is all but lost in an advancing shower moving up the Sound. The shower spreads a filter of diffused sunlight—not hiding Kerrera, but rather superimposing a misty yellow upon the greens and transmitting from the ledges an ephemeral tint of red.

The mountains of Mull were not visible when I began to make these notes. Now they gradually appear from behind a screen of showers. These far curtains of rain are a soft gray, washed with rose. The heights are mauve. A range of peaks is swept clear. It stands boldly before a lemon world of distant cloud. In the passing of minutes the distant scene has changed, and the mountains are again lost in the sweeping mist.

The Sound of Kerrera fills with shaggy wreaths of wind-spread vapors. The rain reaches the window, and the gleaming slates of the rooftops reflect the sky. The harbor has become a steely gray, flecked with a suggestion of lavender cast from the heavy clouds passing above. Two sailboats, one with red sail, are tacking home. The grain field of Ardantrive Farm on Kerrera[*] reappears—a rectangle of yellow below the rising moor, which is greening in the returning sunshine as if spring were swiftly spreading on the hills.

Now the whole sky is an arch of light-filled clouds that pass a misty lavender between the gray-blue of their bases and their buff, rolling

---

[*] Ardantrive Farm was acquired by the Campbells of Breadalbane from the MacDougalls of Dunollie prior to 1751.

summits. Through a chasmed rift there shines a watery turquoise sky, pure and undefiled. Even as I look upward, the raindrops fall again upon the windowpanes. They join and rejoin to form rivulets down the glass.

I am thinking about Highland manners.

"Will you not bide a little and have a pancake? The tea is almost ready. Or would you rather a drop against the damp?"

There would follow talk of the weather, not because there is nothing better of which to speak, but because, truly, there is no subject more worthwhile. It is a sad race who has forgotten the elements that nurture both the land and the psyche. As Emerson—that grand American man of letters—said, "clouds, the bread of the soul."

A Wet Evening

[Edited from notes taped on site, 1994.]

Standing inside Dunollie's old keep, there is a fine wind blowing through the seaward openings—wet but not chill. What a glorious experience to be here on this wet evening. The wind is rising and probably is bringing a harder rain with it. I have never been here when the wind was whistling about this old hall as its does now. A flight of swallows wings past the tower like fall leaves driven. The ivy rattles like sleet on a window pane.

The rain sweeps in from Kerrera, and that world of sea and island is now lost in the grayness. *'Se oidhche fluich a th'ann a-nochd!* "This is a wet night!" A night for a fire in that great open fireplace, the kettle on the crane, and the windows fastened tightly.

Back at the B&B, I arrive with the front of my pants soaked from the driving rain. A few people still mill about Oban despite the night.

Changed into dry clothes and a sweater, I sit on the window box looking up Albany street at the car lights shining on the wet pavement. It is quarter past ten and some evening light still finds its way through the murk. The big boats are moored for the night. The harbor is a dull gray and all about is hung with wet cloud. A hot cup of tea at last.

Soft Evening

The evening seems to be quietly remembering this splendid day of piled cumulus floating above the hills of Lorn. The sun sets slowly over Kerrera; the soft ocean winds blue the harbor with their passing. From across Oban's harbor comes the deep ring of the Cathedral bells, and all around the birds are singing.

Kinds of Weather

A bit about the weather we have been experiencing—there are numerous kinds of "wet" weather here on the west Highland coast. There is "high-damp weather," when one can see most of the higher mountains, and "low-damp weather," when for instance the top of a hill like Cnoc Carnach is planed off flat. There is mist, slow rain, rain, and torrents. We have had all these, singularly and in mixtures, as this sodden weather continues.

Another variety of rain is waves driven before the sudden wind. Several times in the last half hour, here in the front bedroom of Glen Morvern House, has come a succession of moods—the weather almost clears, and then with a great rush the new stormlet smashes ashore, tumbling over the chimney pots and coming with dancing fronts of rain, across the slates of the house across the road, to slam into the windows.

Bright Morning

The sun is up and there is bright color everywhere. Fine breakfast.

Saint Swithin's Day

Nancy and Isabel Black are resigned to the persistant rain. It rained on Saint Swithin's Day (July 15th), and you know the old rhyme, "St. Swithin's day if ye do rain, For forty days it will remain."

Hail

It is a dramatic June day of sun and wind-driven showers. It seems what we would call "sleet" is termed hail in Oban. It hailed today, which reflects the temperature. The evening, while chilly, is clear as if God were starting all over again.

Snow on the Mountains

Astonishing how much snow remains on the deep clefts of the mountains in mid-May. Waterfalls are splashing down. Nancy MacDougall Black says the snow has lasted a long time this year.

Night

At 1:00 A.M. there is a spatter of rain on the window. A trawler made known by her two mast headlights and red sidelight is going down the Sound of Kerrera. Four flashing markers like great fireflies flash on and off toward where Kerrera must lie, and there, where the channel runs between island and shore, two more markers punctuate the blackness with their red warnings.

Sunset

We went up to Torwood, the home of Nancy Black. From her yard one looks down on Oban, rising in terraces of lights above the dazzled reflection of her waterfront. It seems a Mediterranean paradise. Nancy lives on the brink of sunsets. This evening, the west is a world of gold and pink, and the Sound of Mull is filled with the red aura of the setting sun. I wonder if in Lorn the weather saying about "red at night" holds?

Morning Mists

It is a gray morning of enfolding mists. History seems to have lost her way. As I walk down the Shore Road, there comes the pungent smell of coal smoke and, from beyond Kerrera, the deep-throated sound of a ship's horn.

Lightning and Landslide

A night of rain and storm. This morning, as we walk down to the Post Office, a bolt of lightning hits along the top of the ledge behind Albany Street. It is immediately followed by a thunderous cannonade and then a stunned silence.[*]

There has been a landslide on the railway line below Crianlarich and only one train is running today, and then only to that station. A bus will take us from there to Stirling, where there are rail connections to Edinburgh and Glasgow.

---

[*] In my experience, lightning is not a common occurrence in the Highlands.

Long Golden Evening

The evening continues perfect in its conception. We go for a drive in the last golden sunshine. Each mountainside is a pastel masterpiece of shadowed lavenders and lighted pinks. We stop on the road to Seil to look back at Cruachan rising a solid blue above the nearer hills, which are aglow with greens and russets from a last long light. The warm air passes around us filled with the smells of day—warmed earth and an aroma like heliotrope.

Kerrera in November

There is a slight breeze rippling the low swells that move up the Sound of Kerrera. A grand quiet rests over all, as if the earth were waiting and listening. There is a music in this stillness—a great counterpoint that the soul hears and knows. To the north, the mountains of Benderloch are swathed in cloud. To the east and across the Sound, the eroded uplift of mainland and the steeps of Dun Ormidal are clothed in the muted yet richly dyed colors of fall—the tawny red-brown of the bracken contrasting with the green of grasses and the burnished bronze and pastel yellows of leaves still clinging to the trees and bushes. Hope MacDougall tells me that this longevity of fall colors is rare. Usually the gales, breathing salt spume, wither and blow all the hues of fall away. So the world waits for the gales that will come.

Chapter 21
Glen Lonan

This is my last day in MacDougall Country. There is much I have not seen and one place in particular that I have wanted to visit. Always, when studying the topographical map of the Oban area, my attention has lingered over Glen Lonan, which lies within the heartland of Lorn and east of Oban—a place of ancient habitation through which threads the "Road of Kings." I have read that the family of Dr. Livingstone, the explorer, and the Highland forebears of Burns came from this glen. Whether or not this is true, I cannot say, but certainly many a member of our Clan family saw the first light of day—and the last—in this glen.

The morning dawns with rain drumming upon the skylight above the Heatherfield's upper hallway. This rain ceases, however, by the time I turn to the left from Combie Street and onto the road that leads up Glen Cruitten. This road begins at the base of the old shoreline cliffs. As the road climbs, the cliffs continue to the left, while on the right the links of Oban's golf course rise green upon green, interspersed with clusters of trees. The glen is at first suburban and well-manicured, but it becomes less so as one goes upwards and the hills close in.

The road to Glen Lonan turns off to the right at the top of the golf course, but I keep on to the head of the glen where the road and the railway line run side by side. I am not sure just why I have walked this way. One could, of course, follow the track toward Connel until one could see Loch Etive, Beinn Lora, its grand neighbors to the north, and the white sand arching around Ardmuchnish Bay, but I have no intention of doing so. I seem to be led by that natural inclination to follow this glen to its head as one might climb a mountain to its top. Here at the beginning of Glen Cruitten, the moor steals in upon the hot water taps, the electrical switches, and the glass storefronts of Oban. A twenty-minute walk from Argyll Square and one can be out upon the high, wild moors of inner Lorn.

Rather than retrace my steps to the Glen Lonan road, I take to walking the ties of the West Highland Line (this probably constitutes trespassing). I try walking the rails as well—a person has grown truly old when he or she does not try this stunt with outstretched arms and one foot placed just in front of the other. The rock cuts along the line are gardens. Every crevice is filled with crimson bell heather and buttercup. Above these lower flowers rise spikes of foxglove.

The railway crosses over the road to Glen Lonan just as the latter begins its steeper climb over the west side of Glen Cruitten. It would be difficult to find a road that provides a more pleasant walk. Beyond a roadside plot of yarrow sits an abandoned cottage, once white, but now graying to match the blackened doorway and the open windows. The roof is but partly covered with sheathing tins—ocher red with rust. Where there is no sheathing, the chuck frames show a skeleton that once may have supported a roof of thatch.

Once, this glen held a considerable agricultural community known as Balure.* Perhaps this abandoned cottage is a remnant of this settlement.

Two swans ride the still surface of Loch Coille Bharr, which lies close by the road. In their rippled wake paddles a gray-tufted "swanlet." The map indicates that the woods through which the road mounts is called Coille Dharaich which, I think, means "Wood of Oak." If this translation is correct, then the name no longer fits, for here is a fine, tall stand of spruce, fir, and Scots pine.

Now the woods are behind, and the road runs downward toward Loch Nell, still hidden by the hills. The road crosses a tapestry of green, olive, and golden-brown moor sweeping down to the white farmhouse of Barranrioch, which stands at the junction of this road and the highway running north from Loch Feochan to Connel on Loch Etive.†

The Road of Kings leaves the Connel Road, perhaps half a mile south of Barranrioch Farm. This byway runs eastward and threads its way through Glen Lonan. On this particular day, a small house trailer is tucked in the corner between the Lonan and Connel Road, and brightly colored laundry blows on a line tied between the little van and a clump of bushes. Several children are playing near the burn that tumbles under the roadway. They return my greeting with looks of suspicion. I wonder if there are still gypsies in Scotland?

---

* Oban as a busy port was a "late bloomer." Bleau's map of 1637 shows that what now is the low, flat area south of Argyll Square and west of Combie Street and the beginning of Soroba Road was a loch connected to the present bay by a tidal stream. Oban's first industry began there. The name Loch a' Mhuilinn, as this pond is called, indicates the presence of a mill. Southward there was the "township" of Glen Seileach, with its inhabitants being careful to build above the floodplain. East was the "township" of Glen Cruitten. In 1617, the Campbells of Dunstaffnage acquired Glen Cruitten, and later, Glen Seileach became part of the Duke of Argyll's Oban holdings. In 1760, the Duke had the custom house moved from Fort William to Oban. Through such influences, the coming of the steamboat, the romanticizing of the Highlands and islands, and the commercial ventures of such energetic families as the Stevensons, Oban quickly eclipsed and incorporated the surrounding "townships." See Charles Hunter's *Oban—Past and Present*.

† On the left before reaching the intersection is now located the Rare Breeds Park, which includes a number of interesting animals including red deer. There is a place to eat as well.

Chapter 21

The Road of Kings passes between the wide marsh through which Dig Bharrain finds its wandering way and the rocky swell of Meall Reamhar. Rising and dipping over the moor, the road reaches the flat plain at the head of Loch Nell. Across the grassy plain, close beside the road and just before the road enters the hills once more to follow River Lonan up the glen, there stands a great granite finger of stone. [4]

For a very long time this monument has been known as "Diarmid's Pillar." How often legends, arising half a world apart, use the same mechanics of myth to tell of human foibles! Diarmid was a great warrior whose body was immortal in all its parts except the soles of his feet. He had the passions of men, however, and unwisely fell in love with the lordly Fionn's wife, Grainne. [71]

Together, Diarmid and Grainne fled to Glen Lonan. Fionn found their bower, but being a crafty fellow, feigned forgiveness.

It seems that there was in those far-off days a huge fanged boar that roamed the Glen Lonan, laying waste both the land and the inhabitants. Fionn convinced Diarmid that, together, they should rid the countryside of this beast.

"Now," said Fionn to Diarmid when the boar lay dead upon the plain at the head of Loch Nell, "walk along the creature's back and pace its length, that there shall be no doubt in generations to come as to the size of the boar you have killed." Fionn knew that the boar's bristles were deadly poisonous, but he did not mention this fact to Diarmid. Up jumped the barefooted Diarmid and down he fell, dead. The great stone, so this story goes, was erected to his memory. [85]

That is the Celtic myth, but the true significance of the standing stones and the stone circles was known only to the men of the age of bronze who buried their dead in silent cairns and left us with a mystery.

Just east of the standing stone in Glen Lonan is the remains of a kerb cairn[3] once ringed about with large rocks among which the ancients scattered a quantity of quartz chips. Excavation has revealed that cremation was a part of the burial rite associated with this cairn.

Across the field and south of Strontoiller Farm, which sits among a group of trees at the head of the plain, is the only stone circle in mainland Lorn. Like the larger circle at Dunadd, a more descriptive term would be "boulder ring." The standing stone appears to line up with the two largest boulders in this circle. My pocket compass gave a rough bearing for this alignment of 165 degrees magnetic.

Beyond the level fields and the ancient monument, the road continues through the glen, skirting the steep sides of Deadh Choimhead and keeping close to the rapid river, first upon the north bank, then crossing to follow the south side.

Less than a mile and a half beyond the standing stone, one comes to Glenmachrie, a place with tantalizing legends. There is supposed to be a standing stone, but the only unusual stone I could find was about four feet tall and very near the road. According to tradition, the children who died at Dunstaffnage were buried here. If this is true, it would be fascinating to know why this spot was chosen.

Madam MacDougall has told me how many gates there used to be on this road through the glen when she was a girl. I have forgotten the exact number, but there were many. When out on a drive with their parents, Madam MacDougall and her sisters would scramble to see who would open and close the most gates. No money ever changed hands, but the tally was excitedly kept at a shilling per gate. Now there are no gates. It is open range, with cattle and sheep often sharing the one-lane passage.

A little beyond Clachadow Farm, I turn right and begin to climb the south heights, which wall the glen. Having gained some height, I recline on a cushion of moss above the Glen Lonan Road. Across the glen rises the fortress-like Deadh Choimhead. Hope MacDougall tells me that when she was young the graduating class from Oban climbed that craggy height as a celebratory outing. This too is a moment to celebrate. It has cleared for the moment, with a blazing sun and a stiff wind sweeping this hillside. I am partially sheltered by young spruce trees, but above, all around, and with the music of water rushing, there passes a clean, eager wind.

Now I am standing in the bright sunlight and wind, higher still above the glen floor. Just ahead a high valley runs to the southward. To my left, the heath falls away steeply into Glen Lonan, where the road is a narrow ribbon rising and falling northward between groups of cattle and the white dots of sheep. Beyond the glen range the Highland peaks of Benderloch, and beyond that the mountains of Glencoe. Swinging right, there are the sharp peaks of Ben Cruachan. Closer to hand, the east walling of Glen Lonan rises in a steep sweep of upland moor, mounting through outcroppings of ledge and rock to a jagged profile against the blue sky and tufts of white cumulus.

Here beside me, delightful groves of birches intermingle with spruce, providing glades of shadow and light. The omnipresent sheep graze in small groups. In the distance a cuckoo calls its oft-repeated benedictus, and a Gaelic phrase comes to mind, *glasadh na cubhaige*, the "cuckoo's greeting."

The clouds return as I retrace my steps down the glen. Crossing the level fields beyond the standing stone, I find a perfect seat on the first elevation above the plain and just south of the road. It is a rock whose top has apparently been chiseled in a concave arc. Here I sit and eat my lunch in the fine and steady rain. To sit dry and well content in a world of rain brings a wonderful feeling of self-containment. I have a large plastic bag over my lap, a hooded raincoat for a tent, and my pack sheltered between my legs.

The rain follows its own errand, and there follows another splendid transmutation—an expanding of horizons left overspread with a blue atmospheric filter. I leave the road again and climb Meall Reamhor. The climb is an easy assent between the quartz-veined outcroppings upon a hillside of heather, sedge, and fern, while sufficient rushes grow in the wet runs to light the rushlamps of the world.[86]

All the while, the sky is clearing and the view grows more exhilarating. I keep thinking (and reverently, too), "Oh Lord, how glorious will be the view from the top."

Upon the bald head of the Meall, the view *is* glorious! The full length of Loch Nell shimmers below, aquamarine behind a ridge of yellow broom. Southward there is the glint of Loch Feochan. Across Loch Nell, the sun brings vibrant life to the green hills while the cloud shadows pass, darkening with purple the ragged tors and cliffed hollows. North and eastward the Road of Kings mounts and descends the moor. The near hills are rich in ochers and golden greens. Their slopes are white-speckled with sheep. The folds of the hills are filled with dark woods. Here and there is the chimneyed gable of a farmhouse. Beyond, a patchwork of pastel shades softly blends into blues. The mountains of

Benderloch are sun-touched with pink. More distant, the heights of Morvern are a misty blue and a pale lavender where light floods the corried steeps. Here is MacDougall Country in all its spectral beauty.

It is actually warm. Back in Oban, the "change in the season" has filled the sidewalk and half the street with happy people. Who would have thought there were so many in this seaside town?

Chapter 22
Benderloch

The days encircled upon the calendar have run their rapid course, and my journey in MacDougall Country has, but for an evening, come to its inevitable end. It is the kindness of a clanswoman, Nancy MacDougall Black, that makes this last evening memorable. Nancy owns and runs a chandlery in Oban's Argyll Square.[*] Her shop is piled from floor to ceiling with fascinating gear. It is a busy place, and it was after a long day of work that Nancy took her evening to show me the land of Benderloch.

Nancy's MacDougall family left Oban in the fourteen hundreds[†] but, unlike so many families of the Clan, they returned. Her ancestors include the pipers of the Clan—champions of pibroch, composers, and pipe-makers whose craftsmanship produced instruments that have been likened in quality to the violins of Stradivarius.[24]

It is an evening that would have inspired these pipers, for the gentler spirit of the Highlands is upon the ocean and the land as we drive north toward Connel Bridge. The lowering sun is sweeping the hills with long shadows and rich radiance. The Firth spreads blue and sparkling to the islands, under a spectacular sky. The pale vault is crossed with high pink cumulus, while lower huge masses of cloud hasten inland—shaggy, blue-gray, and newly born at sea. Across Loch Etive, Benderloch is drenched with both sun and showers. The evening seems to be shouting Tennyson's lines:

> The long light shakes across the lakes
> And the wild cataract leaps in glory.
> Blow, bugle, blow, set the wild echoes flying.

We cross the Falls of Lora upon the old railroad bridge's narrow web of steel and drive north on A828 past the level and tawny Moss of Achnacree, dotted with lochans and with ancient cairns. The village of Benderloch is guarded by the high rock of Barr nam Gobhan. The ancient hill fort whose scattered remains top this rock is the stuff of which myths are made. Some say that this was a capital of the Picts, while others claim that here was Selma, the fort of the sons of Uisenach

---

[*] As of the second edition of this book, Nancy Black has retired, but the shop continues with the same name.
[†] The population of Glen Lyon in Perthshire was decimated by the plague. Ewan (John), seventh Chief of Clan MacDougall, sent some of his people to replenish the farms. See Lore of Lorn, Note 23, "MacDougall of Glen Lyon." See also Nancy Black's *From a Hollow on the Hill.*

who were heroes in the Ossianic sagas. We would think of Ossian again before the evening passed.

Just beyond the rock, we turn left to pass through Keil Crofts. The narrow road runs through a level countryside of fields that must have been one of the bread baskets of the Clan. As if in sign of fertile richness, an intense rainbow, matched by a second, higher ribbon of color, arches upwards from a golden field.

Beyond the solid tower of Barcaldine Castle[33] opens a splendid view up Loch Creran—a vista which ends with the mountain wilderness south of Glencoe. Among the farthest peaks, a beam of light illuminates the flanks of Beinn Fhionnlaidh and moves downward into a misty valley. Nancy stops so that I may photograph this view, with a foreground of foxglove glowing red in the light of the setting sun.

Rejoining the main road to Appin and Ballachulish, we drive beside Loch Creran. In every kelp-wreathed pool left by the retreating tide lies a molten reflection of the sunset fires in the west. Halfway up the loch, we turn inland on B845, which runs upwards through Barcaldine Forest.

These planted forests are changing the face of the Highlands in many places. The results may be closer to the Caledonia of our distant ancestors,[64] but the landscape will certainly be different from the naked moors that later generations have known, which give an open view on every side.

We talk of this change and of the old days of crofts before the emigrations denuded these hills and glens of hearth and thatch. Nancy's relatives, for instance, are spread across Canada, Australia, and New Zealand. Nancy thinks the fact that so many Highland families prided themselves in being able to read contributed to the continued exodus. Many Highlanders not only read, but wrote and received letters. Those who left the glens wrote of places where the soil gave livelihood less grudgingly and where one could own his own land. What Nancy is saying makes sense and must be added to the stories of the clearances and of the vanquished sold upon the indentured market. The majority of Highlanders did not come to the "new world" as beaten and bitter exiles, but rather as a people who folded their identity, their spirit, and their treasured memories of home in their tartan plaids and sought a land where one could stand with a warranty deed in one's hip pocket.

Those who remained seemed to the outsider terribly isolated, but they were often remarkably well informed about the world at large. Nancy met a woman in Skye who, in all her eighty years, had never traveled as far as Portree, yet she knew much about foreign lands and could converse with insight on current world events.

Chapter 22

A traveler through the glens could always find an open door and, if he or she brought news, a welcome indeed. Nancy's aunt used to walk seventy miles to visit relatives, and never did she want for shelter or for food along the way, nor for ready ears. She was an unusual person, but perhaps not so unusual among Highlanders as one might think. She had been a servant in the household of a laird, had traveled to France, and knew French and English along with her native Gaelic.

We descend Glen Salach with Loch Etive before us. The waters are wind-roughed and a deep blue, matching the clouds overhead. A last ray of sun, finding its way across the loch, shines orange on the distant houses of Taynuilt. Twilight is on the expanse of Achnacree Moss when we drive out upon the level plain to visit the great chambered cairn, which stands in an island of trees upon the wastes.

Above, the steep brow of Beinn Lora lowers. Fresh-cut banks of peat form black earthworks and, in the fading light, seem the habitations of the ancient ones.[3] At any moment it seems we might be encircled by some dark rite.

It has been claimed that the body of the Celtic bard Ossian was laid in the cairn of Achnacree,[88] but he is probably as much a myth as the sagas associated with his name. Regardless of its source, the legend of Ossian and of Tir nan Og (the "Land of the Forever Young") has struck a cord of imagination throughout the years. According to the tale, Ossian's gifts of song and verse won the love of Niamh, who washes her golden hair in a crystal spring amidst the bowers of that other land beyond the uttermost western sea. She is the fairest of all the fair in a land where death never visits and where old age never comes. To this place of joy and feasting Ossian was taken, but time and human longing had hidden in his sporran and troubled him so that he missed his home and the sight of his kinsmen. So Niamh gave him a wondrous horse to carry him over the sea. On his cheek she lovingly laid a kiss and implored him to remember that he must not touch his foot to mortal soil. But Ossian was overcome at seeing the changes that had come to his home during his absence. Youthful, he sprang from the saddle, and, as his foot touched the ground, old age wrinkled his body and left him lame, blind, and stranded in a world that had forgotten his generation.

We leave the chambered cairn to drive to the Ossian Inn on the shore of Loch Etive. There is laughter around the tables and a man playing old airs upon an accordion. The proprietor seems to me the epitome of a Highland host, though Nancy told me that he had been born on a tea plantation in Ceylon. He, himself, tells us that he would gladly wear the kilt if he weren't so thin. He moves with a quiet courtesy, making clever use of understatement, and serving without being a servant. There is humor in his conversation and, underneath, something sharper that had made acquaintance with the melancholy.

Nancy explains that we had been talking of Ossian, at which the proprietor produces a copy of the book over which scholars have debated for so many years.

"Its all in the introduction," he says.

Having read the section pointed out, I press him as to whom he thought the author might have been.

He laughs quietly, "I suspect MacPherson concocted the whole tale, don't you? A fine background he must have had in the old lore. Yes, it was probably MacPherson who spun the tale, but we make the most of Ossian here."

We come out of the inn to find a nearly full moon shining upon the waters of Loch Etive. It is a night of high, grand quiet permeated with the sweet scents of summer.

Chapter 23
Journey Epilogue

The morning is charged with sunshine. A cloudless vault rests upon the bluer mountains of Mull. The island of Kerrera rises from the sea rich in living greens. The water rippling against the hulls of the fishing fleet is a dazzle of reflecting color. The harbor front is a crescent of luster and shadow. This morning sings a carol. One can almost hear the words proclaiming: This too is Oban; this too is Highland weather!

The shops of George Street have not yet opened their doors, for commerce keeps decent hours here in Scotland. There are few abroad as I trudge to the railway station. The railway coaches are not crowded. Oban on such a morning is not a place that one would wish to leave.

With a rush for the climb up Glen Cruitten, the train rounds the southern outskirts of the burgh. As we thread the rock cuts at the head of the glen, the wind of our passing sweeps a spray of silver droplets along the crimson walls from one thick bed of bell heather to the next.

Now the familiar scenes slip past the heights of Benderloch and Etive still crowned with morning mist, the reverberating cliffs of Brander, the hillocks of Dalrigh, and the surrounding peaks of the Grampians.

A Gaelic admonition finds its way from memory to consciousness: *Cuimhnich air na daoine o'n d' thàinig thu*—"Remember the men from whom you sprang." It seems to me that this approbation contains a riddle, and as the train rumbles southward, I search for the answer. How are we to "remember" those whom we have not known?

My grandfather, when a small boy, must have traveled through this very glen when going north from Glasgow to spend the summer on his grandfather's Highland farm, but I never saw my grandfather Macdougall, for he died shortly after I was born. What I know of him I have been told—bits and pieces of folklore in the making. I can recall such stories, but I can't "remember" my grandfather. As for his grandfathers and my ancestors, the atoms that once commingled in their beings are now part of this place called Scotland. How can we remember those from whom we sprang?

My translation may be faulty. Perhaps this old saying should be rendered "Honor those from whom you sprang." Perhaps, but such a translation does not give answer to the riddle, for what substance does our "honoring" have when reality recedes with each generation into the mists of myth? There is a deeper enigma in all this. Within us runs a more subtle undercurrent that, though not adequately described as "remembering," is more significant than any sentiment embraced in the act of "honoring." There is an inner sense, a mystery that we, for all our analytical capacities, can no more explain than can the salmon as it swims from the borderless ocean back to the streams of birth.

What stirs us in our journey through MacDougall Country is neither a veneration of those long dead nor the memory of faces we have never seen, but rather the presence of the "communal they" within us. Is it not their shiver we feel running up our spines when we stand in their holy places beneath the burning stars? Is it not their courage as much as ours that surges when the *cath dath* (the fighting colors) pass? Why are we so moved as we kneel before the crosses broken in their wars unless it is that for us as much as for them the sky of a new dawn is forever seen through a dark tracery? When our spirits rise at the sight of the mist flowing upwards upon the mountainsides, is it our faith, and ours alone, that takes wing? Who among our kindred has not felt the communion with those from whom he sprang—the timeless haunting of the race—when the far call of pipes lingers in the evening lavenders?

For those of us who are of the extended family of Dougall, a journey in Lorn is an exploration in the syntax of the *present* within that context which is a continuum of the *past* forever moving onward into whatever *future* there shall be.

Humankind is always upon a journey of exploration and a journey in quest of belonging. We search for that fabric woven from both the past and the present and dyed with the essences of our own indwelling heritage. Every man and woman must find belonging in the shuttles passing through and back, weaving the sett of identity, not by the ell, but by the centuries upon the looms of his or her humanity.

Only as we discover the inner and outer wealth of our own belonging can we come to appreciate the inalienable right and the imperative need of others to take heart and pride and purpose in what is for them their own significance.

SUBSEQUENT SKETCHES

1987–1998

LOCHEN CRAIG NA CAILLEACH

Chapter 24
Blessed for a Second Time

Blessed for a second time, I am again journeying to MacDougall Country—that Highland world that long, long ago a poet described as a "lovely land to the eastward, Alba with all its wonders."*

The train is climbing its highroad from Glasgow to Oban. I wonder if the thrill felt during my first experience can be sensed a second time. Certainly the weather has no intention of assisting by casting enchantments. It is July, *an t-Iuchar* in the Gaelic calendar—the month of light and brightness—but this July offers, at best, watery glimmers in a summer that thus far has been so rainy that a MacDougall wit observed she couldn't see what Noah had to fuss about.

This weather does not welcome one at the gateway of romance but rather at the iron-bound door of reality, and I am grateful. It occurs to me that one must be on guard in Scotland against enchantments, for under the spell of the romantic and of the charming, one can miss the Highlands altogether.

Of course, one could do worse than enter and leave the Highlands by the gateway of romance. One could, for instance, end such a journey as did the urbane and clever Samuel Johnson, believing that "Seeing Scotland is only seeing a worse England." All the same, the best assurance against such a dismal waste of opportunity is to enter the Highlands with no "Brigadoon" illusions.

One must acknowledge that the riches of the Highlands are not those of the coffer-box or the larder. Passing the window of the railway coach is a country where the green layer of physical sustenance is thin—like a threadbare carpet often broken and showing a floor of stone. One can sense the austerity of this land passing by, and one can meet the naked truth face to face as it once came to me on the stony heaths of Degnish.†

No romantic caricature with which I am familiar serves to explain the Highlander's love for his homeland. Perhaps it was Matthew Arnold who best placed the poet's finger upon the pulse and the sinew of the Highland Scot—a spirit he described as a "passionate, turbulent, indomitable reaction against the despotism of fact." To feel such a stalwart reaction within oneself is to know something of the resonance between the Highlander and the "grim-splendor" of his homeland.

The "despotism of fact" dwells in the Highlands forever twined with a sublimity beyond description. The train labors northward amidst a

---

* *Lay of Deirdre.*
† See Chapter 14.

mountain grandeur—the sweeping, uplifting magnificence of the Highlands—where the creative command, "Let there be light," still reverberates between the dark crags. The far mountains are the color of ultramarine and those farther still, a cobalt purple. Upon the slopes there shines the tinsel of waterfalls. Close by, the hills are somber with earth colors until a shaft of sunlight, striking sideways and as a beam of faith, lays a swath alive with the radiance of an emerald on dark velvet.

Here is Alba with all its wonders under a mantle of ever-flowing mist and changing cloud. Clouds are as much a part of the Highland topography as are the hills. Of course, there are days that are cloudless—days when the landscape is bald—but the Highlands were not created for such "fair weather." They are stage sets for a more dynamic counterpoint of mist and rainbow, of dark cloud and coruscating waters. Consider *ceò*, the Gaelic word for mist; it has a double significance. The word also means "amazement." This evening is filled with amazement. Like wraiths of white dragons, the mist explores the secret recesses of the mountains and descends the corries as the ghosts of great waterfalls seen in the slow motion of another world.

The clouds do not clear as daylight grows dimmer. They part in ragged rifts to show the blue above. An unseen sun is burnishing those misty regions. Here close at hand, the woods and the moor are a nether world dimly lit by reflections from that higher realm above. From a cluster of trees on the far edge of the moor, windows glow with a homey warmth—shining from a lone house below the smoking mountains and the darkening sky.

I am surprised by the religious turn my thoughts are taking. Have I let down my guard and failed to keep the steel of logic, that blade of realism, between my mind and the enchanter? Is this some unexpected and more clever trick? Or am I realizing what in my excitement I had failed to fully comprehend during my first journey?

Here in this chiaroscuro land—this place of light and darkness, of grim-splendor—the Highland chalice is forever being raised in communion above the despotism of fact. I should have realized why Christianity took deep root here among a race of Gaels—those Gaels the English poet G. K. Chesterton, speaking half a truth, described as a race "that God made mad, for all their battles are merry and all of their songs are sad." Strange misfits for a gentle gospel, one might think, yet the Gael would understand a story of how a band of disciples once sang a song and went out into the night and how there dawned an Easter. The old Gael would understand, for he lived in a hard and stony land where eternal mystery is wrapped in the wonder and amazement of the mist.

Chapter 24

The train comes to a stop beside Oban's wooden station[*] in a dingy evening of palpable grayness. Across the rain-ringed water and as yet hidden by a dark slope rises Dunollie, high-seated above the sea. There, before the ruined tower, we shall stand on a new morning. We shall look outward upon a world of wonders—upon a new testament of beauty. We shall look upon the expanse of blue sea, fading to near-whiteness where the mountains of Mull rise to wall the horizon. We shall look to the world of cumulus where the Hebrides keep the rim of this Highland world. And the gulls will rise and turn into the wind with only the slightest tremor in the arch of their wings as they feel the unseen current that lifts them.

---

[*] Sadly, Oban's old wooden station was replaced in 1986.

Chapter 25
Artists and MacDougall Castles

Mendelssohn

In the early 1800s, increasing numbers of devotees to Romanticism were discovering the Scottish Highlands and the Hebrides. The solitude of the glens, the wildness of the crags, the sweeping dramas of light and shade, the ruined towers reflected in silvered lochs—all were seen as expressing (to borrow from Wordsworth) "something far more deeply interfused." Engendering this new enthusiasm for the Highlands were the poems and novels of Sir Walter Scott, the tour guides published on the wave of Scott's popularity, and MacPherson's Ossian epic. The latter had introduced a world of Celtic myth and heroes, all clothed in the bright mist of the Highlands, to an international audience. In Germany, Goethe, inspired by this epic, went so far as to learn a little Gaelic; while in France, Napoleon had scenes from the Ossian saga painted on his bedroom ceiling.

Ossian's epic was a favorite of Felix Mendelssohn's father, while his mother was especially taken with Scott's works. With such a background it was not surprising that the young Felix and a friend, Carl Klingemann, decided to make a walking tour of the Highlands. On reaching Scotland (the easier part of their trip), they set out on a necessarily round-about route from Edinburgh to Oban. This route can be traced through Mendelssohn's delightful sketches and the descriptions written home by these two adventurers.*

At that time, it was adventurous to tour the Highlands, and arduous as well. Sometimes these two young men rode in a carriage; often they walked more than thirty miles a day, and nearly as often in the rain. Mendelssohn wrote, "The weather is really discouraging. I've invented a new way of drawing specially for it, by rubbing in the clouds and painting gray mountains with my pencil."

They saw Birnham Woods, viewed the place where legend tells us Ossian sleeps by River Braan, explored the Falls at Bruar above Blair Athol, and found shelter in an inn at the Bridge of Tummel, where as Mendelssohn describes, "Wet trickles down the walls [while outside] the storm howls, rushes, and whistles; doors are banging and window shutters are bursting open." Near Aberfeldy, they bought a horse and cart and alternately rode and walked thirty miles to Crianlarich. The next day

---

* Sebastian Hensel, *The Mendelssohn Family (1729-1847) From Letters and Journals.*

they did fifty miles, often walking beside the cart as it bounced down the rough track through Glencoe. Klingemann describes their progress as

> ...stalking onwards through heather and moors and all kinds of passes...under clouds and in thick drizzling rain through the Highlands. Smoky huts were stuck on cliffs, ugly women looking through the window holes, cattle herds with Rob Roys now and then blocking the way, mighty mountains were sticking up to their knees...In clouds and looked out again from the top, but we often saw little.

Still and all, the passage through Glencoe was not completely disheartening. They made up a jolly song about Ballachulish in honor of the village from which they took a ferry and crossed Loch Leven. Their immediate destination was Fort William, where Mendelssohn, who was particularly keen on that new wonder called steamboats, hoped to take passage to Oban.

Perhaps it was the *Maid of Morvern* that took Mendelssohn and Klingemann down Loch Linnhe. The date was August 7, 1829, a day of magnificent sunshine. A fellow traveler provided a good deal of misinformation as they steamed into Oban harbor. He called the Dog Stone "Bruce's Rock" and then to add insult to injury confused the MacDougalls with the MacDonalds when telling how the Laird now "goes home with his ladies to a new house which stands behind the ruins of the old castle." It is there, they were told, that the silver brooch of Bruce is kept. (The Brooch of Lorn is now kept in a bank vault.) Here was the Highlands Mendelssohn had come to see. The resplendent sunshine continued, and his spirits were up.

Having several hours to spend before boarding the boat for Mull, Mendelssohn walked up the drive toward Dunollie Castle, climbed the crag on his right, and sketched the view that spread before him of castle, sea and islands. While it is unfinished, his sketch is remarkable in detail—including the flagstaff rising from Dunollie's keep (a feature in place until very recently) and the mountains of Mull and of Morvern correctly labeled.

This view and the trip across the Firth of Lorn to Mull were an inspiration. That evening Mendelssohn wrote, "In order to make you understand how extraordinarily the Hebrides affected me, the following came into my mind." There followed twenty bars, which were to become the principal theme of his *Hebridian Overture*. The visit to Staffa, that island of caves with which this overture has been so long associated, was still to come. It was not to be a pleasant occasion for Mendelssohn.

Mendelssohn Sketch of Dunollie
By permission of the Bodleian Library

The trip out to Staffa from Mull started out well enough. There were aboard, as described by Klingemann, "two beautiful, cold daughters of a Hebrides aristocrat" who seemed to Mendelssohn worthy of further notice, but unfortunately the trip took a dismal turn. The small vessel began to roll and Felix became very ill. This condition was not alleviated when the passengers were put off in smaller boats to be rowed to the island. Klingemann writes:

> We were...lifted by the hissing sea up the pillar stumps to the celebrated Fingal's Cave. A greener roar of waves surely never rushed into a stranger cavern—its many pillars making it look like the inside of an immense organ, black and resounding.

Mendelssohn made no sketches of Staffa or of Iona, which was next on the itinerary. He was feeling better by the time they returned to Tobermory; however, the passengers' discomforts were not at an end. The Captain decided to anchor for the night, leaving the passengers to sleep on deck as best they might. It was half past six on a rainy Sunday morning when they returned to Oban. Mendelssohn and Klingemann hired an open cart and left immediately for Inverary—as Klingemann put it, not wanting to listen to a sermon in the Gaelic.

Mendelssohn's happy memories must have been of the trip down Loch Linnhe, of the hour he spent sketching Dunollie, and of the trip out across the Firth of Lorn to Mull, all on that day when the *Hebridian Overture* first took life in his mind. Close your eyes and listen to that music. See Dunollie on its rock, see the clouds building castles above the mountains of Morvern and Benderloch. See their reflections in the Lynn of Lorn. Feel the expanse of sky and sea. Sense the light-filled distance, and hear through the genius of Mendelssohn the call of fairy horns from island to island in a magic Land of Lorn.

Turner

Nine years after Sir Walter Scott's staging of George IV's state visit to Edinburgh, which did so much to inaugurate the romaticization of the Highlands, J.M.W. Turner made the second of his two trips to Scotland. He came collecting scenes and impressions to be used in illustrating Scott's *Poetical Works*, and his destination was the western coast and isles, which he had not seen on the earlier tour.[*]

It was late on an August afternoon in 1831 when Turner approached Dunstaffnage from the east, having traveled from Glasgow by way of Inverary and Taynuilt. A contemporary of Turner once observed that one could recognize this great landscape artist by the pencil he always had in his hand. While this must be an exaggeration, Turner seems to have made sketches with the frequency that the avid tourist now snaps photos. His first sketch of Dunstaffnage shows this old MacDougall fortress all but lost in what Scott once called "gigantic scenery"—in this case an immensity of sky and loch, and a backdrop of mountains. In the next sketch we are closer to the castle (Turner, despite his penchant for working unobserved, would probably forgive this "we.") The next sketch is closer still, drawn with the descending sun appearing from below the edge of a cloud. Turner, the genius of light and color, is thinking watercolors, with his pencil noting the hues as he sketches. Inside the castle he draws a wide-angle view of the structures around the courtyard, and then, outside once more, he searches out a view from the southwest that includes both the castle and the nearby chapel. This sketch is engraved as the frontispiece of Scott's *Tales of a Grandfather*. His next objective was Dunollie.

---

[*] On Turner's first trip he sketched scenes along Loch Awe; however, he does not seem to have reached Oban.

Turner Sketch of Dunollie, 1831
By permission of the Tate Gallery

Scott had noted in the "Lord of the Isles" that "nothing can be more wildly beautiful than the situation of Dunollie [Castle].[*] The following day,[†] Turner sketched Dunollie from a number of perspectives: across the bay, where the castle appears in the background while people with their baggage disembark from a steamboat in the foreground; from the proximity of Pulpit Hill; and from a more distant perspective on the shore of the Sound of Kerrera. His close-up of the castle is the "classic view" drawn from where the war memorial and the small lighthouse now stand at the head of Oban's Esplanade. The sketch includes the Dog Stone, suggests the walled garden at the foot of the cliffs, and places Dunollie upon the top of that height of rock, deftly drawn with a master's economy of line.

Turner sketched the little mill that was situated on the shore of Carding Mill Bay just south of Oban Harbor and then crossed the Sound to Kerrera. He crossed the island to the old port of Bar na Boc (Barnabuck) and sketched the expanse of the Firth of Lorn with the mountains of Mull and Morvern rising and walling the west and northwest. It was, however, Gylen Castle that seems to have fascinated him. The guidebook he was using, *The Steam-Boat Companion and*

---

[*] Sir Walter Scott, *The Poetical Works of Sir Walter Scott*, Vol. III, "Lord of the Isles," p. 371.
[†] The author has not seen an account of Turner's daily itinerary and is making an assumption here.

Stranger's Guide to the Western Isles and Highlands of Scotland, may have stimulated his curiosity. Of Gylen the guide had this to say: "A small beautiful and picturesque ruin, perched on the extreme verge of an almost perpendicular precipice." Turner must have been impressed, for he did a series of twenty-five sketches of the castle, starting with his first glimpse of the tower as he approached from the west.

Turner Sketch of Gylen, 1831
By permission of the Tate Gallery

Gylen's spell captivated Turner as it has so many of us. While he appears to have been in a rush throughout this trip, and despite the fact that he was not physically well in this period of his life, he took his time at Gylen. He circled the castle and sketched from the high ground to the east and then, by an arduous descent, from the rocky shoreline. His sketch of the four sides of Gylen is extraordinary. The more one studies it the more one is astonished at the detail, the rendering of proportion, and the surety of execution.

One might wish that these sketches had been utilized to produce a watercolor such as Turner did of the rainbow over Loch Awe, or a powerful work such as his depiction of Staffa, but his sketches of MacDougall castles are too special to allow any regrets. They bring the viewer the sense of seeing these places for the first time, and they take us back to a time when the Highlands were being discovered anew and when romance did not feel it must walk between the dark, draped dwarfs of human disillusionment and materialism.

Chapter 26
The Avenue

Gate House - Dunollie

The driveway to Dunollie House is affectionately known as "the Avenue." That name dates from when the drive elegantly began with an impressive, hexagonal gate house situated on Oban's principal thoroughfare, just east of where Christ's Church Dunollie now stands.

Mrs. MacDonald was the last gatekeeper. She and her two daughters lived in this guardian tower, and one of them was always present to open the gate. Mrs. MacDonald was an interesting woman. She was supposedly related to Flora MacDonald, though (it was rumored) through an illegitimate connection. It was a fact that when one of her daughters played the part of the Highland heroine in a pagent everyone remarked on the resemblance. It was jolly Mrs. MacDonald who taught Jean and Hope, the daughters of the twenty-ninth MacDougall Chief, how to dance the *Dashing White Sergeant*, to *Strip the Willow*, and do the *Highland Fling*.

During World War II, countless eggs were gathered from the islands by the *Light Ship* crew and brought to the gatehouse. There the Chief's wife and other volunteers preserved them by rubbing them with butter and packed them for the troops. By that time the iron gates had been sacrificed to the scrap drive.*

---

* During and following the Second World War, the gatehouse fell into disrepair. When Madam MacDougall of MacDougall, thirtieth Chief of the Clan, inherited the estate there was no option but to dismantle this landmark.

From the gatehouse the Avenue ran north behind the present line of hotels to gracefully curve through an open grove of sycamores.* When the sun shines, one walks through a world of dappled light and shadow. The road crosses a small burn on an arched bridge with crenulated side walls, follows the base of the conglomerate cliffs that rise to the right, and passes through a cleft in the rock. Thus, the view of Dunollie House and the castle are delightfully delayed until one reaches that portion of the Avenue still serving as a driveway to the home of the MacDougall Chiefs.

From this point, the drive runs through a living nave of trees: towering beech, a mix of softwoods, and a large chestnut. Pink campion line the margins, and the white blossoms of wild onion spread into the shadows.† Light comes through the leaves as through the five green windows at York Minster. To the west, past the Dog Stone and a green field, vistas open to the Sound and Island of Kerrera and the mountains of Mull and Morvern. Ahead, Dunollie House is half hidden in its trees and shrubbery. Above it stands the old stronghold. And so one reaches a cattle grid and the "windy corner."‡ Another sharp turn, this time to the right, and one makes a gentle ascent to the house.

I had the privilege to help sweep this last section of the drive in preparation for the Clan gathering in 1994. The rhododendrons were opening their cone-like buds, the crimson azalea close by the old tennis court was already dropping some of its petals among the narcissus and the wild hyacinths. Adding its rich color, a golden chain tree was arching its yellow fringes beside the drive. We swept to a constant chorus of birds and the occasional startling call of a gull as it rode the river of wind inland from the sea, swept over the Avenue, and wheeled upwards along Dunollie's cliffs.

Four hens made a busy, pecking procession behind us. Miss Hope MacDougall of MacDougall remarked that we were stirring up "small beasties" for them to eat. In so many ways, the Avenue takes one to a world very much in contrast with the crowded streets of Oban.

---

* This section of the Avenue is a well-used footpath and a delightful walk.
† Nancy MacDougall Black remembers being sent to gather wild onion shoots to be put in the shoes of her sisters who had the whooping cough.
‡ Dunollie's promentory to the west and the cliffs to the east of the Avenue funnel the stream of air that flows inland off the long Sound of Kerrera. The result is the wind that gives this corner its appropriate name.

Chapter 27
Pulpit Hill

Morning

There is a moment in the celebration of the Eucharist when the priest lifts the chalice above his head in anticipation of a miracle. This is a morning of miracle—a moment to uphold the cup of one's being so that it may be filled with joy.

Last night was crowded with sweeping wind and a washing rain. It has left a world fresh and gleaming. Above the town the bright eastern sky is shining through the arches of McCaig's Tower. The milkman is about, clinking his empty bottles, and a few trucks clatter over the ramp and into the open maw of a MacBrayne ship, but it is early yet for Oban. The burgh still sleeps. I climb Pulpit Hill alone.

This morning I mount the stairs, which leave from Villa Road, through a chorus of bird songs and a sweet atmosphere of yellow azaleas. The stairs climb between walls of shrubbery filled with fluttering and music. Just ahead a chaffinch, russet and blue with white wing tips, pauses on a twig. And there is the song of a robin hidden in the thick foliage. Naturalists, in a *reductio ad mechanimum*, explain that birds sing to stake out their territory, but on Pulpit Hill in this miracle morning, amidst the rhododendrons and azaleas, the birds seem to be singing jubilation to the dawn.

Breathing hard, I top the hill and stand before the spreading magnificence. To the north and eastward, above the harbor and the terraced houses, the gorse of the high moor invades the town. It seems to soak up whatever light there is and to transmute it into gold.

A MacBrayne ship has just cleared the northern point of Kerrera and is heading westward across the wind-darkened Firth of Lorn. Its white superstructure gleams and then the ship passes into shadow. A moment ago it was nearly summer; now it seems early spring as wintry cumulus cover the rising sun. There are showers blowing in from the Atlantic and the wind is cold. I stand with my hands stuffed into my pockets.

From minute to minute nothing in the enchanted panorama is twice the same. The sunshine, when it returns, has a watery beauty and then is gone. Long veils of rain sweep inland—hanging gossamer curtains with a pale yet glowing rainbow trailing down the streamers of mist. And all the time, from the treetops below, come the songs of the birds.

To the west, at the entrance of the Sound of Mull, the island ferry again reflects the sun. The same shaft of light reveals Duart Castle on Mull's shore. The mountains of Mull are clearing except for a band of white mist that stretches across their tops, while northward the showers hide Morvern's heights, which but a short time ago stood out clearly.

There is a spatter of rain upon my back. A great raft of gray and mauve-touched cloud is passing overhead. I wait with my camera sheltered under my raincoat. Far over the Firth, the waters have taken on new life as a flooding of sunlight moves shoreward. It makes landfall on the crown of the Dutchman's Cap (that singular island just west of Kerrera), sweeps Kerrera with a living yellow-green, and then lights Dunollie's ancient tower. And now in a crescent below Pulpit Hill, gardens of azaleas shout with color. All around and up from below, the birds redouble their chorus.

Evening

After the rain and sleet earlier today, this evening has a pristine clarity as if the world were new. Before us is a view of gray and silvered sea, motionless and spreading between gray-blue islands. Below the brow of the hill, blackbirds and robins are singing from leafy layers descending to the town.

The harbor is filled with masts. A full-rigged ship is tied up at the old steamboat wharf and a bark is moored to the railroad pier. Oban delights in playing with time and in mingling one era with another. The new lighthouse tender has just arrived at her birth below Pulpit Hill. High above the harbor, merging past and present, Moira MacKenzie has been watching her husband bring his ship to port.

Mrs. MacKenzie was born on Uist. Often there is a special quality about these women from the Outer Hebrides—a beauty created by a blending of the Celt and Norse. And something more enchanting—a natural grace, a kindness of manners, and a laughter in the voice like the melody of a gentle little burn filled with the pure waters of the mist. Moira MacKenzie makes one feel that one has been invited out of the chill and asked to sit a moment by the fire.

She went to college in Glasgow and then returned halfway to her birthplace to work in Oban at the office of Leslie Grahame MacDougall, architect and husband of the thirtieth Chief of the Clan.

"He was a real gentleman," she says, and then she is away, intent on having supper hot for her husband.

Alone, I watch the vast evening draw its cloud curtain about the day. There will not be one of those famous Oban sunsets when the whole Firth of Lorn is a punch bowl beneath a flaming sky. Instead, as the poet Browning once described, "the quiet-colored end of evening smiled."

The Sound of Mull filled with an atmosphere of pink-gold light. Duart on its distant headland was silhouetted against this glowing world.

At about half past nine, the last red spark of the sun appeared through a narrow slit in the clouds and then disappeared behind the mountains of Morvern. For the moment that spark lingered, there was a burnished path of light seven leagues across the Firth, and then the wide waters were left a blue-gray and once more were traced by the silvering paths of wind and currents.

The "Lismore" light blinks.[*] Mull's mountains are blue cut-outs seen against a smoky rose that fills the west. Dunollie stands dark against the sea, and the expanse of water from this Highland coast to Morvern's distant mountains lies silent below a vast firmament of cloud.

---

[*] Although the light is actually on Muisdale, the locals call it the Lismore light.

Chapter 28
Lismore

The Fire Knoll (Cnoc Aingeal).

Alastair Livingstone is a wise guide and a kind gentleman. He has clambered up rocks to find another flower to add to my sister's list, pointed out the plover flying above the moor, searched for a very special orchid, and scrambled to find the last primrose. Now he has brought us to an ancient and special place, Cnoc Aingeal, the "Fire Knoll."[*]

The Royal Commission on Ancient and Historical Monuments classifies the Fire Knoll as a cairn—a very large cairn, as it rises to a height of some twenty-four feet. Shaped in a rounded cone, the Knoll is obviously piled by human hands from corbels and rough stone.[†] The Knoll is partially grassed over and, on the summer day we climbed it, profusely decorated with white daisies. A dry wall fence of much more recent origin passes over the top, and by the wall we stood amazed at the surrounding panorama. To the south one can see Achadun Castle and, swinging clockwise, up the Lynn of Morvern flanked to the west by the mountain wilderness of Morvern, across the silver reach of Loch Linnhe to the blue masses of Glencoe's mountains, beyond to Ben Nevis, down the mainland coast of Appin, past Tirefour Castle and Lismore's remarkable broch, and so back to Achadun.

Surely it was to create such a vantage point that so much labor went into piling this huge cairn. On this high spot where we are standing may have been built the bonfires of religious festivals during peace and a warning signal beacon during war. *Aingeal* is a Gaelic word used to mean "fire," "messenger," and "angel." One thing is certain, we stand amazed by this full compass of beauty, as did those humans who worked so hard to build this giant cairn.

Lime and the Appin Ferry

Look at a map of archeological sites or ecclesiastical remains along the western coast of Scotland and you will find Lismore richly endowed. There are also many places of historical interest that are not all that old. One of these is situated at Port Ramsay on the northern tip of Lismore. Port Ramsay is the finest anchorage on the island. On the day we visit, the harbor lays glassy calm, sheltered by islands scattered with large

---

[*] See Map 4, p. 275.
[†] In their second authoritative archeological volume on Argyll, *Lorn*, the Royal Commission suggests that the Knoll may have been erected around some natural outcropping.

trees and covered with a bower of blossomed shrubs. Close to the shore is a line of connected cottages—all copies of their neighbors, with whitewashed walls and black slate roofs. These were originally the housing for the workers of the nearby limestone quarry and the lime kilns. The cottages are now occupied by summer folk.

Two ferries serve Lismore—one from Oban, and the other from Port Appin across the seven-tenths of a mile of the Lynn of Lorn to the very tip of Lismore. The north end of Lismore features hills of no great height but they are often abrupt, and the road to the ferry winds downward to the Lynn and its many islands. The ferry is an open boat with an inboard engine and a long-handled tiller. A canvas screen rigged in front of the cockpit gives some protection, though two passengers get a lap full of water when a wave slaps over the gunwale. The boatman and his helper are stalwart fellows, with weathered faces protruding from under hooded oilskins. The helper has a full beard. It takes little imagination to travel back a thousand years and see two Vikings standing at the tiller.

Chapter 29
Gallanach

Invited to Gallanach

[Taken from journal notes, 1985]

As we let ourselves through Gallanach's gate, the taxi driver, with a touch of nervousness, asks if we are expected. None of us anticipates the reception that is waiting. At the second gate, an old man, short and stocky, straightens up from his ditching spade, knuckles his forehead, and stands watching us swing open the gate.*

There is the sound of the Highland pipes as we drive up to the front door. Our taxi driver later remarked that very few have the privilege of such an experience. He is right. There atop the battlements of Gallanach House, against the sky and before the ringing hills of Gallanach stands Major James' handsome and kilted son piping us in.†

Marie Claire, the Major's vivacious and delightful wife, meets us at the door. We learned later that she was very busy that day preparing for a sale to raise money for the local Life Boat Unit, but nothing seems to hamper her kindness and attention. The Major joins us in the high-ceiling drawing room. He is tall man with a suntanned face and a gray, closely trimmed beard—rather as one might picture a Highlander.

I like him immediately, and more so as our visit continues. His reserve serves to accentuate his wit, and he is frank even about his ancestors who spent themselves into financial problems building Gallanach House. From 1939 until he retired in 1959, the Major served in the Royal Scots Fusiliers. During World War II, he saw duty in Madagascar, the Far East, Middle East, Sicily, France, Belgium, and Germany. From 1954 to 1957, he was stationed in Malaya. The latter was a terrible place. In a rare reference to his military experiences, the

---

* I met this man again when I was walking along the drive. We had a few words about the amount of water. Then quite suddenly, he gave me a side-cast smile and his hand.

† In 1987 the author's family traveled to Lorn, and again we had a gracious invitation to visit Gallanach. As we drove up the curve of the gravel drive, Major James Williamson-MacDougall came out to meet us in his kilt. As he did, there came the music of the pipes as if carried on air from out the past. "There are your pipes," greeted the Major, pointing to the top of Dun Ormidale. At the edge of that great bastion of stone, a piper was silhouetted against the sky and cloud. Again, Charlie MacDougall was playing us in and filling the amphitheater of Gallanach with music born of the clifted mountain and the misty sky. Marie Claire, her pretty daughter, and her two grandsons joined us and we listened together.

Major described wading in a swamp where snakes and sniper fire combined their deadly effect. He was wounded three times and awarded the Military Cross for bravery.[*]

A life in the military has been the lot for many of his ancestors. One commanded the Royal Scots at Waterloo. His sword and medals are in a glass case. When I comment on a photo of a soldier wearing a canvas apron over his kilt, the Major responds that the man is his father and adds that the apron was an invention of the Boar War. It was designed to cover the bright regimental sporrans, which were being used as targets by the enemy with devastating results.

The Major is a working laird, with some one thousand sheep and problems galore. His last shepherd proved to be a slovenly chap and had to be dismissed. On top of labor problems, the wool market fluctuates and holds the producer at its mercy. There are deductions for dirty wool but no refunds for substandard shepherds. His wife works with seemingly ceaseless energy. She makes jams for sale from produce raised in a large garden and sees to the holiday guests who rent the old servant quarters.

Amidst all this work, a fine dinner had been prepared and the table spread in the dining room. A chocolate mousse and a lemon trifle sets the ladies to talking recipes, while the Major takes those interested into the billiard room to see the original order of General Wade demanding that all the "tribes of MacDougalls" surrender their arms.[†] Obviously, this order, despite its impressive royal coat of arms and seal of authority, was not entirely effective, as MacDougalls led by the Chief's brother joined the Rising of 1745.

The billiard room also has an instructive feature for those of us who visit Argyll during the milder months. A paneled alcove with a huge fireplace can be enclosed by drawing curtains. The Major tells us that it is a pleasant place of seclusion away from the winter's damp and chill.

Before leaving Gallanach, we walk down to the remains of a tenth century fort situated on a finger of rock that reaches out into the ocean. Behind us and to one side rises silent ramparts and before us the ocean rolls in. The bay just to the north of the old fort is called Cuthaich Port, the "Mad Bay," because there are always sea sounds there even when the waters are calm.

---

[*] I was to learn the latter from his obituary.
[†] This proclamation is dated 1723, and was found folded in a book at Ardtornish Castle and given to the archivist J. Peterson-MacDougall around 1902.

Gallanach and Iain Ciar's Cave

Fortified by a magnificent tea, two of my sons, Malcolm and George, Major James of Gallanach, and myself set out to visit one of the caves in which Chief Iain Ciar may have hidden, a fugitive in his own land. We go down through the chicken yard with the red hens clucking and converging upon us. *Gallanach* means "wild rhubarb," and the Major wants to introduce us to this plant, which grows in profusion at the bottom of the hen yard. It reminds me of American burdock without the burrs.

Having made the wild rhubarb's acquaintance, we strike out along the rocky shore below the cliffs and talus slopes of Ard na Cuile.* This is a wild coast where the Atlantic swells rise darkly among the boulders, turn a pale green upon the ledges, and recede in a tumble of white froth. One could well be stepping into the world of a Scott novel—a wilderness coast frequented by smugglers in a world apart from the law. And such an impression is not all fantasy. There are smugglers about, and Major James met two suspicious characters not long ago nor far from this spot. This afternoon a small boat with a powerful outboard motor bounces across the swells heading for a group of lobster buoys. The Major keeps his eye on the boat. There has been lobster "rustling" going on as well as drug trafficking.

It is easy to envision that we are on patrol—I always travel with a Stevenson-like adventure brewing in my imagination, and I hope my boys will do the same—we are a single file of MacDougalls led by the Major in his kilt of muted tartan.

Our path is no more than a sheep track, the makers of which are feeding along this rock-strewn shelf between the sea and the cliffs. One comes up to us. "Bottle-fed as a lamb," explains Major James. "They never go quite wild."

We make our way around, down, across, and up over the cleaved slabs of stone and the tumble of broken boulders. Now our path is largely barren except where it enters a patch of waist-high bracken—"useless stuff," the Major says. Perhaps a mile below Gallanach House, as the raven would fly, is a large bay that lies partially protected from the sea by a craggy point covered with large stones, hunch-shouldered like a silent convention of spell-bound trolls. The bay, Port na Traigh-linne, is backed by a steeply rising beach of corbels well-rounded by the relentless wash of the sea. High on the beach is a driftwood log battered white except for a black charcoal scar. Someone has lit a fire—probably one of the major's guests, such as the fellow presently fishing in the deep

---

* The "Heights of the Rocky Corries" is a fitting translation. See Map 3, p. 274.

pool at the foot of the beach. The Major calls down to this fellow, asking the fisherman if he has had any luck, but the angler's back is to us and a yell is lost in the sound of the grating cobbles and the surging sea.

Having rounded the bay, we make our way precariously along the top of the cliffs, which plunge to the ocean. To our left, the talus slopes sweep upwards to a wall of perpendicular ledge split by deep crevasses. Major James tells us that once one of these deep breaks in the ledge secreted an illicit whisky operation. From the top of the crag, the revenue cutter could be spotted as it left Oban Harbor. There was time to dampen the fire and hide away the spirit-making apparatus. Major James knows the way up through the crevasses to the top of the crags. But no matter how well one knows this country it remains dangerous and tricky, especially when the thick Highland mist and fog comes rolling and wraps one in a directionless world. This happened to the Major once.

There is a large sea stack just to our right whose south side has the profile of a man with a large mustache. We are, at the moment, skirting the edge of a great gash in the rock, between whose vertical and narrowing walls the ocean swells mount and surge inward to break resoundingly at the end of the chasm. Just beyond the sea stack, we climb around a ledge to find a cliff wall facing southward and, in its base, a natural rock shelter. At the extreme west end of this shelter there is a small cave. It is like a side pocket but large enough to hold two men. Significantly there is a "squarish" rock on the floor of the cave that makes a good seat. We all take our turn occupying the cave and sitting on the rock seat.

Major James feels that Iain Ciar, the exiled twenty-second Chief of Clan MacDougall, used this shelter during the time he braved capture and possible execution to be near his wife and his home.[*] It seems a likely hideaway, so perhaps it was from here that Iain Ciar rowed across the Sound of Kerrera to visit his long-suffering Mary.[†]

From where we are standing, in front of the rock shelter, the southern tip of Kerrera lies a mile to the westward across the steel-gray sea. It would be a hard row as tidal currents run strong, and it would be dangerous were fog to suddenly materialize. Major James had a relative who went fishing down the Sound. The fog came in and when he finally

---

[*] The MacDougalls of Gallanach did not join the Stuart cause in 1715. However, they certainly turned a blind eye to having the exiled Chief of the Clan hiding on their lands and were probably a major source of his support while he was there.

[†] By this time, Dunollie was occupied by government troops and Mary was living in a cottage on Kerrera not far from the burned-out shell of Gylen Castle.

landed, he was on the island of Mull. It could have been worse—he could have missed Mull and found himself bobbing in the open Atlantic.

On our return trek, we traverse the steep talus slopes, considerably above the way we have come. To our left, the level expanse of sea stretches away to the blue mountains of Mull, while the high arch of the sky rests on steeps to our right and high above us. It is a world of wild grandeur and of history this man of quiet humor is showing us. One feels in him the strength of our best forebears.

Our way takes us close to another cave associated with Iain Ciar. It is situated high up in the clefts of the crag and at the top of the talus. But Major James reports that what appears to be a hole in the cliff, on close inspection, does not seem a sufficient cave to house a fugitive.[*]

Back in that bay with the cobbled beach, we are shown a spring and a rowan tree in a level area. The Major thinks a house was probably here at some time. From this site, a steep-sided valley opens, rising northward in the direction of Gallanach. It has another interesting name, Bealach na Nighinn or the "Pass of the Maiden or Daughter." Whose maiden or whose daughter? one wonders. Near the head of this valley and rooted in the talus slope stands a lone, spreading sycamore.[†] Beyond this tree, we come to a place where we can look down on Gallanach House. The descent is through an open woods and across the fields behind the house. Such a dry pasturage does not occur naturally. There is a network of stoned-up drainage tunnels below our feet. The Major shows us where one such tunnel is caving in. We can hear the water trickle below the broken sod.

On leaving Gallanach, Charlie MacDougall of Gallanach pipes us out of the yard. A stirring finale to a grand adventure.

---

[*] Hope MacDougall of MacDougall writes that there was a tradition of a third cave near Lerags on Loch Feochan. Due to a rock fall, this possible hiding place is no longer much of a cave. It is likely that Iain Ciar moved about while in hiding and that he occupied more than one cave.

[†] This is not an uncommon sight—some combination of root-hold and protection from nibbling sheep.

Chapter 30
From Loch Gleann a'
Bhearraidh to Gallanach

[Transcription from tape-recorded field notes, August 1998]

Astride the wind, the rain has been carried off. The sky returns to its tattered clouds and fragments of blue sky. I am standing above the western margin of Loch Gleann a' Bhearraidh.[*] Looking north, there are the mountains of Benderloch. Swinging to my left, there are high, sculptured hills. The loch swings around in a fishhook shape, and I have to go west and south to round this gray sheet of water before I can start up the pass to Gallanach.

A group of sheep are watching my slow progress through the high bracken, which is mixed with nettles. The side of my hand burns from an encounter. A curlew is whistling. Several streams flow down the rough hillside on the south end of the loch; I can hear their tumble down the steep ravines.

At last, I reach the south shore, having forced my way through bracken that was over my head in places! Looking north up the "shank" of the loch, the Mountains of Benderloch (or perhaps Morvern) are nearly lost in the mist. This seems like the beginning of the steep pass that leads to the rounded notch and down to Gallanach. There is a sizable brook falling through a cleft in the rock to the east, and a good place to spread out a plastic bag on a rock and eat my lunch—a rich fruit bread, water, and an orange.

Walking toward the burn, my leg suddenly sinks into the ground up to the knee. I am lopsided and amazed. Retrieving my leg, I find that one can trace an underground brooklet by its hollow and the hidden babbling until it joins with the larger burn.

Heading up the steep valley, there is a light lavender cast of heather on the ridges. There is the sound of the wind's passing and the continual falling songs of the burns. Here again is the underground brooklet welling up from hiding in a miniature fountain.

This seems to be the old track used to haul peats to Gallanach. Underfoot, deep sphagnum moss is saturated like a sponge. Here is the skull of a sheep. I come to a waterfall of about twelve feet. Its peat-stained water pours over a rock face. Bell heather is growing in profusion along with the ling wherever there is a foothold in the ledge. Looking back through a notch, I can see the sea somewhere above Oban and the mountains to the north.

---

[*] See Map 3 on page 274.

I near the top of the pass. Wind-driven rain is sweeping over the top. It is funneled and pelted through the notch. Mist mixed with rain is blowing in successive curtains past me as I stand sheltered behind an outcrop of ledge. I hope this does not settle in and obscure the view waiting at the top.

This is clearly the old track, and I think I am about to reach the point where I shall be looking down into Gallanach Park. The round notch is just ahead. What a thrill! I have seen this notch so often from Gallanach. And since sighting it eighteen years ago from Loch Gleann a' Bhearraidh, I have wanted to come this way. And here I am, praise be to God.

Now I am looking southward down through a steep ravine and out over the ocean toward the Holy Islands. The view draws one into itself. I start down into the huge cup that holds Gallanach House, finding the track and losing it again in the bracken. The view remains magnificent—the sea breaks white on every shore and rock. On my right, I look down on the entrance to the Sound of Kerrera, and on the left, to the gray tallus slopes sweeping up to those creviced ledges that circle Gallanach. In the foreground there is a lone pine tree and a red-berried rowan, both set before the sweep of ocean and the distant islands. The sky has not cleared, but it is dry with a high cloud cover. Now I hear the throb and beat of the ocean rolling in. The sea is a light blue sheet, quilted with whitecaps. On the horizon is a line of white mist. At last, I see the towers and gray block of Gallanach House sitting in its green basin.

By a fence and gate, the heather purples the shoulder of hill and a rowan tree leans outward over the steep drop. There is a lovely patch of ling mixed with bell heather, and in the midst of this profusion of blossoms, a true bluebell. The gate is securely tied, with a sign that this is not a public thoroughfare. I climb the gate and start down the curving track through the stumps of what Major James once told me had been a juniper forest that was sacrificed to make posts for mines during World War II.

Major James drives in as I ring the front doorbell. He has three dogs with him—two large black retrievers and a very friendly and excitable black and white sheep dog.

"Do come in," the Major says.

Chapter 31
Crossing Mull

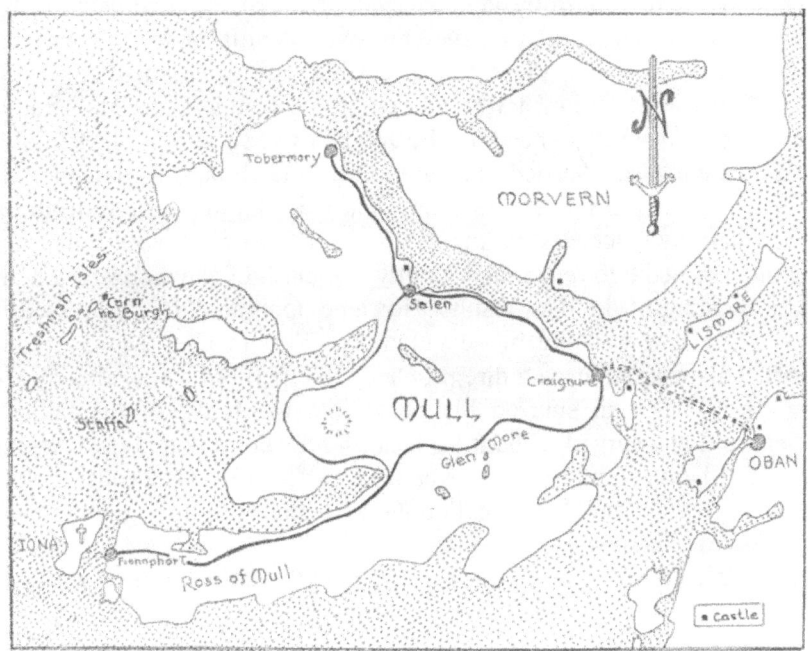

Via Glen More

H.V. Morton, who spent several days wandering over Mull back in the early 1930s, described the island as a solemn and beautiful place.[*] Morton wrote "Iona has made the sign of the cross over Mull...I feel that a man might meet an Irish Saint, his sandals brushing through the drying heather." Beautifully written; yet I would envision such a meeting on Iona itself rather than Mull. The chances are better, or so it seems to me, of encountering a blind catechist with the butt of a pistol protruding from under the folds of his ragged coat, as did David Balfour in his journey across this island.[†] A Celtic world lingers in Mull, especially in Glen More (*An Gleann Mòr*).

Mòr in Gaelic signifies "big," and Mull's Glen More is big. Its expanse commands the eye. In its great hollow, the rivers Lussa and Coladoir gather the waters from innumerable burns. The Lussa flows eastward and the Coladoir west down the full length of the glen to the sea. On both sides of this river the valley floor sweeps upward, matching

---

[*] H.V. Morton, *In Search of Scotland Again*.
[†] See Stevenson's delightful description in *Kidnapped*, Chapters XIV and XV.

in reverse the great vault of the sky. Glen More is open—open as if nothing could be hidden from something that is watching.

It has been claimed that, mile for mile, there is no place in the Highlands more plentifully inhabited with tales of the supernatural than Glen More, which means that such tales are plentiful indeed. Riding the night winds, so it is told, is Eogan a Chinn Bhig, "John of the Little Head." Just what was meant by this epithet is now immaterial, for John the ghostly rider has no head. In life John was younger son of MacLaine of Lochbuie. He married an ambitious and beautiful daughter of MacDougall of Lorn. His wife's ambition led John to ask more from his father than the latter was willing to give. A rift grew between father and son that ripened into rancor and, finally, the clash of claymores. But John had a warning of the fatal results. He came upon an old lady dressed in green. She was washing bloody clothes in one of Glen More's many burns. This women made a dire prophecy, but perhaps it was already too late. In 1538, John spurred his horse into the midst of his father's adherents and emerged without his head. John's horse bolted on, carrying away the body of its master. Over the years, horse and headless rider have been seen and heard galloping in vengeance through the wide darkness of Glen More.

There certainly is a presence of the grandly natural in the great glen of Mull. On this day there is the promise of clearing. From the lip of a nearby ridge, a waterfall plunges into a hollow to reappear tumbling white among the rocks. Its broken path is embroidered with crimson bell heather. Above, the mist passes. Its falling tresses explore the cliff face and, condensing, fill a dark chasm with whiteness.[*]

West of Craig, Glen More flattens. The Coladoir runs seaward, gay with white cataracts, spilling under the twin arches of a fine stone bridge. Beyond the bridge, its final rush completed, the river wanders to Loch Scridain. North of this coastal plane rises Ben More—a blue pyramid topped with cloud. Once a volcanic giant, Ben More still reaches 3169 feet. As one travels down the Ross of Mull, the dark basalt, in up-thrust masses like the remains of primeval forts, gives way to a granite of a contrasting rich pink. The few buildings at Fionnphort are set amidst outcroppings of this stone, which is mixed with patches of olive green sedges and clumps of bell heather.

We arrive at Fionnphort in a moment of bright sunshine. The cottage above the jetty is gleaming white against the background of color-swept water—wines and liquid greens, with a streak of surf over the bar midway across the Sound of Iona. There is the cry of gulls and the

---

[*] See Chapter 43.

rhythmic pulse of the sea washing in and out between the red granite blocks. Across the Sound, Iona's dark dun rises below a shower-filled sky. The Abbey looks small from this distance. It is like an altar set in a cathedral of sea and islands.

A sudden shower sends us into the eatery. As we sit drinking tea and eating sandwiches, my wife suggests that perhaps we should be aboard the ferry that is now halfway to Iona. No matter, the ferry makes frequent trips. Life is too short to hurry; especially here, overlooking the Sound of Iona.

Having spent the greater part of the day on Iona, we recross Mull with the long light* of the descending sun at our backs. Under these conditions, one sees a different Mull. Showers and a vivid rainbow arching over the road and ending in Loch Scridain precede us. In Glen More, the grasses and sedges are bent, both from the wind and from the weight of the newly fallen rain. The moor has a silver sheen as it sweeps down to Loch Airdeglais and Loch Squabain, and there the silver spreads across these waters cupped in the mountain shadow. The bare top and cliffs of Beinn Fhada are flooded with the yellow light of the dropping sun.

It rains as we board the Caledonia at Craignure, and then clears as we leave the pier. Another rainbow climbs over Duart Castle. Across the cobalt water to the north, the Eilean Musdile Light is a shaft of shining white. Beyond and up the Lynn of Morvern, Achadun Castle is silhouetted on its headland.

Now the sun is hidden behind dark cumulus with molten edges. Below this bank of cloud there spread curtains of fanning sunbeams, which touch the sea and turn the waters gold. Thus, "trailing clouds of glory" we return to Oban.

Via Tobermory

[In 1990, through the great kindness of Nancy MacDougall Black, my two sisters, Leah and Jean, and I had the privilege of being driven across Mull by way of Tobermory and of spending the night on the sacred island of Iona.]

In this land of ruined castles, smoke still rises from the chimneys of Duart, that prominent guardian at the entrance to Sound of Mull. It is the home of Sir Lachlan Maclean of Duart and Morvern. At scheduled times it is open to the public, and a visit allows one to step back in time and experience what Dunollie and Dunstaffnage were like before they

---

* See Tennyson's *The Princess*: "The long light shakes across the lake, / And the wild cataract leaps to glory..."

became empty shells. In particular, Duart's kitchen and domestic quarters display the old fare and practices.

The earliest mention of Duart dates from 1390, but its original structures are much older than that, especially the rectangular curtain wall, which was thirty feet high and nearly ten feet thick.[40] The castle was bombarded by English ships rather ineffectually, but increasingly fell into ruin after it fell, along with the lands of the Macleans, into the shrewd hands of the Campbells. In 1911, the Chief of the Macleans and his wife, with the support of Macleans from around the world, began restoration. At the castle are photographs taken at the commencement of this undertaking. These attest to the task the rebuilders faced.

From Duart we travel northward on route A849, which closely follows the shore of the Sound of Mull. At Salen Bay, halfway up that water passage, Aros Castle[32*] is strategically placed at the mouth of a river that bears the same name. It stands on a grassy knoll spangled with buttercup and atop a conspicuous headland of rock. There is a fine view from Aros. From the battlements one could have watched westward up the full length of the Sound and eastward until the view of its broad silver path is hidden by blue mountains. From the castle hall, through a large window with a pointed arch, one could have looked across the Sound's historic passageway and watched the galleys come and go. Few features of Aros remain, other than that window opening in the ruined wall.

The town of Tobermory faces its harbor and the sea, its reason for being, with a bright face—a solid row of stone buildings, their backs to the island cliff and their fronts painted pink, yellow, and light blue. In the MacDonald Arms, the local pub, we find a wonderful map hung upon the wall that portrays the west Highland Coast and the Hebrides. The clans' old territories are delineated, while around the border in resplendent gold leaf are arranged the full arms of the major clan chiefs whose galleys once plowed the Sound of Mull. History has often anchored here in the sheltered harbor of Tobermory.†

From Tobermory we take B8073, which crosses to Dervaig and from there winds on to Calgary Bay. The narrow road skirts Loch Tuath and Loch na Keal, and finally cuts across the mountainous peninsula of Ardmeanach to rejoin the road to Fionnphort at the head of Loch Scridain. At the Gruline Estate we visited the Tomb of General Lachlan Macquarie, who became Governor of New South Wales in Australia and

---

* This was an important fortification when the MacDougalls held Mull.
† Storm-disabled ships of the Spanish Armada sought shelter here, including the pay galleon with its treasure, so we are told.

who was known for his efforts in helping transported convicts become good settlers. This place among the hills of Mull seems remote; yet the people who lived here have touched the world and been grasped by it. I once talked to a woman while waiting for a train in Glasgow who was born in the northeast corner of Mull. There were three brothers in her family, but they were killed in the "Great War."

Beside the road are hillsides of rhododendrons in magnificent upsweeps of blossom, reaching to the barren crags. Then the road finds the ocean once more, and the way opens to sweeping seascapes. Increasingly, the road must cling to the fringes of Mull's rugged mountains. Leaving Loch na Keal, there seems nothing to the west but the ocean with its islands and, above all, an immensity of sky. Close to shore, the chapeled isle of Inch Kenneth rises amidst the shoals, while away out on the gray sea lies Staffa. To the left, the talus slopes of Creag Mhor and Beinn Chreagach sweep upward six hundred feet in a litter of boulders and broken rock. Nancy tells us of a newly married couple who were spending their first night together in a cottage by this road. A huge boulder came crashing down, obliterating the cottage and its occupants.

Beyond Balmeanach lies the "Wilderness" where the cliffs rise from the sea. The road leaves the coast, as it must, to follow a mountain-cradled glen down to the gentler shores of Loch Scridain.

Chapter 32
Evening on Iona

It is a privilege to be spending this night upon the sacred and misty island of Iona. The shore is beautiful in its wetness. There are lights across the Sound of Iona at Fionnphort and a few warmly lit windows along this rain-soaked road. By arrangement with Nancy Black we visited the MacArthurs. They still speak the Gaelic among themselves. Their parents often spoke the old language, especially when there were things they didn't want their children to know. A peat fire burned; we sat drinking tea and eating scones, and spreading honey on homemade bread. Talk turned to the days when the steamboats, the "puffers," arrived regularly from Glasgow. The boats stopped at all the islands as they headed north for Skye and via the Caldonian Canal to Inverness. Traffic was heavy, and barter often took the place of cash.

I asked about the trophy cups lining a cupboard shelf. Mr. MacArthur was a runner in his younger days and had competed at many Highland Games on Mull, often winning three years in succession and thus allowed to keep the cup. The prizes were donated by the MacLeans of Duart.

The MacArthurs remembered when Iona had six hundred inhabitants. There was then farming with horses and crofting. There were many shops, and the community had its own weaver, whose ancestors had plied the trade before him. Fishing employed many, especially when one includes drying and smoking the catch. But that was the old days. We are told that young people won't stay upon the island now.

We walked back to our B&B in an early and complete darkness, under heavy cloud. The sound of the sea upon the beach filled the night, and a fresh wind incessantly drove the rain into our faces. It was a night for monks to pray in the candlelight and for smugglers to row ashore at the swing of a signal lantern.

Chapter 33
Staffa

Galley and Staffa. oil 22x16 Macdougall

A couple of old tires keep the *Land of Staffa* from chafing her fiberglass hull (black and fire-engine red) against Iona's granite pier. With the help of the captain, his mate, and a wooden crate for a step, a dozen passengers board for the adventure. Our captain is one of Iona's sons just graduated from Oban High School and in hopes of going to university in the fall. My sister Jean comments on his handsome sweater and observes that it must be hand-knit to be so fine.

"Not a bit of it," our captain answers with a grin, "It's just the way I wear it."

He does wear it fine, and he can handle a boat "chust sublime," as Para Handy would have expressed it.[*] The captain's skill becomes obvious as we clear the protection of Iona and meet the high swells rolling in from a storm that lays far out to westward. When the dark blue Atlantic, wind-roughed with purple, rises higher than usual across our

---

[*] A fictional skipper created by the journalist and writer Neil Munro in a series of stories published in the *Glasgow Evening News* under the pen name of Hugh Foulis.

bow, the captain eases off his course, and we go plowing down slantwise across the swell in a wash of foam.

To feel the adventure—to sense the sea as our ancestors did—one needs to be in a boat such as this and have the spray in one's face and the salt on one's lips. One must stand, not sit, swaying in counter-rhythm with the motion of the boat, while ahead the black cliffs of Staffa grow higher and the Treshnish Islands—outposts of the MacDougall Lords of Lorn—appear and disappear behind the mounting sea. Then there is a song in the heart born of the water and the sky and not of the shore or the hills.

So we cross the seven miles of ocean to the island of the caves. An equal number of miles to leeward and all along the eastern horizon stretches the blue-green wall of Mull, from the headlands of Ardmeanoch with its landmark waterfalls plunging into the sea to Loch na Keal. On top of the sea cliffs of Mull rise the layered hills—those eroded lava flows whose step-like sides rise like a giant's terraced vineyard. And so we sail on under the blue eye of blessing—a circle of sun ringed about by piling cumulus.

Now a white band of surf can be seen climbing and falling back from Staffa's dark columns. Word is passed around that with such a sea running we shall not be making a landing. Everyone is prepared for such a disappointment. Landings on Staffa are often canceled. Just to see the island close at hand is a wonderful experience.

The giant wall of basaltic pillars, Staffa's famed geological feature, appears nearly black but with a tinge of red. Lichens yellow the bases of the columns, which are topped by a pediment of tufted volcanic rock, which in turn supports the green rooftop of the island. The great openings of the caverns in this pilastered facade are dark with the mystery and the shadows of sacred places.

One should listen to Mendelssohn's *Hebrides Overture* before visiting Staffa, for it will sing in one's ears again: the call of fairy horns sounding from island to island, the musical portrayal of sky and sea, and the inner reverberations of surging waters within the chasm of Fingal's Cave—all are heard. Mendelssohn, writing of his visit to Staffa, tells how a "hissing sea" lifted their boat towards "the immense organ, black and resounding." And so this same sea carries us toward the island and Fingal's Cave.*

The shore is a fantastic array of smaller broken columns—columns in great piled heaps like firewood staked on end and left to dry, columns in ranks, and columns scattered by the sea. Among the rocky fringes, the

---

* See Chapter 25.

ocean rises, turning a light-filled green to shower in white foam and retreat in cataracts. Now there appears a concrete ramp in a sheltered cove. Our boat turns in toward it. We are going to land!

At some time in the past considerable work has been done to build a concrete walkway along the shore to Fingal's Cave. There was once a cable railing as well, but many of the iron stanchions have rusted away, and the concrete pathway is eroded away as well. Still, on this particular day I have no problem in making my way across the tops of the broken columns, which provide closely packed, hexagonal stepping stones.

At the portal of Fingal's Cave, a causeway of eroded shafts slopes downward and disappears under the spilling silver and green of the sea, like pilings for an ancient roadway that, it is said, rises again from the sea on the coast of Ireland. Beside this causeway, the sea rolls through a narrow channel toward the cave, where it surges into the shadows of a pilastered nave. For two hundred and twenty feet the sea surge rolls inward, to leap upwards against the far end of the cave. The flooding and receding pulse fills the great cave with the sound of thunder heard reverberating among high hills. A narrow pathway within the cave runs like a high balcony midway between the water below and the chambered arch above. The ceiling has the same hexagonal jointing as the columns and resembles the comb of giant wasp's nest. Minerals leaching downward from above have added a rich mosaic of yellows and greens. Underfoot there is wonder. Coral-pink algae flourishes in hexagonal pools created where one column has eroded faster than its neighbors. Reflected light from the shining world of sea and sky beyond the portal flickers upon the shafted walls—a procession of dancing lights into the depth of this subterranean cathedral.

From the landing site on Staffa's eastern shore, stairs zigzag up the cliff, leading to the island's top and a spectacular view. North and west range the Treshnish Isles. The line begins with Bac More or the Dutchman's Cap, whose circling brim shows the relentless work of ancient waves, followed by Lunga (Norse for "longship"),[*] then Fladda, and finally the Carnaburgs, once fortified by our ancestors. North and east lies the island of Ulva and the upper claw of Mull. To the southward lies Iona and the Ross of Mull. Near at hand, one looks across Staffa's rolling tabletop. A prow-like arm of the island reaches outward to the west—held up by red-brown columns rising from the surf. Across the green carpet, at the far end of the island, cattle graze in their summer retreat.

---

[*] This is not the Lunga from which the MacDougalls of Lunga take their name.

There are neither trees nor shrubs upon this windswept top of Staffa. Life keeps close to the rock—grasses, sedges, and everywhere, flowers: wild thyme, tormentil, lousewort, and small yellow buttercups. We look up to find ourselves watched by three puffins who have poked their heads above the edge of the bank. They are followed by others, all with their bright bills like great red noses and dressed in their formal attire as if going to another party. They have an "important" walk, like sea captains with their arms clasped behind them.

Below us the *Land of Staffa* seems a toy upon the ultramarine and wind-scudded sea. It had anchored offshore, but now we see it is once again making for the pier—a signal that it is time to leave. Certainly Staffa and this far-flung island world do not lie beyond the reign of time, but the clocks here seem those of the tides and the seasons, whose arms swing upon the pivots of the moon and the sun. As we climb down to our waiting boat, I remember a story recorded by Kenneth MacLeish. A business-like land owner arrived on the island of Coll and being impatient to get his affairs under way asked a native what time it was.

"It's August," was the answer.

Chapter 34
Loch Awe and the Islands of Inishail and Fraoch Eilean

From Taynuilt the road winds over the hills and down Glen Nant to Kilchrenan and Taychreggan. In bygone days, this route would have been crowded with cattle and the air filled with the shouts of the drovers. Kilchrenan was a busy place in those times and the site of a widely attended fair. It is quiet now, and the road ends at Taychreggan in a grassed-over stone ramp that disappears below the dark waters of Loch Awe. This is, by reason of its long use, a public quay, for it was from Taychreggan that a busy ferry transported cattle and sheep across Loch Awe on their way to market at Balloch and Falkirk.[*]

While we wait for Colin Lindsay-MacDougall of Lunga and for the launch that will take us up the loch, we have tea in the lounge of the Taychreggan Hotel, which stands close by the old quay. It is warm and an "out of the damp wind" interlude, touched with Victorian grace.

When the launch comes down the loch, she has the wind at her stern and parts the gray chop with a high prow that looks as though built to be adorned with a dragon head. She is just the craft for our adventure—an open wooden boat that has not seen varnish for some time.

The inboard is housed in a box well forward, the forecastle has a short deck set between low bulwarks. There are bench seats along the sides as well as at the stern, from which flies a small, weathered red ensign. She is, as our skipper explains, a working boat that he has "tidied-up a bit for this excursion." Launch and skipper seem to belong together. He is a quiet, accommodating fellow. He wears a reddish sweater and a tweed deerstalker hat, below which longish hair hangs down to merge with his brown beard. He has on a pair of green Wellingtons and sits with one foot tucked under him with apparent comfort. He spends a good deal of his time exchanging bits of news with Colin. Now and then he makes an adjustment with the wheel. We are alone upon the loch and making our steady way up the center of Awe's broad highway into the mountains.

We travel easily with the wind, keeping pace with the white-capped waves. The waters of the loch seem full to its brim and lap the overhanging shrubbery along the shore. The banks are largely wooded, green and lush. Before us, Cruachan's great bulk rises into thick cloud. It threatens rain as we pass the Black Islands and approach the forested shores of Inishail. Beyond that island and to the northward, the Pass of

---

[*] A.R.B. Haldane, *The Drove Roads of Scotland*.

Brander is a great, steep-sided cup filled with dark storm. The mountainsides that press in on the loch are gray shapes; their steep sides are all but hidden in mist. Above this lower world of vapor, the clouds droop wet and heavy.

Colin and our skipper discuss where best to land. Edging closer and choosing a graveled indentation, our skipper runs the launch up on the bank and we climb over the high prow and down to the water's edge with the help of a narrow, folding ladder.

Colin has brought us on a pilgrimage to one of the holy places in Argyll, the island of Inishail. One might figuratively say that all such sacred enclaves in ancient Scotland were islands often surrounded by a sea of war, lit by lurid fires fueled by avarice, pride, and hunger. These holy places held civilization in a chalice.

Here is the site of the old Parish Church of Inishail,[55] but worship here goes back to early Christianity in western Scotland. Here too, in medieval times, may have been a priory of the Knights Templar.[1, 46*]

A light rain falls as we climb the short distance to the highest part of the island and the oblong ruins of the church. Little remains except a shoulder-high section of the west gable wall. A relic of the early Christian occupation of this island stands reerected inside the ruined walls. It is a cross-decorated slab weathered by the centuries. Most prominent are the bosses that decorate the intersection of the cross. They stand out like four eyes, watching us with a stare more primitive than Christian. The modern wheel-crosses, which stand in the gray rain to the west of the ruined church, mark the present burial ground of the Dukes of Argyll.

One side of these holy precincts is ringed by ancient cedar trees. At one point, three cedars grow close together, as they sprouted from a parent tree now long gone. A fourth cedar in this group has been recently cut. We count two hundred rings in the stump!

We begin exploring the grave slabs, which lie partially buried in a floor of spills and cones shed from the sheltering trees. It is a fascinating occupation. Each person discovers some detail; each new angle allows some feature to be recognized. One tapered slab displays the galley with up-swept bow and stern. A line of conical-helmeted figures peer over the gunwale. Close by is a rectangular slab that may have been a frieze from the altar. Two helmeted knights hold up what appears to be a crown

---

*Also see Michael Baigent and Richard Leigh's book of fascinating speculations, *The Temple and the Lodge*.

above a shield emblazoned with the galley.* To the left, two priests in long robes flank a crucifix. One carries a censer, caught in its upward swing. The face of Christ, now mysteriously sculptured by the elements, seems to be resigned in sleep. To their left are two knights. One has a spear in one hand while the other hand grasps the hilt of his sword. His conical helmet appears to have two plumes. The second knight has a battle-ax and rests one hand on his drawn sword.

The sword is the ubiquitous symbol. It is never more eloquently displayed than when incised alone upon a grave slab, with no name, no other mark to identify whose life ended here. The best example of such a stone lies within the old church. On this rainy day, the details of the sword's hilt stand out in a mirror pool of water. Is this the resting place of a Knight Templar who had known the parching Mediterranean sun before he came here to rest beside the silver waters of Loch Awe?

The work of time and the stillness of sanctity surround us. On one reclining slab all is erased except a wonderfully executed design of interlacing circles, and on another are the remains of a chalice. The grail? One feels the miracle, the far-traveled story that whispers to the heart "that he who believeth shall not die...."

Colin points out the many shrubs growing close around the ruins—hawthorn, myrtle, and rowan. Before the coming of Christianity, he tells us, places like this were often associated with a sacred spring around which were nurtured and protected those plants with special properties and purposes. We stand for a moment in the soft rain, amidst the green lushness and beside an ancient ivy. Centuries of branches fantastically twist and intertwine to form one massive trunk—a tree of spells, as from a Tolkien story.

Under the shelter of the ancient cedars, we eat our lunches.

Our skipper, who has "stood-off" the island while we explored and ate, now comes back to fetch us. We all stand near the stern, to raise the bow while the skipper backs the launch off the gravel. A "working boat" is a good craft for island exploring. It has stopped raining. Dare we hope that our pilgrimage to Inishail has blessed us? Is the mist rising up the sides of Cruachan and is the sky brighter? Our next port of call is Fraoch Eilean, the "Heather Island,"[46†] which lies less than half a mile northeast

---

* One wonders if this may represent an early Arms of the MacNaughtons, who were related to the MacDougalls of Lorn (thus perhaps the galley) and were the hereditary keepers of the castle on nearby Fraoch Eilean for the Scottish crown.

† *Argyll: An Inventory of the Ancient Monuments, Vol. 2, Lorn*, published by the Royal Commission on the Ancient and Historical Monuments of Scotland (1975), calls Fraoch Eilean a two-storied "Hall-House" (There may have been an additional loft.) A fragment of sandstone casement with filleted roll molding

of Inishail. Above the island rises the massive backdrop of Cruachan. The island is heavily wooded with tall pines to the left and hardwoods on the right, their leaves turned silver in the wind. Between these trees rises the brown wall of Fraoch Eilean Castle or Hall-House.[*] That steeply pitched ell must look much as it did when Chief Iain Bacach[†] anchored his galley off this island, but now the three windows, one over the other, are filled with the brightness of the sky behind and bushes grow where slate roof should meet the wall. There is a landing place below the Hall-House on the south side of the island, and a pathway leads upwards through the remains of the curtain wall and outbuildings. A doorway gives passage through the five-foot walls of the Hall-House's undercroft. Inside there is little left. Sometime in the early sixteen hundreds, a dwelling house was set in the east end. There is a mural stairway from the undercroft to what was the hall above. Some beveled window casings in purple sandstone have survived. In the northeast corner there is a small chamber that has been identified as a prison cell. Robin MacDougall Morley and I take refuge there when another sudden shower drenches the island. Robin thrusts his unopened umbrella through the small window and then opens it to keep out the wind-driven rain.

The rain proves to be a clearing shower. From the remains of a round tower at what was the northwest corner of the curtain wall, we watch the mist rise in flowing tatters above the Pass of Brander. It is clearing!

It is a privilege to be on Loch Awe—that twenty-four-mile waterway upon which the galleys of the MacDougalls maintained the inland safety of Lorn. It is lovely to see such a body of water, but to be *on* it—pushing forward with the waves washing along the sides—is to be part of history and to feel gloriously alive. Our trip from Taychreggan had been through gray, wet-wind weather known well to our ancestors. Our return passage is under a glorious clearing that thrills our hearts as it must have gladdened theirs. A marvel of white clouds still hide the top of Cruachan. Their light-filled masses stretch away in long ranks to the eastward. The water of the loch is alive below this clearing sky—pale blue, crossed by the dark blue backs of the waves. There is still much moisture in the air,

---

and dog-tooth ornamentation apparently from an arch window has been found. As there is no provision for an intermural fireplace in the hall, a central fire was likely used, with the smoke vented through louvers in the roof.

[*] The castle is not only defensively well placed but controls Loch Awe as it reaches northward into the Pass of Brander. Iain Bacach is supposed to have anchored his galley off this island during the battle within the Pass. Also see Lore of Lorn, Note 15.

[†] It is not clear that Iain Bacach was Chief at this time, as his father was still alive. He was probably serving as *Tosheadeor* or "Commander" of the Clan.

and its filter whitens the blue mountains east of Loch Awe and pales the olive roughness of Cruachan and the dark green shadows of the passing clouds.

Once again, in the middle of the loch, we strike the waves head-on and the wind blows the spray in our faces. Let fly the standard of the MacDougall Chief and bend the ashen oar!

Chapter 35
Glencoe - a Second Look

From Loch Leven and between the conical peaks that mark the entrance, Glencoe leads eastward under a solemn spell of mountain walls. To appreciate this glen, one must walk beside River Coe as it splashes to the sea and climb, if only for a short distance, to some vantage point above the glen's floor.

The lambs are frolicking. They seem to be wearing white stockings with black bands, and these flicker as the lambs romp upon the banks of the Coe. Their exuberant play and the river's flow accentuates by contrast the monumental stillness held in the hugeness of mountain walls. The Coe never rests. The lips of blue pools continually break in flashing ripples over white corbel stones. As for the mountains that sweep upward on both sides, they seem the foundation of forever.

Below the mountain rampart a white cottage gleams in the sun. It is a miniature below a titanic backdrop. Behind it, a rock-punctured hillside rises steeply—green in the sunlight until the vertical walls of crag rise in shadow. A white web of water plunges down from a high corrie where a touch of sunlight whitens a distant and broken ridge of rock. Beyond the corrie there rises another eminence, the mist caught on its jagged top.

Higher up the glen, the Coe falls between dark ledges and churns white amidst the boulders. This may have been the spot Stevenson had in mind when he had his two heroes in *Kidnapped* cross this river by daring leaps.

We stop near the place poetically called "The Study" to climb up a natural stairway of tumbled stones. Our way takes us past a stone hut whose roof is tied down with cables. Winter winds must be severe. But in today's calmness, we climb on. Never have I been seized with such a feeling of exhilaration. Each step from one rock to the next brings an increased sense of freedom in this immensity of purpled heights (no poetic license needed).

And then one turns to look out over the glen. Down to the sea, in increasing blue haze, winds the glen. The river glints, disappears, and then runs once again, a thread of silver. Opposite Beinn Fhada, Buachaille Etive Beag and Mor sweep upward their shoulders and backs hunched by age. On the right, the sunlit green sweeps upward to meet the blue shadows and the lavender cliffs of Aonach Eagach.

There is a great, wild strength here and a solemn beauty like the roofless nave of a titanic cathedral built by God before he bothered with man. If all this were suddenly to become music, then there would surge upwards an overture such as not even Wagner dreamed.

Chapter 36
Rannoch Moor and Glen Orchy

One late evening as we stood in the yard of Torwood House above Oban Harbor, Nancy MacDougall Black pointed out the soundless flashes of lightning upon the northeast horizon. There is a storm over Rannoch Moor, Nancy told us.

Rannoch is a primitive place—a high plateau of desolation. Once a great mass of ice sat upon Rannoch and ran its glacial fingers down Glencoe and down the glens of Etive and Orchy. Much later there was a forest there, perhaps as late as Roman times, but now it is an expanse of dull purple heaths, olive green rushes, and countless pools that are deep and black except when they reflect the wide arch of cloud and sky above. Away off, there appears a range of mountains, but the Rannoch is an expanse of tundra and a profusion of rocks, as if some ancient race had gathered them intending to build a thousand stone circles and then never got around to doing so.

The moor is a great empty place. Two red deer spring across the highway; otherwise we see no life.

In contrast, the road (A82) soon leaves the waste behind and passes between blue lakes spread out in a green land* and then winds south through forested hills and above the silver sheet of Loch Tulla. Over this loch, one looks west and northwest into the mountain fastness of Clach Leathad and Stob Ghabhar.†

Less than a mile below the Bridge of Orchy, B8074 branches toward the southwest to follow River Orchy's tumultuous course toward Loch Awe. The road is narrow and twisty and Glen Orchy is not spectacular, yet it contains country beautiful in its seclusion. My journal reads:

> A white cottage with light blue trim, orange chimney pots, and a blossomed rowan tree stands against the rough hills—a background of lavender shade, sunlit green, and blue cloud shadows that flow across the ridges dipping into the depressions and riding up the craggy tops.
>
> The glen seems all that is left of the world that was, its boundaries kept secure by the high hills, above which white cumulus with feathered edges rise up to support a cerulean sky. If the glen is not spectacular, River Orchy is. It thunders between the ledges, dropping into a profusion of spray and white-churned torrents.

A little over two miles east of Dalmally, B8074 joins A85 as it heads for the Pass of Brander.

---

* Including the sizable Loch Ba (Cow Loch).
† "Peak of the Goat." Elevation is about 3553 feet.

Chapter 37
View Over Lunga House

To appreciate the situation of Lunga House, one must climb the high hills that rise just to the east. I take the dirt road that leaves Lunga House and travel eastward to Ardfern, then shortly turn right to follow a deeply worn bridle trail that climbs steeply under a dense arch of trees. The bridle path rejoins the road to Ardfern, which bears southward along a high ridge. What appears to be a path beckons. It winds westward a short distance over peaty ground strewn with rock and decorated with the tossing heads of cotton grass, and ends at the edge of an escarpment with nothing in front but this glorious view.

From many vantage points, one can look down and see the tower, ells, black slate roofs, and chimneys of Lunga House rising above the trees, and the green park land sloping down to the sea. The sun is warm, the breeze strong, the foreground is purpled with rhododendron, while in front there opens a vast view of island in a wind-crossed sea. Haunting all is the calling of a cuckoo.

Between the outcroppings of glacier-scoured ledge there grows a low thick mat of heather with mattress qualities. There I lie and attempt to absorb the majesty that opens in a grand half circle. Here spreads the southern portion of the Kingdom of Lorn—the kingdom that fell to Dougal when Somerled died in 1164.

To the south, perhaps fifteen miles over a tide-churned sea, rise the Paps of Jura, the commanding feature of that island that was another home to MacDougalls. Turning clockwise, there is the mountain island of Scarba, a landmark along this coast, then the island of Shuna and behind it Luing, where the early MacDougalls of Lunga lie buried at Kilchattan along with the MacDougalls of Ardlarach and Arcafolla. One can see that narrow raceway of the tides that separates Luing from Seil. Just to the east of this thoroughfare is the island of Torsa, home of the MacDougalls of Torsa.[22, 34] Seil has the remains of Ardfad Castle and the later home of the MacDougalls of Ardencaple. And then to the north-northwest, there is the peninsula from which the MacDougalls of Degnish sent their men to fight and die at Dunaverty. Beyond low-lying Luing rise the high, red cliffs of Mull, and above them, walling the west, are the mountains of Mull, with Ben More's cone highest of all.

The foreground drops away in two plunges to Lunga House. Down below, from the foot of the first cliff toward the walled garden beside the house and as far as the ear can hear, a choir of birds is singing.

I am absolutely comfortable on this bed of heather, cooled by the sweeping wind, transfigured from my common self by the immensity and magnificence of the view, and mesmerized by the call of the cuckoo.

Chapter 38
Craignish

It is an exceptional spring for flowers. Just outside the window at Innisaig House in Ardfern, the crimson-flowered tree is in flaming bloom, and in the garden behind the house, roses and azaleas keep company with an exotic palm tree. There are flowers everywhere in this exceptional spring.

We exclaim about this beauty at breakfast, and Katherine Lindsay-MacDougall comments that each spring and early summer month has its favorite color: February is white with the carpets of snowdrops, March tends to the yellows of daffodils and primroses, May is the time of bluebells and forget-me-nots, and for June, the choice is pink or mauve with the willow herb, foxgloves, and bell heather.

We find the bluebells (wild hyacinths) spreading profusely from the sides of the road into the shadows of the trees as we climb a hill above Ardfern's town hall. Beyond the farm to which the road leads, we climb a high knob to look out over Loch Craignish. A cuckoo intones its solemn mantra, and from the woods below come faint bird songs. Otherwise, it is so quiet here that one can hear the cattle in the pasture below pulling up grass from around the tufted sedges.

The late afternoon sun finds and warms the gables of the farm below and of a house nearly hidden in the trees. The many hulls of sailing boats clustered in Ardfern's harbor gleam white.

Away off across the loch, the corkscrew road climbs toward the Pass of Kintraw. The windshield of a car gleams momentarily as a motorist negotiates a tight turn. At the head of the loch, the tide-bare flats are a dark background for gliding bits of white, as gulls sweep out over the shallow water and the yellow-green reflections of the steep shores beyond.

The waters of the loch are split by the high back of Eilean Mhic Chrion and by the lower-lying Eilean Righ, the "King's Island." What king? one wonders. Four miles or more down the loch, the light blue waters merge with a distant whiteness and mystery.

Chapter 39
Ardencaple House, Seil, and Luing

Seil Island

The banks of Seil round in a rich golden-green in the morning sun, and the waters of narrow Clachan Sound mix blue with the same bright hue. Over this colored ribbon of the sea, Clachan Bridge arches its graceful span.

Car up and car down over that narrow bridge and we are on the Island of Seil, with an invitation from Mrs. Frances Shand Kydd, the mother of Princes Diana and the present owner of Ardencaple House,[28*] to take photos of this once MacDougall home and visit the ruins of Ardfad Castle.[29]

The road to Ardencaple House leaves B8003 at Oban Seil, where a long time ago lived Robert Grant, factor for Campbell of Ardmaddy. The story goes that Grant went out to Mull to collect rents for his Campbell laird and failed to return. Animosities between the MacLeans of Mull and the Campbells ran deep and strong, and Lord Neil Campbell became alarmed. He asked MacDougall of Dunollie if he would go out to Mull and make inquiries. The Chief of the MacDougalls was received by MacLean of Duart, the table was spread, and the two men sat down to eat. After these amenities, MacDougall broached the subject of the Campbell's factor. MacLean strode over to the sideboard, uncovered an object that had been covered by a cloth, and there was the head of Robert Grant. Well, that's the story. It is known that MacDougall of Dunollie was able to convince MacLean to return the body and that it was buried at the churchyard at Kilbrandon on Seil.

Ardencaple House

We stop at the gatehouse of the Ardencaple estate and explain our presence. The gate-lady evidently calls ahead, for Mrs. Shand Kydd, tall and naturally elegant, meets us on the gravel drive in front of Ardencaple House. She points out the high rock formation upon which Ardfad Castle had once stood.

"There is not much left of the castle," she tells us, "except its wonderful situation."

---

[*] Ardencaple House has since changed hands. Mrs. Shand Kydd has now passed away.

We set out following the path indicated, accompanied by Mrs. Shand Kydd's dog, which is anxious for the excursion.

Ardfad's long rock rises some thirty feet as a cliff-sided island from a sea of closely cropped grass, clumps of straw-colored rushes, and cotton grass. A bit of wall rises in the center and a tree with wide-spreading branches is silhouetted against the sky. The old entrance to the stronghold was from the southwest, up what appears to be a man-contrived ramp through a purposefully widened gully to the top of the rock. The old curtain wall followed the perimeter of the rock, while the principal tower was twenty-five feet north and south and spanned some forty-five feet east to west across the width of the rock. At the southwest side of the ruins is a well-defined foundation of what probably was a round stair tower. One needs to walk around the base of the rock to see the few remaining courses of stone, which rise from natural rock.

The site has been likened to a miniature Stirling. Mrs. Shand Kydd is right about the situation, both strategically and from the standpoint of the view! She is writing by a front window when we return and again joins us. Had we seen the wild goats? They were grazing earlier that morning, but have a way of disappearing.

South of the road to Ardencaple House, B844 branches from B8003 and heads west to Easdale. There is another Kilbride on this road to Easdale. It was the site of a Gaelic center of learning presided over by a family of MacLachlans who possessed manuscripts from the monastic library at Iona.[*] Beyond Kilbride one rounds (preferably slowly) a switchback to suddenly face one of those views where one seems poised on the edge of a new world of sea and sky. A dramatic coastline breaks into rocks, each ringed with white, breaking waves. The ocean reaches outward—at first green-gray, and then a silver sheet holding the dark-shouldered islands of the Garvellachs. Above, an immensity of sky is filled with cumulus floating shoreward like titanic dirigibles.

The quarrying of slate once made Seil a prosperous place, with Easdale the center of the industry, until 1881, when a terrific storm swept waves ashore and filled the quarries. The rows of cottages are again freshly painted and snug below the Gibraltar-like heights of Dun More, but the industry is no longer black slate, but people.[†]

---

[*] Màiri MacDonald, *The Islands of Nether Lorn*, West Highland Series, No. 3.
[†] For an intimate and nature-wise description see *Island: Diary of a Year on Easdale* by Garth and Vicky Waite.

Luing Island

The tidal currents sweep like a swift river through Cuan Sound, which separates Seil from the island of Luing. The ferryman tells me that a four-knot current is usual, rising to eight knots on a spring tide. The ferryboat crosses on the bias, struggling against the flow.

Luing is one more jump removed from the crowd. As on Seil, slate was once the big industry, but there was much farming and cattle-raising as well. Once six hundred crofting families made a subsistence living and a substantive existence on Luing. There "Luing cattle" once had a special reputation. Now Cullipool, one of two villages on the island, caters to holiday seekers. We eat at the "Buttery," a freshly painted cottage dining room.

The road to Cullipool leaves Luing's central road, turning to the right a scant mile from the ferry. The way that turns left takes one to Ardinamar Bay and the site of Dun Ballycastle, one of Luing's Iron Age hill forts. We drive to the end of the road and an old, comfortable cottage by the shore. We are obviously intruders to the woman who answers our knock. The view from her front step seems the best way to open a conversation. I mention my interest in Degnish Point, which rises across the Sound, and in the Island of Torsa,[22, 34] which lies at the mouth of the Bay, and then add our desire to visit Dun Ballycastle. At that moment, an overfed cat comes sauntering down the road. "That's right, Philipi," the woman called to the cat, "size them up!" Obviously the "them is us," but already the woman's voice is softening; she turns out to be full of stories and anxious to talk.

"So you know Degnish Point," she said. "Now-a-days people don't know what is right under their nose. Now, you'll have to be careful getting through the electric gate when you go up to the fort."

We climb a steep ridge to Dun Ballymore, commanding a splendid view. Across the Sound, the chimneys of Degnish House appear above the steep line of hill; northward, Ardmaddy Castle sits at the head of the bay; and behind it, range on range of mountains reach into the haze. To the west, narrow Cuan Sound threads between the islands; beyond is the blue wall of Mull's crevice-scarred cliffs and corried mountains.

The dun appears at first to be a colossal tumble of rocks some ten feet tall and spilling down the sides of the ridge. Here and there, the large facing blocks can be seen rising a few rows above the rubble. On the east side there appears a laid-up corner, marking the old passageway though the thirteen-foot-thick walls. On closer inspection, we find one of the inlet door jambs in place.[5] Inside the oval ring of stone (104 feet on the longer axis), the sole occupant is a knurled tree.

I have read that Dun Leccamore, located less than a mile to the south of Ballycastle, is even better preserved. There, a large slab of slate serves as a door jamb and bears the mysterious indentations known in the archeologist's jargon as "cups." The gateway has a bar hole and there are two intramural chambers. Luing must have been an important and impressive place during the Iron Age.

To Kilchattan and Ardlarach House

Running down the center of the island, Luing's main road passes through Glen Dubh Leitir, the "Glen of Dark Slopes." According to folklore, the glen was once inhabited by a *glaisrig*,* a creature of the mist and the night that preys upon travelers. On this afternoon, it is hard to imagine any threat. The landscape lies open under the hot sun, and the only menace is a species of fly that favors the sheep droppings but could take time to bite.

Still, this story speaks of Luing's past, which is so much a part of its fascinating present. Mairi MacDonald writes in *The Islands of Nether Lorn* that there was once a boulder just north of the schoolhouse in Glen Dubh Leitir that bore the imprint of the beast's claw. Nearby was a Fairy Knoll, which she describes as "a small grassy hillock about four feet high." She adds the delightful information that people still leave a votive offering such as "a hair or a thread of clothing." We would do so, except we are not sure which hillock to choose.†

A ribbon of fireweed marks the burn that has cut its path southward toward Kilchattan and Ardlarach House. One of the last of the old water-driven grist mills in Argyll is at Achafolla Farm. The large iron wheel no longer turns, but the stones and machinery remain. Its tin roof seems an anachronism, but even that is showing its age—its red-rust contrasts with the green ferns covering the bank nearby.

Kilchattan sits in the quiet of its centuries amidst a lovely countryside of rolling green fields. To the south the mass of Scarba's sea mount rises, and to the west lies the island of Lunga. A heavy, gray cloud of smoke rises from this island, and for a moment one is reminded of that era of sudden terror when the "sea wolves" came in their Viking boats to burn and pillage. This afternoon, someone is burning the heather to increase pasturage. The yellowish smoke trails toward the mainland like an old story.

---

* A Celtic Gorgon.
† On the map provided in Màiri MacDonald's *The Islands of Nether Lorn*, the school shown is on the wrong side of the road, at least in regard to its present location.

Kilchattan Church probably dates from the twelfth century. Three walls survive, and the flat surfaces of their outside stones display a singular array of old graffiti, which the Royal Commission on Ancient and Historical Monuments suggests may have been incised by children.* Predominating are the outlines of medieval galleys—long, sleek, and high-prowed. A fleet of galleys appears to have been engraved on one large stone. I feel I am looking at a scene that the engraver had just seen and, in excitement and awe, had reproduced. Whose fleet? I wonder. Perhaps they were King Haakon's ships, or Somerled's.

The surrounding graveyard holds the table monument to the MacDougalls of Lunga, emblazoned with the differentiated MacDougall Arms. The names of many other clanspeople appear on nearby stones: MacDougalls of Killchattan, Ardlarach, and Archafolla; Livingstones; MacCullochs; a past master of the Masonic Lodge; and Campbells too—including Alexander Campbell, revivalist Covenanter who dug his own grave "like Jacob did," as the inscription says. A typical stone with an interesting spelling of surnames reads:

In Memory of John MacDougall
Son of Finlay and Mary McDougall, Cruachan
Who died 5 October 1837
Age 24 years

West of Kilchattan, a road runs past Ardlarach House,[30] which sits long, two-storied, and white against the dark background of the surrounding trees. Beyond this house the road ends at Black Mill Bay. Today, the bay lies quietly reflecting the white clouds and the shadows of the steep headlands on its northern shore, where, at the entrance to the bay, stand three sea stacks called the "Cobblers of Lorn." This whole world of land and sea lies washed by soft, warm sunlight. Perhaps it is impossible to adequately describe such moments, when one stands by the sky-reflecting sea. For a moment the world seems to hold still in one solemn quietude. Two days ago I stood on a height above Degnish Farm in the drenching rain and looked across to Luing as it lay half veiled in the mist. Today, in this sun-blessed solitude, I look across the Firth of Lorn to the omnipresent mountains of Mull, clear and blue on the horizon, and think, "This also is the west Highlands."

---

* *Argyll: An Inventory of Ancient Monuments, Vol. 2, Lorn*, pp. 144–146.

Chapter 40
Tigh Cuil and the Stones of Duachy

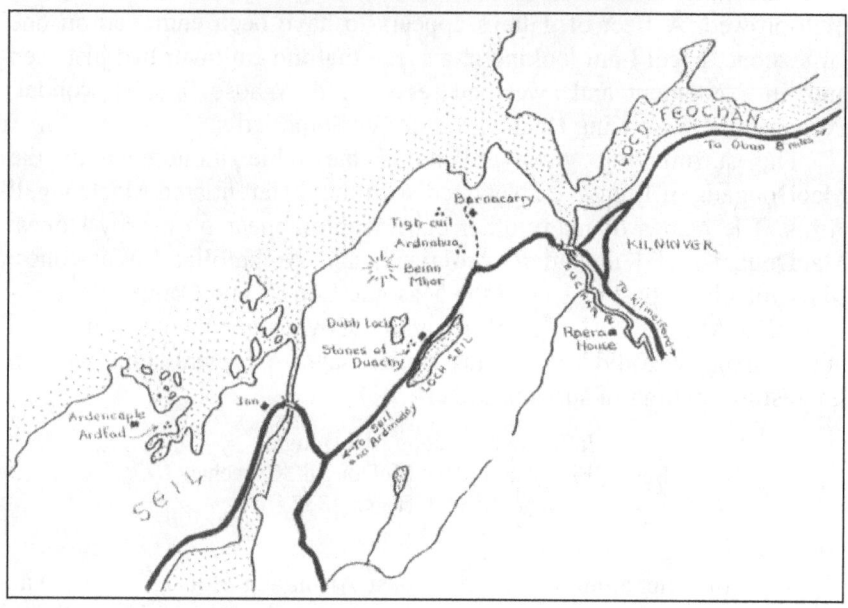

Barnacarry House and Tigh Cuil

In 1723, in pursuance of "An Act for the more effectual disarming of the Highlands," General George Wade issued an edict to "the Clans and tribes of the McDougall and their followers" demanding the surrender of their weapons. Kilninver is listed in this edict along with the other parishes[*] and islands then considered MacDougall country. Since then, Kilninver, in answer to the more effective mandates of social and economic change, has delivered up a goodly portion of its native people. The salmon waters of River Euchar, upon whose bank, it is said, the MacDougalls of Raera once had their stronghold, still fall to Loch Feochan, and the road westward to Seil and Ardmaddy still runs over the hills, but those hills are now largely inhabited by sheep, the stray holiday seeker, and the past. Between this road and the coast, and west of the narrow road that leads to Barnacarry, lie Ardnahua and Tigh Cuil. These two villages are now marked by roofless gables and tumbling walls.

---

[*] Other communities listed are Kilbride, Kilmore, Ardchattan, and Mocharn.

Chapter 40

Mrs. Kerr, who owns Barnacarry House, meets me at the door with a heavy walking stick in her hand that might well serve, it seems to me, as a cudgel. But it is her eyes that draw attention. They show she had made the greatest of human discoveries—how to get the most out of life. How did I know about Tigh Cuil and would I not come in for coffee? For forty years she and her husband have enjoyed living at Barnacarry. Their children grew up here. Now they are far away. She and her husband used to keep the way to Tigh Cuil marked, but that was years ago. Still, she can give directions to get me there.

Mrs. Kerr's direction, or rather, the way I actually go, leads through woods and rough pasturage, with glades here and there in which the bluebells spread the color of the sky into the shadows beneath the trees. In one narrow ravine, a roe deer is suddenly up, bounding ahead, and as suddenly gone. I might use the deer as an excuse for wandering from Mrs. Kerr's directions, but that would hardly be fair. I come out on high ground to the west of where Mrs. Kerr intended, but with a magnificent panorama before me. The Firth of Lorn lies an Aegean blue, fading until it reaches a band of white vapor. Away off, the mountains of Mull with their pink striations rise in great masses and range westward. Over this expanse, the sky is cloudless except in the north, where long, long feathers of cirrus fan outward from the upper pole of the heavens. Below, where the rock-broken heath rises after sweeping down from where I stand, are the gray gables and tumbled walls of Tigh Cuil.

Descending the steep hillside, I find an old track scooped out from the hillside, leading through scrub oaks down to the brook Mrs. Kerr had mentioned. Ahead, a wall crosses the brook, which flows dark and clear under a linteled arch. I am back on the way Mrs. Kerr has detailed—

"cross the brook and follow the wall." The wall to the left is shoulder-high and masterfully laid-up. To the right, a field rises gradually from the brook—the major piece of fertile ground for the hamlet above. Mrs. Kerr told me that in the winter one can still see the moldings of the lazybeds.[77] The blackbirds are singing in the woods beyond the wall, a cuckoo calls from somewhere up the far hillside, and a skylark rises into the wind—its wings a blur—to hover momentarily above the old garden plots.

One enters the village of Tigh Cuil under an arch of living oak. The old tree leans outward from the top of the wall, as if long and patiently sculptured by oriental gardeners. A hundred years ago, one might have spoken with a grandmother spinning in the doorway of her byre-dwelling or passed the news with a man (a MacCowan, let us imagine, for that was once a common name in this place) returning from his patch of garden. One would have been told that the young folk were away to the shielings of Glen Risdale tending the cattle, and one might be asked if he or she had heard of Breadalbane's intent to turn the high pasturage into a sheep-walk.

This morning, only sheep greet the visitor to Tigh Cuil. Three ewes and their black-faced lambs come out through a lintelless doorway. There are few things more disconcerting than a sheep's stare. It is filled with such complete disinterest.

There is more remaining of these houses than I anticipated. The buildings stand on ground that rises above a strip of swale running down through the center of the hamlet. They are protected from the western gales by the rising heath.[*]

There are pink-spotted orchids growing by the path to the largest house. And here, just outside the doorway, sits a stone mortar, ready after all these years to be used in grinding the staff of life. Crossing the stone threshold, I stand in what was a room with a fireplace in the gable end, a cupboard built into the thickness of the wall, and a window—all set apart from another room that must have been the kitchen. A second gable wall with another fireplace separates that room from the byre. From the window, one could not have seen the neighbor's smoke rising into the morning, but had one wished reassurance that he or she were not alone, then a few steps from the door would have brought the entire hamlet into view.

---

[*] For a wonderfully informative account of how some of our Scottish ancestors lived and left, see the fairly lengthy entry on Tigh Cuil Township in *Argyll: An Inventory of the Ancient Monuments, Volume 2, Lorn*, of the Royal Commission on the Ancient and Historical Monuments of Scotland. There is also a map and floor plans for several houses on pages 273–275.

It seems that something within these walls has been waiting while the stones fell—waiting for a visitor in whom it might make its questions conscious. It asks, "Where are the descendants of the folk who called this 'home' and kept their Bible in the niche above the fireplace? Are they half a world away or long since dead? Have all the days when the rain has fallen where once there was a roof and the years of wheeling sun and stars made meaning of all this?"

Perhaps it is the Firth of Lorn's Aegean blue that has reminded me of Euripedes, for in imagination I hear, from outside the window opening, a chorus repeating:

> There be many shapes of mystery,
> And many things God makes to be,
> Past hope and fear.
> And the end men looked for cometh not,
> And a path is there where no man thought.
> So hath it fallen here.

There are paths that lead from here—paths to where no man thought. They lead down across the brook and out of sight around the corner of the hill. There is a feeling of transience, as though the last resident had scratched the Gaelic word *d'fhalbh* upon the stone windowsill, "gone away," "perished." The same root word resides in the Gaelic name for the swallow, *fabhaich*—the departing birds whose flocking tells of the end of summer. Was it a swallow or a sparrow or a skylark or some nameless little bird that figures in the Celtic analogy of human life Bede set down in his *Ecclesiastical History*? A little bird enters the lodge flying in from the darkness. Swiftly it passes through the firelight and the warmth and then is gone out into the darkness. "Gone away" is the message left at Tigh Cuil—the forever going away of human existence. A whisper in my mind echoes in the corners of this gray rocked room; a whisper saying we are but brief eddies in the stream of things, and all is cupped in the hollow of a vast enigma.

I leave Tigh Cuil. Once I look backwards to see at the top of the rising heath the citadel-like ledge called Losgann Lathurnach, the "Toad of Lorn," which crowns Beinn Mhor. It is a wall of rock from which a giant bite has been taken from one side, leaving two jagged pinnacles. They stand like pointed teeth against the sky.

Seil and Duachy

Reaching Barnacarry House, I head south down the road to Seil, bound for a rendezvous with the Stones of Duachy. The residents at Tigh Cuil were not the first here among these hills to pile rock on rock, to tie down the thatch, and to call the results of their labors "home." Long before them, people of the Iron Age built a fort on top of Beinn Mhor. Before these builders were the Bronze Age cairn makers, while earlier still came and vanished those who buried their dead in passage graves, and so back to the dwellers of the caves along the west Highland shore.

It may have been the people of the Bronze Age or the passage grave builders who raised the Stones of Duachy. Archaeologists speculate, but do not know who erected the standing stones or why they went to such prodigious labors.

The road to Seil and Ardmaddy skirts the shore of Loch Seil and runs between the loch and the present farm of Duachy. The farm house sits above the road and is approached by a steep drive, which leads to a courtyard between long ells at the rear of the building. In celebration of this fine afternoon, the courtyard is bedecked with washing hung out to dry. A small, white dog meets me the moment I step from the car. His game is "attack the pant cuffs," and together we make our way to the door left open to the sunlight.

"Go through the gate at the end of the drive, turn left, and follow the path up the hill," are the directions given by the young woman who answers my knock.

The path leads westward and upward to the top of the rounding pasture that lies between Loch Seil and the smaller Loch Dubh—the "Dark Loch."

The Stones of Duachy stand like giant exclamation points. They are mysterious punctuation marks under an immensity of sky. Until recently, there were four standing stones upon this hilltop—three aligned and running northwest to southeast, and a fourth, an outlier, located some one hundred and twenty-five feet to the east. Of this latter stone, only the stub remains in place. It was knocked down when a natural split threatened to topple the stone upon some back-scratching cow. The middle stone of the triad now reclines among the buttercups, watched over by its two giant flankers.

Beinn Mhor looked down upon the men who sweated to raise these nine-foot shafts and upon the people and the tribal priests who came in procession up this swell of heath. Did they come to assure themselves of the sun's faithfulness or to propitiate the powers of good fortune? Did they assemble here to bury men who longed to be remembered? It was so long ago, yet the Stones of Duachy seem to have some meaning still.

Two men are fishing in silence from a small boat on the breeze-purpled waters of Loch Dubh. Except for the tell-tale ripple, time appears to have stopped momentarily about these fishermen, as it does here beside the standing stones, where I too am angling.

The sober mood has come with me from Tigh Cuil. The stones seem sentinels before an old, dark passageway, and I feel a communion with countless souls groping for some answer to the enigma. We are endeavoring to touch, if only for a moment, that which is certain and everlasting.

Then, slowly, my spirit is filled with exaltation as if infused by some fresh current descending from Beinn Mhor and now swirling around the Stones of Duachy. Whatever the ancient and particular significance of these pillars, they have to do with our human reach, with the drama of human existence, however tenuous, and with the adventure.

To hear the perennial note of sadness, to sense the renewing of joy, to see the beauty around us, to feel the bravery of the race, to be touched by the mystery, is to know the privilege of being.

Chapter 41
A Day on Kerrera

[Transcribed and edited from tape-recorded field notes, 1992]

I am on the Shore Road to Gallanach and walking down to the ferry. It is a cloudless day, with the sun warm enough to make the cool azalea shade welcome. The anchorage here in the Sound of Kerrera is filled with white-, blue-, and red-hulled boats, all facing Oban in an out-going tide. To the right on the shore is the Brandy Rock,[78] and ahead rises the deeply scalloped face of the Swallow Rock. It is the first abrupt palisade of the Ardbhan Craigs.* The white cottage that once stood on the shore of Carding Mill Bay has been replaced by an ugly structure. They tell me that the old cottage was "very damp." Still, it belonged.

Behind, across the harbor, Dunollie rises from its promontory—dark on the seaward side and lit by the morning sun on the eastern wall. Now the Swallow Rock is past and the road is flanked to the left by great perpendicular cliffs, which tower above the road like some great fortress of Fingal and his giants. These rock faces are constantly weathering away. As recently as last year, tons of rock gave way and plugged this road for weeks.

The light blue waters of the Sound are crossed with darker ribbons where the morning breeze and the tide are playing games. There on Kerrera's bright green shore is the chapel/schoolhouse† standing high above the jetty. And there is the ferryman's house, white below the spreading sycamore trees.

A number of cars are at the landing and a group of people waiting. Kerrera is now an Automobile Association (AA) Walk. A friendly person waiting on the quay shares a copy of the colored brochure, which features the island's attractions. This is an interesting collection of people—picnickers with hampers, serious-looking walkers, and one large man with a big walking stick and two dogs straining on the leash. One thing that has not changed is the ferryman. He is as dour as ever—a cousin of that fellow who is to meet us at the River Styx.‡ I wait for the second boatload.

---

* Nancy MacDougall Black advises the author that the natives speak of these as the Ardbhan *Rocks*.
† In 1990 there were 34 people living on Kerrera and 11 enrolled in the school. We arrived at the ferry just when a happy group of schoolchildren with knapsacks on their backs were disembarking for a trip to Oban and perhaps beyond. In 1997, the school was closed for want of sufficient children.
‡ In November of 1997, the ferryman was a young fellow and very pleasant.

Chapter 41

The gravel road leads steeply up from Kerrera's stone pier. Just beyond the schoolhouse and to the right of the roadway, the land continues to rise abruptly, giving a chance for a good picture from the top of the knoll. One looks down on the ferryman's cottage and out across the sparkling Sound to the steeply rising mainland and the Ardbhan Craigs. Behind me there is a fertile-looking pasture dotted with sheep, and then the central spine of the island rises to block the view westward.

Inland among the hillocks, it is a bit too warm for comfort. The road rises over the ridge, and there spreads the sweeping view of the Firth of Lorn, backed by the mountains of Mull and Morvern. Despite the size of the group waiting at the ferry, I can see no one in front or behind me. Evidently the brochure directs the travel clockwise around the island rather than the way I have chosen. Thanks to the sheep, there always seems to be a place just made for sitting on the bank beside the road. One always has a front seat to magnificence. Far off on the Isle of Mull, Duart Castle stands, a pink-brown block on its headland. A MacBrayne ferry is returning to Oban, a good-size sailboat heels over in the wind, and the white shaft of Eilean Musdile Light off Lismore marks the passage up the Sound of Mull to the open Atlantic. Suddenly I realize why the school seemed deserted. It is Saturday. Shouts of play come up from the farmyard at Slaterach. And as I listen, a hooded crow rises, cawing its way into the sky.

Ahead on the left is a little grotto with a small burn and greenery. It is the narrow entrance to what I call the "Hidden Glen." Its real name is Gleann na Curra ("Glen of the Mowing" or "Glen of the Heron"?). What a happy privilege to take one's time, to wander and to wonder, or to tape the sounds of the burn as it comes splashing down from the glen. There is a rising wind at my heels. It rushes past me into the glen, rippling the tall reeds and grasses that grow rankly in the wet basin of this rounded valley. Sheep bounce along ahead, their backsides waddling with a bustle of wool.

About halfway up the glen, and located upon the eastern valley wall, is a large rock fall. It is a landmark one cannot miss. Directly across the glen from the tumble of stone, one turns to make a "four-legged" scramble up the steep western slope to reach Lochan na Circe, the "Little Loch of the Water Lilies." Where the rock face is exposed, one has the impression of climbing over a manmade wall of cemented rock. The turf on the top of Kerrera is thinly spread over red conglomerate bedrock—the same rock that forms the Ardbhan Craigs.

It is a short climb. One stands on the western rim of the glen looking across at Lochan na Circe, which is windswept to a cobalt blue. The lilypads turn up in the wind, yellow-green against the nearly violet wavelets. Looking across the lochan, there seems but a narrow brim holding the water from dashing four hundred feet down the western side of Kerrera to join the Firth of Lorn. Indeed, it appears that half an hour with a spade would turn the lochan loose, but a solid ridge of rock must be interposed.

The wind at the top of the glen is strong enough to shift my pack and cause me to brace my feet as I photograph. I find a sheltered spot at the lochan's bank and sit in the lee of a rock outcropping. At my feet the myrtle grows half in and half out of the water, and the ground about me is rich in small flowers: lousewort, tormentil, violets, and a small yellow buttercup. Across the lochan the wind sends dark scuds of waves, now breaking white along their edges. A thousand silver crescents dance among the lilypads.

This lochan has another name: Lochan nan Seachd Crioch, the "Lochan of the Seven Boundaries." What boundaries—physical or the meeting of powers unknown? If a third name were needed, I would suggest the "Chalice of Lorn," for this gem of a lochan seems lifted up in celebration to the sky and encircled with a glorious world of sea and mountain—the sacred, shining center of the old MacDougall Kingdom of Lorn.

My reverie is jolted by the sound of a human voice. It seems to come from afar, but still I am startled and soon to suffer disillusionment. Gleann na Curra is not as "hidden" as I thought nor the "Chalice of Lorn" as private. More voices, then a group of clamoring schoolchildren and their chaperones arrive to picnic and leave their wrappers on the banks of Lochan na Circe. I remind myself that it has been the practice of our recent Chiefs to welcome Boy Scout campers at Dunollie and on Kerrera. Yet in the ruins of my solitude, however unfairly, I also recall that one such group burned the roof from the cottage here on Kerrera that had served as the dower house for Chief Iain Ciar's faithful wife. It was the last thatched-roof cottage on the island.

Turning southwest and climbing above the lochan, one reaches a place where one looks down on the green fields of Barnabuck and Kerrera's west coast. Lounging comfortably on the carpet of the moor, I eat my lunch. There is too much wind here to record the skylark's song as it mounts vertically into the sweep of air, and there is no way to express the grandeur of the world that spreads south and west. Southward across the Island of Seil rises the mass of Scarpa, the mountain island, and as if floating on the white band of haze that rims the sea, the Garvellachs. Further out to sea is Colonsay, and further south still and all but lost in the misty distance are the Paps of Jura. Westward, the cliffs of

Mull rise to wall the Firth of Lorn. Mull's Ben More, once a giant volcano, rises in a hazy cone. The closer mountains are a pale green crossed with pinks and blues. To the north and northwest, the purple-topped heights of Morvern join in a wilderness of peaks.

I wander inland a short distance and suddenly find that I am looking down a deep notch in the hills to see Gylen Castle by the sea. There is no end of wonderful surprises here on Kerrera.

The picnickers have gone when I return to Lochan na Circe. Two brilliantly white gulls are riding on the dark blue waters. The gulls appear over the western crest and sweep out across the lochan, apparently having ridden the elevator express of the winds from the coast to this elevation without a wing beat.

Today, descending into Gleann na Curra, every step takes one into a different climate—out of high wind into a balmy, even hot, afternoon. I follow a track that separates the upper from the marshy, lower section of the glen. The track crosses a little burn and begins the climb up the eastern side of the valley. The white plumes of the cotton grass toss in the wind, and again the seasons change as I climb from the nearly tropical to the cooler and windy highlands. My object is the highest point on Kerrera, that precipitous knob called Carn Breugach, 619 feet above the Sound of Kerrera. Unless one keeps one's mouth shut, it is literally and forcefully filled with air like a balloon. At times I find myself leaning into the wind as though against a cushion.

Here amidst the heather bushes there is a beautiful little orchid—pale pink, nearly white. Another shallow glen, and then I am high enough to look south and out to sea and to those distant "Holy Islands," the Garvellachs. I have been looking for evidence of past peat cutting on these uplands, but none is evident.[*]

Now my attention turns to the really serious climb ahead. I would guess there is a 45-degree grade in front of me and a hard scramble through the clumps of burned-over heather.[†]

What a stupendous view on Carn Breugach's narrow top! Northwest, one looks high over the top of Oban—over the top of the Ardbhan Craigs, which from the eagle's roost look unpretentious. To see Dunollie, one has to know where it stands, almost lost in this gigantic scenery. To the west rise the twin peaks of Cruachan; nearer at hand, the cloud

---

[*] Miss Hope MacDougall of MacDougall's book, *Island of Kerrera*, relates that a shortage of peat became a real problem for those living on the island.

[†] I traveled by compass bearing from the eastern rim of Gleann na Curra to Carn Breugach, as that destination was often out of sight to one traversing Kerrera's irregular interior. My route was, therefore, as near a straight line as possible, and there are doubtless easier routes. However one goes, the last ascent will be steep.

shadows move across the landscape of knobs and declivities so distinctive of the country west of Oban. The Sound of Kerrera stretches below. Standing on the eastern edge, Carn Breugach drops in vertical cliffs and then tumbles downward in a series of steep descents to the road that skirts Horse Shoe Bay. The total drop is some six hundred feet. The wind is actually swaying me, and I instinctively move back from the edge, glad of the solid of rocks heaped up to form a cairn. Westward, across the Sound, one looks down into Gallanach Park and upon Gallanach House, small in its great clifted cup. Turning around, there are the omnipresent mountains of Mull and the Firth of Lorn. Lochan na Circe, however, is hidden behind the western rim of Gleann na Curra.

Hazy cumulus now float across the sky. The nearer mountains of Mull stand clear, but the heights of Glencoe are indistinct in the haze. On the sea horizon, a layer of white mist makes it impossible to tell where ocean ends and sky begins. It is difficult to take in such a full panorama. I sit in the shelter of the cairn, while around me the wind flows over the top of Carn Breugach and makes its song in the grasses and the rushes.

Hope MacDougall of MacDougall tells me that this site atop Carn Breugach is a traditional place for celebratory bonfires. The one lit to celebrate the birth of Madam MacDougall of MacDougall, thirtieth Chief of the Clan, burned for three days. Getting that much fuel up here took a lot of dedication! The old were not up to it and the young were too occupied to build a bonfire here in honor of the Prince of Wales. Instead, that blaze was lit near the Hutchinson Monument on the north end of Kerrera.[*]

The next objective is Gylen Castle on the southern shore of Kerrera. Walking diagonally down these steep hillsides is as rough going as climbing upwards. Heather bushes grow in tough mounds amidst inches of moss intermixed with broken rock. Here and there the bracken grows rankly. The map shows several finger-like glens that work their way down to the shore. I am not sure which one I have taken, but it does not matter. Ahead, seen through the notch of the glen, spreads a view of the gleaming sea and the Garvellachs low on the horizon. There is a real sense of adventure, not being sure just where one will come out, but still being sure one will arrive. New turns, new views, and a little burn flowing in its ledgy declivity to my right. Fair weather cumulus define the arch of the sky and float over the dark heather and the scattered rock. I stop. I must keep reminding myself: always stop for beauty. This is

---

[*] Miss MacDougall also told me later that it is the custom to carry a rock up to the top of Carn Breugach to add to the cairn.

really magnificent—the clouds floating above and their shadows running over the wide expanses of the folding moor.

I have come out high up and overlooking Gylen Castle. It stands just off to my left, slender and miniature in the vastness of this spreading view. Below me a buzzard[*] wheels above the road that winds its way toward Lower Gylen Farm. There must be some primeval instinct coded in our genes that senses it is best to be high up and looking down—to be the watcher and not the watched. I never feel more akin to my ancestors than when so situated.

On the rocky ridge above the road, a flock of sea gulls sails past at eye level. The sun is actually torrid. A path switches back and forth across the face of this last steep hillside. At the bottom by the road, as if made as a place to rest, is one of those delightful little spots on Kerrera that afford a relief from the overpowering vistas that sweep one's soul out and nearly away. The little burn comes down between two ledges, bubbling, falling white between mossy rocks, and pooling where the tall yellow flag grows. How I wish it were safe to drink from one of those shaded pools.

---

[*] The largest hawk in Scotland. See Lore of Lorn, Note 66, "Buzzards."

Chapter 42
Dunollie's Eagle

In the fall of 1831, William Wordsworth visited Dunollie Castle. In a letter dated October 27, he wrote:

> At Dunollie Castle, a ruin seated at the tip of the horns of the Bay of Oban, I saw the other day one of those noble creatures [eagles] cooped up among the ruins, and was incited to give vent to my feelings as you shall now see—
>
> Dishonored Rock and Ruin! that, by law
> Tyrannic, keep the Bird of Jove embarred
> Like a lone criminal whose life is spared.
> Vexed is he, and screams loud. The last I saw
> Was on the wing; stooping, he struck with awe
> Man, bird, and beast; then, with a consort paired,
> From a bold headland, their loved aery's guard,
> Flew high above Atlantic waves, to draw
> Light from the fountain of the setting sun.
> Such was this Prisoner once; and when his plumes
> The sea-blast ruffles as the storm comes on,
> Then, for a moment, he, in spirit, resumes
> His rank 'mong freeborn creatures that live free,
> His power, his beauty, and his majesty.

Wordsworth was certainly incited and inspired. His cause was both noble and current, but the poet did not have all the facts. Particulars come to us by way of a letter written in 1908 to Sophie MacDougall by Elizabeth MacDougall, a great-aunt of our thirtieth Chief, Coline MacDougall of MacDougall.

It is true enough that there was an eagle at Dunollie. Its large cage was protected by the section of curtain wall that still rises from the edge of the cliff in front of the old keep of Dunollie. The eagle had been kept for at least five years before Wordsworth's visit, for it was there when Elizabeth's mother was married in 1826. What Wordsworth did not know was that the eagle could not fly. It was brought to The Chief of the MacDougalls injured and permanently disabled. As Elizabeth recalls, when a storm blew the cage apart, the eagle was found

> crouching in a corner and was taken into the house [Dunollie House] until the cage could be mended and there he killed a poor cockatoo who was loose and went too near the king of birds.

Nature is cruel. It had been so for the eagle and it was to die as a result of cruelty. Some drunken sailors prodded it with sticks and, according to Elizabeth MacDougall, "It never flourished after that and finally died."

While it lived and brooded from its high cage at Dunollie, the eagle paid for its keep by being a watchbird. "No, one," writes Elizabeth, "could pass the windy corner without it giving a peculiar cry."[*]

---

[*] The "windy corner" is located on the avenue to Dunollie shortly before the drive reaches Dunollie House. Here the wind that seeps down the Sound of Kerrera flows unobstructed. Often from the protected lawn of Dunollie House, one hears that wind passing as if it were the sound of a waterfall.

Chapter 43
Touched by the Mist

Recently I came across a pencil sketch made one afternoon in Mull's Great Glen. At the sketch's margin was this Biblical-sounding notation: "Who can draw the tendrils of the mist?" It was evident that I could not; however, I can remember vividly what the pencil had tried to catch and the experience that came upon me, and will attempt to describe both here.

Far down the glen and through a window in the gray cloud ceiling, a sun shaft gives birth to a swath of vibrant green and spreads that wonder upwards upon a sweep of blue hillside. This creation comes and goes, while above upon the heights, the mist seems to flow eternally as if materializing from some inexhaustible and primordial store in the west. It travels eastward, as if forever. It explores the faces of the cliffs, as a wedding veil brushes the cheekbone of a bride. It condenses and fills a dark chasm with its whiteness; it holds an intimate relationship with the light—alternately keeping the illumination within itself and then transmitting. It enchants a high valley with a fairy light and then, white as a patriarch's beard, it shadows the heights with an intense purple. But in all this pageantry of beauty, it is the grand silence of its passing that most moves me. The mist flows eastward across the mountaintops with a solemnity of silence, and in the power of that silence a message brings to the inner self a knowing that cannot be put into words.

Below the silent passing of the mist with its timeless persistence and intimacy, I sense within myself another continuity. In that moment, I know I am part of a flowing from those who came bravely before, keeping the faith as best they could, to those who will follow with their own bright hopes.

In some similar but individual and special manner, those both past and present to whom this clan and every clan owes so much must have been touched by a sense of this flowing. To them must have come an understanding of the privilege of belonging to a special heritage, of being part of a challenge and sense of pride. On their shoulders, as it were, is laid the shoulder plaid of a tradition that is both their duty and their happiness to wear. Silent and embracing as the flowing of the mist upon the hills comes that inner knowing of that which is their native own.

LORE OF LORN

About the Notes

The following notes provide historical, geographical, and architectural information that either supports the preceding journal text or gives additional information for those journeying in MacDougall Country. The notes are grouped under subject headings and are preceded by numbers that correspond with the reference numbers given in the journal text.

Antiquity of Lorn

1. Timeline

Chronological Chart:

7500-7000 BCE	Humans in Oban Area.
5000 BCE	Mesolithic man lives in caves along the coast and on islands.
4000 BCE	Agriculture begins in Argyll.
3000 BCE	Neolithic man builds chambered cairns.
600 BCE	Celtic immigrations.
500 BCE	Bronze Age curb cairns with cists, beakers, food vessels, cinerary urns, bronze swords, and other artifacts.
400 CE	Iron Age hill forts, duns, brochs, and crannogs. (Some hill forts may have been built as early as 1000 BCE.)
500 CE	Kingdom of Dalriada founded.
560 CE	Coming of Saints Columba and Moluag.
802 CE	Vikings plunder Iona.
803 CE	Union of the Picts and Scots.
809 CE	Stone of Destiny (coronation stone) removed from Dunstaffnage Castle to Scone.
1069 CE	Marriage of Malcolm Canmore and Margaret; increase of "English" influence.
1098 CE	Magnus Barefoot of Norway claims Western Isles.
1130 CE	Somerled emerges as Regulus of Argyll.
1164 CE	Death of Somerled.

2. Clan Families in Lorn (Other Than MacDougall)

Campbell

The Campbells are descended from Duncan MacDuibhne, a chieftain of the Loch Awe area. They may have been connected with the British Royal House of Strathclyde, but there was a connection with the Dalriadic royal house as well. The Campbells were well enough established in the Loch Awe area by 1292 for their Chief, Cailein Mor, to be listed as one of the twelve barons within the newly created Sheriffdom of Argyll, over which Alexander of Argyll, fourth Chief of Clan MacDougall, was High Sheriff.

Cailein Mor was killed in a fight with the MacDougalls.[10] His son, Neil Campbell, was one of Robert Bruce's staunch friends. Neil won the hand of Lady Marjory Bruce, and his support of Robert Bruce assured the ascendancy of the Campbells in Argyll.

Through a marriage with a daughter of Stewart of Lorn[16] coupled, as Sir Ian Moncrieffe notes, "with cash and a bit of force," the Campbells acquired the title of Lords of Lorn. Intermarriage between the Campbells and the MacDougalls has been frequent and, in the case of the MacDougalls of Raera, pretty much the rule, though one such marriage cost this cadet of Clan MacDougall their home of Ardmaddy Castle.[*]

Though the Campbells looked to their own aggrandizement, they have been often maligned, perhaps because of their success. They were a resourceful people who proved they could stand bravely for those causes in which they believed.

MacArthur

This is a very old line inhabiting the Loch Awe region that has claimed decent from the British Royal House of Strathclyde and even from King Arthur of the Round Table. Moncrieffe suggests that a marriage into the MacArthurs may have given the Campbells their claim to this same heritage.

The MacArthurs seem to have had a special standing in the Loch Awe area granted by the Scottish Crown—a position that may date back to Dalriadic times. Reginald Hale suggests that the "Arthur" from whom this line arises might have been the son of King Aiden of Dalriada. Whatever their lineage, the MacArthurs are an ancient and honorable line in Lorn. A number of this name are buried at Kilbride.

MacDonald

From the standpoint of ancestors, Clan MacDougall and Clan Donald could not have been more closely related. The MacDougall Chiefs descended from the eldest son of Somerled while the Chiefs of Clan Donald descended from Reginald, Somerled's second son. While blood may be thicker than water, it often lacks the viscosity of treasured and envied possessions. The MacDougalls and the MacDonalds began their voyage through Highland history at the helms of Somerled's divided kingdom.[†]

Chief Alexander MacDonald of Islay married Juliana, sister of Alexander, Lord of Lorn and fourth Chief of Clan MacDougall. The marriage provided no strong ties between the two Alexanders in the complex drama in which the leading families of Argyll jockeyed for advantage during the thirteenth century.

---

[*] *The Tartan*, Fall 1982, and Spring 1983, "MacDougalls of Raera."
[†] R. Andrew McDonald, *The Kingdom of the Isles*.

Alexander of Islay and his father, Angus MacDonald, were involved in Bruce's secretive Turnberry Band in 1286. Both of these MacDonalds refused to do homage to King John Balliol in 1293. However, they do not appear to have been particularly pro-Bruce but rather were intent on outflanking the MacDougalls. Alexander MacDougall of Lorn and Alexander of Islay took their dispute before King Edward of England in 1292. Both agreed to bide their time for the sake of peace in the western Highlands. The peace was short-lived. With King John Balliol on the Scottish throne, Alexander of Islay sought the support of King Edward, while Alexander of Lorn and his son John Bacach were only too willing to take the field when directed by their relative, King Balliol, to bring the MacDonalds into line—an errand never completed. Alexander of Islay remained pro-Edward throughout the turmoil over the Scottish throne that was to follow. Both Alexanders were to suffer the consequences.

Angus Og MacDonald of Islay, to whom the chieftainship of Clan Donald was to pass with the fall of his brother, Alexander, was pro-Bruce and anti-MacDougall from the time King Balliol was placed upon the throne. That Angus Og stoutly admired Bruce there can be no doubt, nor can there be any question that in the cause of Bruce he saw the best chance to acquire the island possessions of the MacDougall Lords of Lorn. The galleys of Angus Og, joined with those of Bruce's allies, finally defeated John Bacach MacDougall of Lorn when the latter was acting as King Edward's Admiral of the Western Seas.

It is an irony (or perhaps only an inevitability) that the two forces that most profited by the demise of MacDougall supremacy in the western Highlands were to become bitter foes, for the Campbells were later instrumental in the final fall of the great MacDonald island realm of which Angus Og had dreamed.

MacIntyre

According to legend, the MacIntyres came from the Hebrides. They landed upon the mainland shores of Lorn in a galley that carried a white cow. The significance of this cow is not recorded, but it must have had a special meaning to have been this long remembered. Settling in Glen Noe on Loch Etive in the early fourteenth century, they became hereditary foresters to the MacDougall Lords of Lorn. (*Mac an t-Saoir*, their Gaelic name, translates "son of the carpenter.") In later years the MacIntyres leased Glen Noe from the Marquis of Breadalbane for the unusual rent of a white calf and a midsummer snowball, which they procured from a cranny high up on Ben Cruachan. Interestingly, the Arms of the MacIntyres, as shown on a grave slab at Ardchattan Priory, portrays a rounded object which might well be a representation of a snowball.

MacLean of Duart

The MacLeans were neighbors of the MacDougalls (separated by the Firth of Lorn) and often closely associated. Moncrieffe gives the MacLeans' origin in the person of Gillian of the Battle-Ax, "a thirteenth-century warrior whose lineage is traced through a Celtic abbot of Lismore and the royal house of Lorn." Both Adams and Bain affirm that the MacLeans first sided with the MacDougalls of Lorn before transferring their allegiances to the MacDonalds of the Isles.

Duncan of Dunollie, sixteenth Chief of the MacDougalls, married Margaret, the sister of Sir Lauchlan MacLean of Duart. This marriage evidently did not hamper the cattle raids between the two clans. Sir John MacDougall, seventeenth Chief, married Katherine, the daughter of Hector MacLean of Duart, in 1610.[40]

MacNab

The MacNabs held lands around Loch Tay and in Glen Dochart and Strath Fillan. The latter valley is named for Saint Fillan, who was a prince of the Dalriadic royal house of Lorn. Associated with this saintly name were the powerful Abbots of Glen Dochart, to whom the MacNabs were closely related. Angus MacNab of Glen Dochart was related to the Red Comyn, who was murdered by Robert Bruce. Thus, the MacNabs joined with the MacDougalls of Lorn in the Bruce-Balliol contention over the Scottish Crown.

MacNaughten of Loch Awe

Moncrieffe says that "Nechtan" is an old Pictish name and thinks it likely that the clan descends from a Pictish mother and a father belonging to Cenel Loran or the royal house of Lorn. One branch of the MacNaughtens were the hereditary keepers of Fraoch Eilean Castle,[46] on an island at the eastern end of Loch Awe, as granted by King Alexander III in 1267. Gilbert Macnachten was one of the twelve barons in the Sheriffdom of Argyll, established in 1292 and placed under Alexander, Lord of Lorn.

On Inishail[49] close by Fraoch Eilean is a gravestone upon which is engraved a coat of arms in which two knights in conical helmets hold what appears to be a crown over a shield bearing a galley. Is this the galley of Lorn, and does this stone mark the resting place of one of the MacNaughten Chiefs? Donald, a thirteenth-century Chief of the

MacNaughtens, was related to the MacDougall Lords of Lorn and supported them in their opposition to Bruce. A number of MacNaughtens are buried at Kilbride.

3. Caves, Cairns, Cists, and Burial Urns

Some eighty cairns and barrows have been identified in Argyll with two important centers: one in Benderloch and Lismore, and the other around Loch Nell and the head of Loch Feochan.

Cairns with central chambers (and often with passageways) belong to the Neolithic Period. The chambered cairn on the farm at the south end of Loch Nell and the passage cairn on the Moss of Achnacree are good examples.

Cairns of the Bronze Age are characterized by a ring of curbstones and a central cist or stone coffin. There is little left of the Bronze Age cairn at the head of Loch Nell (mentioned in Chapter 22). A better example can be seen east of Moleigh Farm south of Loch Nell.

Cists without surrounding cairns are also abundant in Lorn. Fortunately many artifacts found in these cists have been preserved in the National Museum of Antiquities in Edinburgh. The artifacts include food vessels from cists discovered on Slaterach Farm on Kerrera and in Corran Park, Oban; bronze armlets found at Melfort House; a riveted dagger from Kilmore; bronze axes found on the Moss of Achnacree and near Dunollie; and cinerary urns found in Glen Seileach and the "gasworks cave" in Oban. Most well-known of all the Bronze Age finds are three bronze swords found in a peat bog on the Island of Shuna.

Before the cairn builders arrived, Mesolithic man was living in rock shelters and caves along the shore of Lorn.[*] They were hunters, fishermen, and gatherers of shellfish. They used flint instruments, although apparently there is no known source of this stone in Argyll. A good deal of what is known about these early inhabitants comes from the remains found in two Oban caves, MacArthur's Cave and the so-called "gasworks cave," both of which have been destroyed by quarrying and the expansion of the burgh.

The levels of occupation uncovered in these caves indicate they were places of habitation over a long period of time. Skeletal remains from a later, though still prehistoric, era were found in a cave just south of Ganavan when it was being converted into an icehouse (this cave still exists). More extensive finds were discovered in a cave below Dunollie,

---

[*] Another cave has been discovered in Oban during an excavation for a house. These and other finds have been so important that archeologists apply the term "Obanian" to this entire ancient assemblage in Argyll.

including four skeletons laid in a cist alongside a sword. Close by the skeletons were a gold brooch and a finger ring.

Caves continued to be important places of refuge in historic times, and there lingers today a fascination for these openings in the earth's rock, as if they were tunnels into the hidden psyche of the race.

For additional information see *The Archaeology of Argyll*, edited by Graham Ritchie, Edinburgh University Press, 1997, and *Argyll, Volume 2, Lorn*, published by the Royal Commission on Ancient and Historical Monuments.

4. Standing Stones and Stone Circles

There is a compelling mystery surrounding the standing stones and stone circles. They evoke the imagination. One visualizes religious rites practiced by men and women enthralled by the unfailing calendar of the stars. Even the unpretentious stone circle on the plain above Loch Nell has this aura. One feels the kinship of human experience, of awe, and of adventure into the unknown.

STANDING STONE - GLEN LONAN

Standing stones of particular interest are a group of four stones west of Duachy farmhouse and close to Dubh Loch on the road to Seil (see Chapter 40), the stone on the Glen Lonan Road above Loch Nell (mentioned in Chapter 22), and the tallest of all standing stones in Lorn, situated northwest of Acharra on the upper coast of Appin. There is also a circle of standing stones at Lochbuie on Mull.

Puzzling, like so many remains of prehistoric man, are the cup-and-ring markings engraved upon rocks. Only one example of cup-and-ring design is recorded in Lorn, and that is on a boulder about a mile east-northeast of Kilchrenan on the north shore of Loch Awe. The most outstanding cup-and-ring examples can be seen at Balameanach below Kilmartin. Cups without rings can be seen at several locations in Lorn. A fine example came from Benderloch and is now in the Oban Museum. Supposedly once both cups and rings were visible on the large granite boulder near the lighthouse at the head of the Esplanade on the Oban waterfront. However, the writer was unable to find any trace.

5. Hill Forts and Duns

At least sixty-two duns and hill forts have been identified in Lorn. The remains of these Iron Age strongholds top many of the headlands around Oban and are frequently found on top of the island heights. While there is often very little remaining of these ancient citadels, their frequency, strategic placement, and structural strength give a picture of the rough and ready era in which Celtic tribes lived and warred.

The surrounding walls of these hill forts were massive drystone structures, often twenty feet thick and interlaced with timbers. Perhaps it was in a ritual of destruction practiced by conquerors rather than a purposeful firing of these timbers by the builders that caused the vitrification of the walls observed at many sites. One can be quite sure the fires that melted rock into semi-molten masses were not accidental, for the firing had to be contrived in order to produce such intense heat.

Duns are distinguished from hill forts mainly by their smaller size. As in the case of many hill forts, the duns were protected by outer works of stone and earth.

Some of the most interesting hill forts and duns are:
- **Dun Ormidal**—just north of Gallanach House, which, though little remains, has the honor of having the largest enclosed area of all the forts in Lorn.
- **Dun Leccamore**—on Luing, where many huge, facing blocks are still in place and where a small room and staircase built within the walls can be seen. The south entrance features a bar-hole and a slate jamb with cup markings (see Chapter 39).
- **Caisteal Suidhe Cheannaidh**—one of the best-preserved duns in Lorn, located about a mile north of Kilchrenan between the road to Taynuilt and Loch Droighinn.
- **Dun MacSniachan (MacUisneachan)**[*]—a combination dun and hill fort located just west of Benderloch Village on Ardmucknish Bay. Standing upon a great rock outcropping, this complex includes vitrified remains of a fort surrounded with an older rampart of stones which rims the entire top of the rock. Excavations have produced a tanged iron sword, an iron dagger, an iron ring (certainly from an iron age!), a bronze ring, and several querns for grinding grain. These are preserved at the Museum of Antiquities in Edinburgh.

---

[*] The site is associated by myth with Ossian's Selma. See J.E. Campbell's *Popular Tales of the West Highlands, Vol. 4*, pp. 223–224.

6. Early and Later Structures

Crannogs

Crannogs are an engineering feat dating from the late Iron Age and early Middle Ages. They are manmade islands composed of stone and timber crib-work, sometimes connected to the shore by submerged causeways. No fewer than sixteen crannogs have been identified in Loch Awe. There is also the remains of a crannog in Loch Nell. Excavations of a crannog in a now drained lochan upon the Moss of Achnacree showed evidence that the living accommodations had turf or wattle walls, a clay floor, and an open hearth. Among the artifacts found were a wooden comb, a piece of wood with a crosslet burned into it (note similarity to crest of Clan MacDougall), a knife, a hook, and fragments of a leather slipper.

Brochs

Of all the dry stone constructions of the Iron Age, the brochs were the most outstanding in both design and execution. These round, tapered towers, which could rise to a height of forty-five feet, were built with two concentric walls, allowing intermural galleries. The door by which one entered the broch was small and led through a tunnel with openings in the roof through which spears could be thrust downward from a chamber above.

These structures were obviously built by skilled masons, and it has been suggested that their plan may have been the work of a "gifted designer" who saw the need for safe refuges from marauding enemies—perhaps southern Celts or Roman slave hunters.[*]

While brochs are associated with northern Scotland and the Orkneys, there is at least one broch in Lorn. This is so-called Tirefour Castle, located on the east shore of Lismore about a mile and a half north of Achnacroish. The remains of what may be another broch is on Lismore overlooking Loch Fiart.

Church Designs

The floor plans of medieval churches in Lorn remained simple. Except for the plan of Ardchattan Priory, which included shallow transeptal chapels, churches kept to the confines of an elongated rectangle.

---

[*] Richard Muir, *Riddles of the British Landscape*, pp. 141 ff.

In the chapel at Dunstaffnage, the nave was separated from the chancel by a wooden screen. This arrangement does not appear to have been common, nor was the degree of ornamentation found in this chapel. The general design featured a single door on one of the long sides and few windows.

Later parish churches followed the same basic design and were usually built on the sites of older chapels, as in the case of both Kilbride and Kilmore. In some cases, the site may have been one of very early veneration, often including a sacred well, as appears to be the case with Kilbride.

With the Reformation, galleries were often added to the older parish churches.

The standard Presbyterian church design became the "T" floor plan, as found in the Parish Church at Ardchattan built in 1836. In this church the communion table runs down the center, thus dividing the pews.

It is worth noting that the three remaining medieval ecclesiastical monuments of major historical and architectural importance—Ardchattan Priory, the Cathedral Church of Lismore, and Dunstaffnage Chapel—were built under the auspices of the MacDougall Lords of Lorn.

Castles, Keeps, and Tower Houses

While most of the medieval defensive domiciles in Lorn are called castles, it is useful for descriptive purposes to categorize them as castles, keeps, or tower houses.

Using this terminology, Innischonnell[49] and Dunstaffnage[45] are *castles*, both taking the form of rectangular enclosures of considerable size having halls, kitchens, and other accommodations built against the inside of the curtain walls. Dunstaffnage shows an advance in design, having rounded corner towers rather than the square towers of shallow projection seen at Innischonnell.

Keeps feature a single tower with the kitchen, hall, and living quarters on successive levels. Keeps usually had out-works, including a postern and enclosed courtyard or bailey. Of the early keeps in Lorn, Dunollie is the most impressive, both in size and in construction. It is also the most important historically.

Fraoch Eilean and Coeffin, which share many similarities, are simpler *tower houses*. Each has an unvaulted cellar. The hall of Fraoch Eilean was covered by a timber roof surrounded by walkways. While Coeffin had a mural fireplace in its hall, Fraoch Eilean appears to have had a central hearth.[37, 46] (Also see Chapter 34.) Later and much more ornamented tower houses are represented by Gylen on Kerrera and Stalker in Appin.

The thick walls of earlier castles and tower houses were built of roughly coursed and unsquared rocks. Corners and openings were dressed with squared blocks of sandstone; often, in the case of door and window facings, these were carved and chamfered. Portals, windows, embrasures, and passageways were either capped with large stone mantels or arched. Some fine pointed arches are found at Dunstaffnage; however, in this castle huge timber lintels were also employed, reminiscent, no doubt, of earlier building practices.

While the first-floor halls of all three structural types were usually paved with stone supported upon the vaults of the cellar, the upper floors were wood resting on joists running from stringers along the walls that, in turn, rested on projecting corbels. In some cases, as in Gylen, floor joists were mortised into the walls themselves. The roofs were supported on timber bents, while the gables were stone, often with the characteristic "crow-steps" construction, which results in a stair-like appearance. Roofs were covered with slates.

7. Decorative Designs

The following designs are a sample of the decorative work used in both castles and churches of medieval Lorn. Similar examples can be found at many locations.

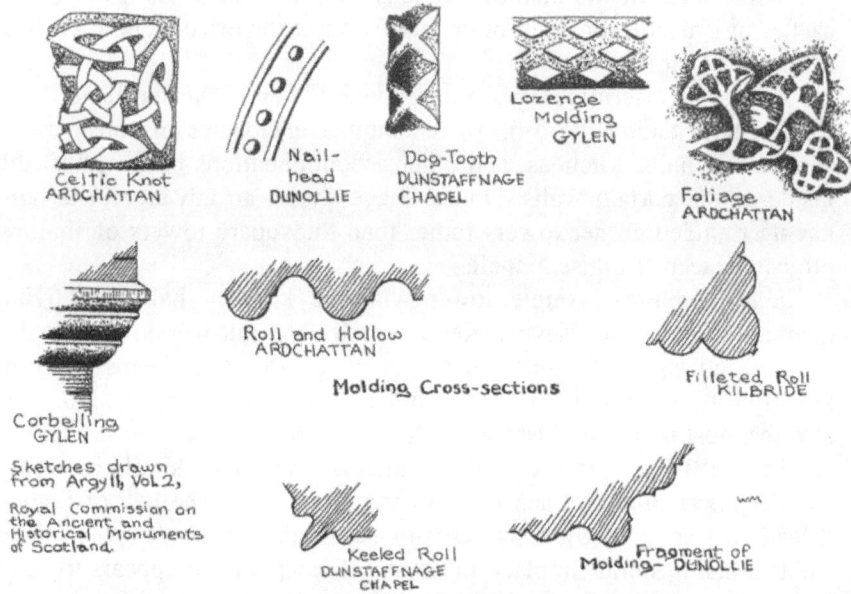

Diagram 1. Architectural Decorative Designs

8. Arrow Slits and Gun Loops

Many castles and tower houses in Lorn managed to survive the transition to firearms. Arrow slits were converted to gun loops, and sometimes provision was made for mounting cannon. Both arrow slits and gun loops were inletted into blocks internally splayed, to allow the defender to cover a wider area below the walls.

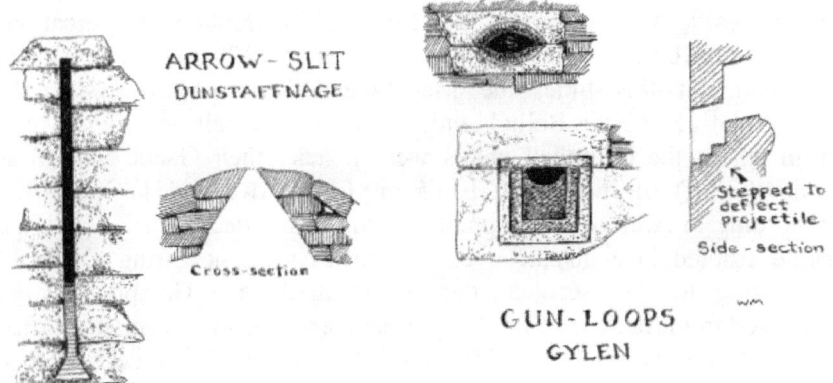

Diagram 2. Arrow Slits and Gun Loops

9. Schools of Carving

Experts divide much of the medieval carving both on buildings and burial markers in Lorn into two classifications: those done by the Iona School and those by the Loch Awe School.

Most of the work accomplished by the Loch Awe School was done before 1500. These artists seemed to travel from job to job and use whatever stone was available. Their work was not inscribed and was usually of inferior craftsmanship compared to that of the Iona School. Typical work of the Loch Awe School is found in the burial slabs at Kilbride, which feature long swords and plant-scrolls.

The work of the Iona School is exemplified in the coffin lid of the Somerled MacDougall family at Ardchattan.

Battles

10. Allt Dearg

It has been claimed that the contest over the throne of Scotland and the contention between the adherents of King Balliol and Robert the Bruce were the issues over which the MacDougalls and the Campbells fought beside Allt Dearg, the "Red Stream." The immediate altercations appear to have been closer to home. The year was 1294; the season is not recorded. At this time, the MacDougall Lord of Lorn was the representative of King Balliol, and Sir Colin Campbell—"Cailein Mor," from whom the Campbell chiefs were to take their Gaelic title—was baile (bailiff) of the crown lands on Loch Awe and in Kilmartin. According to Archibald Campbell, writing in his *Records of Argyll*, the battle erupted in a dispute over boundaries near the String of Lorn.[*] According to this account, the MacDougalls and Campbells were supposed to meet close to Loch na Sreinge and upon a stream still called Allt a Chomhlachaidh, the "Burn of the Meeting." As described in Chapter 13, the MacDougalls were late, having had, according to the tale, a rather disturbing experience upon the shore of Loch Scammadale. Campbell adds another twist to the tale of the talisman consulted by Loch Scammadale. The charm was passed among the MacDougalls present three times, and on each occasion it indicated that a certain clansman in the party would be killed. Kindly, he was sent back to Dunollie with a message and supposedly out of harm's way. Yet he should have stayed, for on his return he met a group of Campbells and was killed.

The Clan Bard, Dugald Gordon MacDougall, who visited Allt Dearg at the turn of the last century, wrote a poem entitled *Fineghleann* in which he mentions a number of cairns in addition to the memorial to Cailein Mor. However, the writer of these notes was able to locate only one other cairn, situated on the south side of stream below the falls and the ford.

It would be interesting to know if the cairn piled to the memory of Cailein Mor marks the spot where the Campbell Chief fell or was merely built on the highest and thus the most prominent spot on the track as it crosses the String of Lorn. If the cairn marks the spot where the legendary and fatal arrow struck down Cailein Mor and if the fight began

---

[*] In another version recorded by Campbell and contributed by Allan MacCulloch of Kerrera, the battle resulted from a raid made by the Campbells into Nether Lorn. According to this account, it was mainly the MacDougalls of Nether Lorn who took part.

at the ford, then one must doubt the Campbell account that the MacDougalls were all but beaten when the Chief of the Campbells fell.

Archibald Campbell's *Records of Argyll* includes a gruesome yet moving version of how the MacDougall march *Brosnachadh-Catha Chlann Dughaill*, "Clan Dougall's Incitement to Battle,"* was first played amidst the carnage of Allt Dearg. According to this tale, it was a Campbell piper who played this tune as a lament for the fallen MacDougall piper.

> My loss! My loss! that I have not three hands,
> Two engaged with pipe and one with sword.
> ...
> My loss! My loss! low lies yonder
> MacDougall with his pipes whose sound was
> Soft and sweet to me.

Archibald Campbell ends his account of this piper's lament with a Celtic gory twist. The Campbells, knowing that the tune was not one of theirs, "ran to where he (the piper) was and chopped his head off. It is said that the piper's fingers played three or four notes on the chanter while his head toppled to the ground." All in all a rather unlikely story, except that, to our loss, the human race is forever cutting its pipers down.†

11. Asknish

Burke in his *Landed Gentry* states that Dugald MacDougall, ninth Chief of the Clan, was killed in a fight with the Campbells at Asknish. The writer of these notes has not been able to determine if this refers to the son of Iain MacDougall, eighth Chief, who was reportedly killed in the fight at Loch Druimnean, or to another son killed in a subsequent battle.[14]

12. Daileag

Daileag is north of Taynuilt and reportedly the site of a prearranged duel of seven men on a side between the MacDougalls and the Campbells. The deadly contest was staged to determine who would take possession of Muckairn. The writer has been unable to confirm this story.‡

---

* Also called "The Battle March." This can be found in William Ross' collection of pipe music.
† See also Archie McKerracher's "The Battle of the Red Ford."
‡ See *Scotland Magazine*, March 1968, p. 28; also *The Highlander*, May/June 1983, p. 38.

13. Dunaverty

Though not within the MacDougall Country of Lorn, Dunaverty Rock looms darkly in the annals of the Clan. Nothing remains of the stronghold that once stood upon this promontory, which reaches out into the sea at the tip of Kintyre (although the author did find what appeared to be laid-up wall filling a small ravine near the top of the rock). Befriended by Angus Og MacDonald of Islay, Robert Bruce spent time at Dunaverty following his defeat by MacDougall forces at Dalrigh and before fleeing to Rathlin Island and Ireland. (The northern hills of Ireland can be seen from the Mull of Kintyre.) Three hundred and forty years later, in May of 1647, a combined force of MacDougalls, MacDonalds, and their supporters, joined in the Royalist cause against the forces of the Covenant, were left (actually abandoned) by Sir Alexander MacDonald, a lieutenant of Montrose, to hold Dunaverty.

The army of the Covenant led by General David Leslie and Alexander Campbell, Marquis of Argyll, spurred by the religious fanaticism of John Nave (who threatened all who showed mercy to the Royalists with the curses that befell Saul for sparing the Amalekites) besieged Dunaverty. The garrison held until the attackers cut the water supply. It seems evident that quarter was promised to the three hundred defenders (some reports say five hundred). They surrendered and were "cruellie and inhumanelie butchered in cold blood."[*]

No less than forty-nine MacDougalls of the main stock of the Clan fell in this massacre, including two brothers and three cousins of the Chief, a nephew of MacDougall of Raera (Raray), MacDougall of Ardmore, and MacDougall of Degnish. With these clansmen died at least forty-one members of the wider Clan family.

According to the story most often repeated, only one defender was spared the slaughter. This was a John MacDougall who was but a boy and perhaps the son of the eighteenth Chief of the Clan.[†]

---

[*] J.R.N Macphail, *Highland Papers*, Vol. ii.
[†] J.R.N Macphail, *Highland Papers*, Vol. ii, pp. 248–257.

14. Loch Druimnean

An account of the fight between the MacDougalls and the Campbells at Loch Druimnean is given in Archibald Campbell's *Waifs and Strays of Celtic Tradition*, Vol. I. According to this story, MacDougall of Dunollie married as his second wife the sister of Campbell of Innischonnell. This MacDougall may be the eighth Chief of the Clan as given in Burke's *Landed Gentry*, although this work mentions only one marriage and that to Christina, daughter of Sir Dougald Campbell, seventh Lord of Craignish. (The discrepancies in these two accounts may follow the first rule of Highland sources; namely, that any two accounts of the same event shall agree in all irrelevant particulars.)

The account in *Waifs and Strays* tells us that the stepsons tried to get hold of the title to certain lands through their stepmother and that she fled Dunollie to Innischonnell and her Campbell relatives. This indomitable lady next married Campbell of Craignish and then MacIvor of Lergychony. In the course of time, she wearied and died. The Campbells decided that her body should be laid to rest at Kilvorie (Corranmore?), but before this could be accomplished, some MacDougalls from Dunollie arrived demanding Christina's corpse.

The Campbells invited the MacDougalls to dinner, and while their guests ate, the body was secreted away. The MacDougalls, discovering they had been tricked, helped themselves to some of the Campbell's cattle and started for home. Alerted, the Campbells overtook the MacDougall party, who had stopped on the shore of Loch Druimnean to feast on freshly butchered steak. In the fight that followed, one of the MacDougall sons of Christina was killed. (The tale follows the usual Campbell formula. First one praises the MacDougalls for fighting bravely and then adds that despite all that the Campbells won. It is useful to remember that the person who writes the account has a great advantage.)

The tale ends with a bit of further revenge. The man who slew the MacDougall was a Campbell weaver. MacIvor, who was a half brother of the slain MacDougall, ordered a pair of hose from this weaver, contrived to get into an argument over the cut, and killed the weaver.

15. Pass of Brander

In March of 1307, Robert Bruce won victories over the English forces in Glen Trool and at Loudon Hill (Galloway). By May he was in a position to march north, subdue the Comyn power, and silence the opposition of the Earl of Ross.

Sir John of Lorn—who had been in Galloway to join forces with his kinsman, Dougal MacDouall, in an attempt to hunt down Bruce—returned to Dunstaffnage. A year later, Bruce had overcome his enemies in the north and, with a force of three thousand victorious troops, was ready to descend upon Lorn and the MacDougalls.

Sir John was in a difficult position. He was ill and confined to his bed. The Barons of Argyll, many of whom could see their own advantage in the defeat of the MacDougalls, would give him no help.

John and his father, Sir Alexander, the fourth Chief of the Clan, did hold three castles. Scholars agree that these must have been Dunstaffnage, Dunollie, and Innischonnell. The Chief and his son could count on a fourth tower house, Fraoch Eilean, which was held by their kinsman, the Chief of MacNaughtens. They had eight hundred men in service, of which three hundred were kinsmen and supporters and the rest under pay. Sir John also had a fleet upon Loch Awe manned by crews upon whom he could depend. Finally, there was a natural ally, the Pass of Brander, through which Bruce must funnel his force if he were to march into the heartland of Lorn.

When word came of Bruce's approach, John got up from his sickbed and gathered an additional one thousand two hundred men of Lorn. As his Gaelic epithet "Bacach" indicates, Sir John was lame, but he was a fighter and even his enemies respected his tenacity. Still unable to take the field himself, John positioned his men in the Pass of Brander and watched from his galley moored off Fraoch Eilean. The exact time of the year is not known, but it was probably August 1308.

It is doubtful that Sir John expected to take Bruce by surprise. He certainly did not anticipate being outflanked himself. It may have been Sir Neil Campbell who led Douglas and his flanking columns up Cruachan and down into the pass, to catch the waiting MacDougalls and their supporters in a pincer.

Barbour, who wrote the glowing and laudatory epic of Robert the Bruce, records that the men of Lorn fought manfully. There was actually no other way to act, as the MacDougalls were outnumbered and had the River Awe to their backs. Eventually, it appears that the MacDougall forces broke through the pincer (or perhaps a part of the forces of Lorn were not caught within Bruce's claw), for a last stand was made in the field above the steep west bank of the river where the cairns of the dead dot the bracken. There is disagreement on whether there was a bridge across River Awe at this time. In a note to the author, Hope MacDougall of MacDougall writes, "I understood that the MacDougalls and Lorn men crossed it [the bridge] and tried to destroy it to prevent Bruce's men passing over, but failed." It is reported that Sir John retreated to Innischonnell Castle.[49] He would fight again, but never upon his own soil of Lorn.

16. Stalc

An inscription upon a monument close by the Scottish Episcopal Church at Portnacroish in Appin reads:

A.D. 1468.

> Above this spot was fought the bloody Battle of Stalc in which many fell when the Stewarts and the MacLarens, their allies, in defense of Dougald, Chief of Appin, son of John Stewart, Lord of Lorn and Innermeath, defeated the combined forces of the MacDougalls and MacFarlanes.

Anyone aware of the close relationship between the MacDougalls and the Stewart Lords of Lorn will be puzzled by this inscription. Why were the MacDougalls joining with the MacFarlanes to fight Dougald (Dougall) Stewart? Why, indeed, when but seventeen years before the Battle of Stalc, Dougald's father, Sir John Stewart of Lorn and brother-in-law of the tenth Chief of Clan MacDougall, had confirmed by charter to John MacAlan MacDougall, the eleventh Chief of the MacDougalls, not only Dunollie but ninety-one merklands that included Kerrera and a large section of inner Lorn.

It seems likely that any MacDougalls taking up arms against the Stewarts of Appin belonged to the band of Alan MacCoul (MacDougall) who had risen against his own Chief. It is regrettable that so little is known about this dramatic period in the history of the Clan. Was Alan MacCoul simply an ambitious tool of the Campbells? Did he draw a following from the restless young among his kinsmen, or did he represent a wider faction of clansmen who felt that the last MacDougall Lord of Lorn and seventh Chief had sacrificed too great a portion of the Clan's common interest when he arranged the marriage of his daughter to the Stewarts of Innermeath?

Apparently Alan MacCoul was closely, though perhaps illegitimately, related to the MacDougall Chief. He may have felt that he should have been chief rather than the title passing to John MacDougall of Dunollie (eleventh Chief).[62] Whatever his motives, Alan MacCoul took a bold and ruthless path. At one point he captured the Island of Kerrera and, in 1460, succeeded in kidnapping Chief John MacDougall, holding him for a time a bound prisoner on Kerrera.

The murder of Sir John Stewart by Alan MacCoul is recounted in Chapter 18. Alan rushed from the bloody scene to seize Dunstaffnage, which he held until dislodged by government troops dispatched by the Estates of Parliament in 1464. It is not clear what became of Alan MacCoul. Did his life end in the bloody Battle of Stalc? If so, the name of this spot where the fight took place, Lagna an Phail or the "treacherous hollow," was a fitting place for his final moments.

Michael Starforth in his *Official Short History of Clan MacDougall*, p. 26, in commenting on conditions in Lorn following the murder of Sir John Stewart, writes:

> There followed several years of intermittent warfare throughout Lorn with Dougald Stewart supported by most of his father's adherents, by the MacLarens, and by some of the MacDougalls against the unholy alliance of Alan MacCoul and his renegade MacDougalls, the Campbells and lowland men-at-arms of the dead Lord's brother, Walter Stewart.

Perhaps the men-at-arms mentioned in this description account for the presence of MacFarlanes at the Battle of Stalc, for there were MacFarlanes associated with the Stewart Earls of Lennox, and Duncan MacFarlane of Arrochar was married to a sister of the first Lord Campbell.

As a final outcome of all this intrigue and strife, a deal was made in which Dougald Stewart received Appin and Walter Stewart, his devious uncle, got the Lordship of Lorn (minus the ninety-one merklands, including Dunollie, held by Chief John MacAlan MacDougall). Walter Stewart quickly gave the Lordship of Lorn into the waiting hands of the Campbells in exchange for lands in Perthshire.

Cadets and Other Branches of Clan MacDougall

17. MacDougall of Ardencaple

The MacDougalls of Ardencaple are descended from either Coll, the second son of John, the fourth of Raera, and Margaret Campbell, or Hugh, the second son of Somerled, the fifth of Raera. One story is that Hugh's mother bought Ardencaple from a MacLean so that her son might have an inheritance. This cadet is associated with the Island of Seil, Ardencaple House, and Ardfad Castle.[29]

18. MacDougall of Degnish

This was an important cadet during the Religious Wars of the sixteen hundreds. Iain MacDougall of Degnish was killed in the massacre at Dunaverty.[13] John MacDougall of Degnish signed the statement concerning this event issued by John of Dunollie, nineteenth Chief of the Clan. There are no known representatives of this cadet today.

19. MacDougall of Gallanach

The MacDougalls of Gallanach are descended from John MacDougall, the son of Allan MacDougall of Torsa.[22] John was granted Gallanach by Alexander MacDougall of Dunollie, seventeenth Chief of the Clan, in 1641.[*] The head of this cadet is Charles Williamson MacDougall of Gallanach.

20. MacDougall of Lunga

The MacDougalls of Lunga are descended from Allan, the sixth of Raera, through the MacDougalls of Craigenicht and of Ardnahoy and Dowacha.[23] They were first associated with the islands of Lunga and Luing and then with Craignish on the mainland.[†] The present head of this cadet is Colin Lindsay-MacDougall of Lunga.

21. MacDougall of Raera (Raray)

This branch of the Clan is considered the senior Cadet of the MacDougalls of Lorn. It is descended from Allan MacDougall, the second son of Ian (Iain) of Dunollie, eighth Chief of the Clan. Some

---

[*] *The Tartan*, Spring 1982.
[†] *The Tartan*, Spring 1981, "MacDougalls of Lunga."

accounts of the Battle of Allt Dearg mention the MacDougalls of Raera. If accurate, these accounts indicate that there was an earlier cadet by this name, but there is no information indicating when such a family may have branched from the line of the Chiefs.

After the loss of their seat at Ardmaddy Castle, the MacDougalls of Raera became associated with Craigenicht on Lismore. From the MacDougalls of Craigenicht sprang the MacDougalls of Mingary. Alan Miles MacDougall, a long-time officer of the Clan MacDougall Society in North America, through descent from the MacDougalls of Mingary, may represent this ancient cadet.[*] Raray Farm, upon which the original stronghold of the MacDougalls of Raera stood, is presently owned by Jeremy Inglis and his brother, who have a strong MacDougall ancestry.

22. MacDougall of Torsa

The MacDougalls of Torsa descend from Allan, second son of Duncan of Dunollie, sixteenth Chief of the Clan.[†] They are associated with the Island of Torsa, which lies between Luing and the mainland,[34] and were the progenitors of the MacDougalls of Gallanach.[19]

23. Other Prominent MacDougall Families Associated with Place-Names

MacDougall of Ardantrive

This family is associated with Ardantrive Farm on Kerrera. Duncan of Ardantrive was the fourth son of Alexander MacDougall, twenty-third Chief of the Clan.

MacDougall of Ardlarach

This family seems to have descended from the third son of Duncan MacDougall, sixteenth Chief of the Clan. They were associated with the Island of Luing. Ardlarach House, built by this family, is situated above Black Mill Bay.[30]

---

[*] See also Note 71, "John Maol MacDougall and His Wives," and *The Tartan*, Fall 1982, Spring 1983, "The MacDougalls of Raera."
[†] Alternatively, Hope MacDougall of MacDougall has suggested that Allan may have been the second son of the fifteenth Chief.

MacDougall of Ardmore

This family is associated with Ardmore Farm on Kerrera's southern shore. Dougall MacDougall of Ardmore was killed at Dunaverty in 1647.[13]

MacDougall of Ardnahoy and Dowacha

These MacDougall families were closely related to the MacDougalls of Raera as well as to the line of the Chief. Alexander MacDougall of Shellachan and Dowacha was the second son of Allan, the sixth of Raera. He married a daughter of Duncan MacDougall of Dunollie and became the Constable of Dunbeg Castle. He was killed in 1615 by Sir James MacDonald and others.

MacDougall of Balichun

This family is associated with the Island of Seil, and some family members are buried at the old parish church at Kilbrandon. Interestingly, the gravestone of Allan MacDougall (son of Allan and Katrin MacDougall, who died in 1759 and is buried at Kilbrandon) bears engraved Arms similar to those used by Iain Ciar, twenty-second Chief of the Clan. Iain Ciar's second son was also named Allan. The similarity of Arms may indicate a connection of this family to the line of the Chiefs.

MacDougall of Corrielorne

A family associated with the area just north of Loch Tralaig known as the Braes of Lorn, halfway between Kilninver and Kilmelford, on A816.

MacDougall of Craigenicht

See MacDougalls of Raera.[21]

MacDougall of Cruachan

A family mentioned in Burke's *Landed Gentry* as being intermarried with the MacDougalls of Craigenicht. They may have been associated with the MacDougalls of Raera, who reacquired the Pass of Brander for the Clan through marriage with the Campbells.*

---

* See Lore of Lorn, Note 71, "John Maol MacDougall and His Wives."

MacDougall of Dunach

An important cadet during the Religious Wars of the sixteen-hundreds. Dougald MacDougall of Dunach signed the statement concerning the massacre at Dunaverty in 1647.[13] This family is associated with the northern shore of Loch Feochan and has no known representatives today.

MacDougall of Ferlochan

This family is said to have been the hereditary pall bearers of the MacDougall Chiefs and are associated with land on the south shore of Loch Creran. Dugald Gordon MacDougall, the Clan Bard, was descended from this family.

MacDougall of Glen Lyon

These MacDougalls went from the Oban area to Glen Lyon to repopulate that glen after the plague had killed many of the inhabitants. The famous line of MacDougall pipers and pipe makers belong to this group of MacDougalls.*

MacDougall of Hayfield

This is a branch of the MacDougalls of Gallanach. Alan MacDougall of that latter family built a house on the north shore of Loch Awe and named it "Hayfield."

MacDougall of Kilmun and Narrachan

This family descended from the MacDougalls of Craigenicht and thus from the MacDougalls of Raera, and is associated with the north shore of Loch Avich. They are said to have buried their dead at Caibeal, above this loch. According to one account, a MacDougall of Kilmun was saved from the massacre at Dunaverty by shouting in five languages "Is there anyone here at all who will save a good scholar?" (Contrast this with the only survivor as given by Macphail.[13]) There are descendants in America.

---

* Nancy Black, *From a Hollow on the Hill.*

MacDougall of Soroba

This family is associated with the Soroba estate, just south of Oban, and was mentioned as early as 1696. The house was bought by Coline MacDougall of MacDougall's maternal grandfather around 1890; however, he was not descended from the original MacDougalls of Soroba. At present Soroba House is a hotel and restaurant.

24. Pipers of Clan MacDougall

The MacDougall School of Piping at Kilbride was founded by Alasdair Mor MacDougall (1635–1709). Alasdair Mor was probably descended from earlier hereditary pipers to the MacDougall Chiefs. Certainly, he served in this office as did his son, Ronald Ban, who accompanied his Chief, Iain Ciar, at the Battle of Sheriffmuir in 1715. It seems quite certain that Ronald Ban composed the famous *Cis an Rìgh* ("The King's Tax"). He also composed *Failte Iain Ciar* and lived to write the lament for his Chief, *Cumha Iain Ciar*.

Ronald Ban's grandson, Ronald Mor, was the last hereditary piper to the MacDougall Chiefs. It was he who composed the lament for young Captain Alexander MacDougall killed in the Peninsular Campaign in 1812. The hereditary pipers to the Chief were granted Moleigh Croit, a mile from Kilbride on the level ground known as Lomaire na Spaid Searachd, or the "marching furrow." Piping classes were held at Moleigh as late as the 1890s under the direction of John McColl (MacDougall).

A horizontal slate slab at Kilbride has this brief inscription: "A. McD Piper 1773." Evidently such a laconic description was sufficient for those who knew the excellence of these MacDougall musicians.

From this line of pipers sprang the family of Duncan MacDougall of Aberfeldy. This family is credited with being the "foremost bagpipe makers that ever existed in Scotland."[*] They held a Royal Warrant: "Bagpipe makers to HM Queen Victoria." For a season, Duncan served as the piper for this queen.[†] Duncan won first prize for piping at the Northern Meeting (the prize was a set of pipes made by his own hand) and later won the Great Champion Gold Medal. His son, Garvin, carried on the manufacture of pipes until his death in 1911.

The Oban Pipe Band wore the MacDougall tartan until 1961.

---

[*] *Piping Times*, November, 1978.
[†] Nancy Black, *From a Hollow on the Hill*.

25. Clan Bards

The family of hereditary pipers to the MacDougall Chiefs also produced Ailean Dall MacDougall, often described as "the last of the true Highland bards." Ailean Dall was born in Glencoe in 1750. His natural gifts, besides those of composing song and verse, included a sharp wit, which, according to story, cost him his eyesight. As a youth, he was apprenticed to a tailor, and while seated sewing with a fellow apprentice, so angered his companion with a verbal barb that his associate lashed out and pierced Ailean's eye with a needle. Infection spread to his other eye, and Ailean Dall, "Blind Allan," was cast into a world of darkness.

Despite the loss of a world filled with nature's images, Ailean Dall would write:

> A thrush am I among Dougall's children
> Singing tunes in the thickness of the branches.

Another poet, Dugald Gordon MacDougall, was appointed as Clan Bard in 1904. He was born in 1845 into the family of shoemakers that charted its line from one of the fifteenth-century Chiefs of the Clan. Dugald was a soldier, newspaperman, and government surveyor as well as an accomplished poet. Ninety of his poems written in the Gaelic have been published in a book entitled *Bràiste Lathurna*, "The Brooch of Lorn."[*]

26. Families Associated with Clan MacDougall

Families with the following surnames were closely affiliated with Clan MacDougall over extended periods of Highland history and have their roots in the land of Lorn.

Carmichael

This name was anglicized from the Gaelic MacGillemichael, meaning "son of the servant of (Saint) Michael." The surname Carmichael is found elsewhere in Scotland, particularly in the lowlands. Recently this surname has been recognized as a clan. Those with this surname whose genealogical lines are traceable to Argyll, especially the island of Lismore, are likely to be associated with the MacDougalls.

---

[*] *The Tartan*, Fall 1982, p. 7.

Conocher, MacConochar, and O'Conochar

These were hereditary physicians to the Chief of the Clan for many years. A number of this name are buried at Kilbride. Records show that between 1530 and 1640, several O'Conchobhairs were physicians to the Chiefs at Dunollie. The Beatons, another famous family of doctors, also attended the Chiefs and their family. At times physicians from these two families lived at Dunollie or at Dunollie Beg, and were involved in translating into Gaelic ancient medical texts as well as tending the sick. There is a record of their attending two Chiefs who died in the "speckled bedroom" at Dunollie, which probably was on the top floor of the castle.

Livingstone

The Livingstones represent an ancient line in Lorn. Moncrieffe describes them as a "small and sacred clan." They are particularly associated with the Island of Lismore, Glen Lonan, and the head of Loch Awe. They were descended from Dunsleave, a son of a Scottish princess, and Aodh O'Neil, a king of Northern Ireland. Their eponymous name in the Gaelic was, therefore, MacDhunshleive, which was anglicized to "MacOnlea" or "MacLeay." The surname "Livingstone" was adopted from a seventeeth-century landlord of Lismore.

From early times, the MacLeays were hereditary keepers of the "Bachuil Mor," the sacred staff of Saint Moluag.[72] This staff, or crosier, was a symbol of great importance in the sea-washed land of Lorn over which the MacDougall Lords presided. Tradition tells that the staff was carried before the forces of Lorn and, doubtless, was prominently displayed at the installation of each succeeding Chief of the Clan.

The close association of the MacLeays or Livingstones of Lorn with the MacDougalls continued long after the Lordship passed to other hands. Of particular interest are the graves of Livingstones buried at Ardchattan Priory.*

Recently, the recognition of a representative of the lowland Livingston family as Chief of the name and the subsequent claim that all those with this surname belong to the same clan has caused consternation to those Livingstones who have an Argyll origin.

MacCowan or Cowan

An ancient line of untraced origins. Associated with Nether Lorn and Loch Seil. Nancy Black notes that this surname means "son of the blacksmith."

---

* *The Tartan*, Fall 1981, p 6.

MacCulloch, MacCullagh, and MacLullich

This line is said to have descended from Somerled's son Reginald and is associated with the lands of Benderloch.

MacDill, MacHale, and MacClintoch

These surnames are included under Clan MacDougall in the little book *Scots Kith and Kin*. Some of these may have been associated with the Macdowalls of Galloway rather than with the MacDougalls of Lorn.

Macdowall and MacDowell

The surnames Macdowall and MacDowell need special consideration. While MacDougall, Macdowall, McDowell, and a host of other variations in spelling all represent attempts to phonetically reproduce the Gaelic MacDhughaill, these generally represent two separate though related heraldic houses: the MacDougalls of Argyll and the Macdowalls of Galloway, each headed by its own Chief.

Chief of the Macdowalls and MacDowells is Fergus Macdowall of Garthland, who bears the Arms of Galloway as senior representative of the ancient Lords of Galloway, while Madam Morag MacDougall of MacDougall bears her baronial Arms as Chief of the MacDougalls of Lorn, representatives of the ancient Lords of Argyll.

A successful alliance of these two Clans has occurred within the Clan MacDougall Society of North America. This alliance is not a fabrication superficially based upon similar surnames. It predates the founding of the society by nearly a millennium, springing from hereditary and political linkages that date back to the 1100s. The Arms of our two Chiefly families show this early interconnection—they share the silver lion on a field of blue and the war cry "Victory or Death."

We know that Affric, the daughter of Fergus, Lord of Galloway, whose line continues in Fergus Macdowall of Garthland, married Olaf, King of the island of Man, whose daughter, Ragnhild, married Somerled, Regulus of Argyll and later King of the Isles. Their eldest son was Dougall, from whom the MacDougalls of Argyll take their name.

During those years when the Bruces wrestled the Balliol Kings and Lords of Galloway for the Scottish crown, the alliance between the MacDougalls of Argyll and the Macdowalls of Galloway became truly a matter of victory or death. MacDougall forces from Argyll joined those of the Macdowalls in Galloway in an attempt to capture their mutual enemy Robert the Bruce, who had intensified the feud by murdering their cousin Sir John (the second Red) Comyn of Badenoch.

Again, the linkages between the MacDougalls and the Macdowalls were strengthened by marriage—Alexander, fourth Chief of the MacDougalls of Argyll, married the granddaughter of Alan, the last of the ancient Lords of Galloway. This marriage connected the MacDougalls of Argyll with two other royal Galloway names: the Balliol Kings of Scotland and the Comyns, who were the new Lords of Galloway.

There is a suggestion of a still closer connection between these two great MacDougall/Macdowall families, who each wore the silver lion on blue. All the Macdowall family lines in Galloway have held that Sir Dougal MacDowyl of Gairochloyne (flor. 1295) was their common ancestor, and Sir Dougal may have been the fourth son of Sir John MacDougall of Argyll. Hopefully, future research will clarify this intriguing possibility. Note that if Dougal MacDowyl was Dougal the fourth son of Sir John of Lorn, he would not have been able to assume the position of Chief of the MacDougalls of Argyll, due to the forfeiture of his father and brother John. However, he would have been heir to the line of the ancient Lords of Galloway, through his grandmother.

MacEachan, MacEachern, and McEochain

A number of families who adopted this surname and who lived in Lorn were supporters of the Chiefs of Clan MacDougall.

MacEwan

The MacEwans were closely associated with Clan MacDougall. They served as bards to the Chiefs, and eleven fell with the Clan at Dunaverty.

MacKichan (MacKickan)

This surname was anglicized from the Gaelic MacFhitheachain, meaning "son of the little raven." One of this surname is said to have saved the charter chest of the MacDougall Chiefs during the devastation wrought by General Leslie in the 1600s. By tradition, the MacKichans were the hereditary charter-keepers of the MacDougall Clan Chiefs. Evidently a number of this surname emigrated from the Oban area to America. There is a MacKichan stone at Ardchattan.

MacLucas, MacLugash, and MacLugais

This surname was derived from the Gaelic MacGillemoluaig, meaning "son of the servant of (Saint) Moluag." These folk were closely associated with the MacDougalls and once a prominent name on the islands of Mull and Coll.

MacNamell

This name was anglicized from the Gaelic Mac na Maoille, meaning "son of the bald (man)." This surname is usually associated with MacDougalls of Jura.

Castles and Houses

27. Achadun

This castle is on the southwest coast of Lismore, with the closest approach being the road to Achadun Farm, which branches west from the island's main road just above the old schoolhouse south of Achnacroish.

ACHADUN

The castle stands upon lands once granted to Bishop William by Duncan of Argyll, second Chief of Clan MacDougall. The castle was probably built in the late fourteenth century by the same masons who labored on Lismore's Cathedral. The castle served as a residence for the Bishop of the Isles until the sixteenth century. In this capacity, it had close MacDougall associations. Sir James Livingstone, from whom the MacLeays took their present surname,[26] may have resided at Achadun in the 1640s.

Achadun can also be seen from the ferry to Mull. After passing the Eilean Musdile Lighthouse on the outward passage, look up Loch Linnhe—Achadun appears on a west shore of Lismore.

28. Ardencaple House

ARDENCAPLE

This house is on the north shore of Seil. The present house was probably built by John MacDougall of Ardencaple, who was the son of Coll MacDougall of Ardencaple and who was alive in the late seventeen hundreds.[17] The house is oblong, two-storied, and constructed around a central passageway and a turnpike stair, enclosed in a semicircular bay that extends from the rear of the house. (See Chapter 39.)

29. Ardfad Castle

The "Castle of the Long Height" is east of Ardencaple House on the north shore of Seil, upon a long, rocky outcrop. Little is known of the history of this castle and very little remains of its structure. The site has been likened to a miniature Stirling. This castle was the seat of the MacDougalls of Ardencaple.[17] The Royal Commission on the Ancient and Historic Monuments of Scotland indicates that the castle may have been built by John MacDougall of Ardencaple, who died shortly before 1615; however, there were MacDougalls of Ardencaple occupying the northern end of Seil from the early fifteen hundreds, and it seems probable that Ardfad was their seat before the time of that John MacDougall.

ARDFAD

Much more of the wall must have been standing in 1895, for a description of that date speaks of the presence of arrow slits. Now only a low fragment of the northwest gable remains. The outer courtyard on the south end of the rock was separated from the inner bailey by the castle building itself. A portion of the inner yard's curtain wall, which followed the irregular perimeter of the rock, can still be seen on the northeast side. (See Chapter 39.)

30. Ardlarach House

This house is situated on the west shore of the Island of Luing, on Black Mill Bay, and can be reached by the road that runs west from Kilchattan. It is a typical eighteenth-century tacksman house and was built by Patrick MacDougall in 1787.*

ARDLARACH

The house is a good example of early improvements in farm houses built in the eighteenth and nineteenth centuries. The design includes a central staircase, two stories, and a slate roof.

---

* See Lore of Lorn, Note 23, "MacDougall of Ardlarach."

Also of interest in this area are the huge rock stacks at the northern end of Black Mill Bay known as the "Cobblers of Lorn."

31. Ardmaddy Castle

This mansion, built in Jacobean style, is on the mainland shore of Seil Sound. The lower story and other interior portions are the remains of a late medieval tower house that was the seat of the MacDougalls of Raera.[21] The tower house was probably built in the second half of the fifteenth century, when this cadet of the Clan became the principal force in Nether Lorn. Ardmaddy was remodeled by later Campbell owners in 1790 and again in 1862, when plans designed by James Graham were employed in the reconstruction.

Several stories describe how John Maol MacDougall lost Ardmaddy to the Campbells. The version most repeated is included in Note 71, "John Maol MacDougall and His Wives."

32. Aros Castle

Aros is on the north shore of Mull, about two miles west of the village of Salen. It held a commanding position overlooking the Sound of Mull—that ancient thoroughfare to the Western Isles. The castle also overlooks the outlet of Aros River, and its name may derive from the Norse *Ar-Os*, meaning "river mouth." The promontory upon which the castle stands was originally rimmed with a wall composed of large, flat slabs set on end and forming inner and outer facings for a rubble fill. Typical of the thirteenth-century fortifications in the western Highlands, the approach was protected by a ditch and the two-story hall house itself. This latter structure was built over an unvaulted cellar and has architectural features typical of thirteenth- and fourteenth-century masonry. A window of particular interest still exists in the remaining side wall. It has a pointed arch and the remains of a mullion, indicating the earliest form of tracery in the form of a pierced spandrel similar to examples found at Saint Andrews (1275) and Rothesay Castle (1350).

There seems little doubt that this castle was built by the MacDougall Lords of Lorn. Following the final victory of Bruce, the island of Mull was granted to Alexander MacDonald of Islay, and Aros became part of the chain of castles held by the MacDonald Lords of the Isles. From them it passed to the MacLeans, and finally to the Campbells in the mid-seventeenth century.

In 1608, the chiefs of the Isles met at Aros, where Lord Ochiltree, acting for James VI, managed to lure them aboard his ship under the guise of attending a church service. Once on board, the chiefs were placed under arrest.

33. Barcaldine Castle

This tower house is on the south shore of Loch Creran, west of A828. It was built by Sir Duncan Campbell in 1609. Madam MacDougall of MacDougall, thirtieth Chief of the Clan, and her husband, Leslie Grahame MacDougall, lived in this castle for a time before taking residence at Dunollie House.

34. Caisteal nan Con

This castle is on the fertile island of Torsa, which lies between Seil and the mainland. The castle appears to date from the fifteenth century and may have been occupied by the MacDougalls of Torsa.[22] The island was originally part of the realm of the MacDougall Lords of Lorn, but was granted to the Campbells of Loch Awe in 1313. During the first half of the sixteenth century, the island seems to have been held by the MacDougalls of Raera under a grant from the Campbells, and to have reverted to the MacDougalls under Allan MacDougall of Torsa in the seventeenth century.

The name of this castle, which translates "castle of the dogs," has been said to have arisen from the use of this tower as a hunting lodge by the Lords of the Isles. It seems more likely that the name stems from the temporary possession by the MacLeans of Duart who were labeled by their enemies with the appellation "the dogs." Colin MacDougall of Lunga has suggested that the name refers to the MacDougalls keeping their famous hounds at this location.

35. Caisteal na Nighinn Ruaidhe

The ruins of this very old tower house are on an island in Loch Avich. The name translates "castle of the red-haired maiden." Just who this maiden was is not clear. Some reports say that she was the daughter of the toiseach of Loch Avich, whose marriage to Duncan Campbell of

Craignish (died in 1220) brought the castle into Campbell hands. This writer was informed by Colin Lindsay-MacDougall, the present Laird of Lunga, that the red-haired maiden was the daughter of the MacDougall who built the castle. She fell in love, much to her father's rage, with an Irish workman employed in the construction.

36. Cairn na Burgh

The scant remains of this stronghold are on Cairn na Burgh More—one of the two northernmost of the Treshnish Isles. This castle was an early outpost of the MacDougall Lords of Lorn. It stood upon a tabletop of volcanic rock that provides some excellent grasslands. The high cliffs of the island show columnar jointing typical of basalt, and a rather spectacular natural arch has been carved by the waves pounding against the island's northern point. These cliffs are inhabited by nesting sea birds, while the rocks below are often the resting place for seals. Little has been recorded of Cairn na Burgh, which was held by the MacDougalls until 1354. King Alexander of Scotland attempted to get Ewan, third Chief of the Clan, to turn this stronghold over to the crown. There is a 1354 indenture between John MacDougall, Lord of Lorn, and John MacDonald of Islay in which Cairn na Burgh was granted to the latter with the stipulation that it should never be given to any of Clan Mackinnon.

37. Coeffin Castle

Coeffin is on the northwest shore of Lismore and is approachable by a road turning westward from the main road of the island, just below the cathedral church. The castle commands the Lynn of Morvern. It was built in the thirteenth century by the MacDougall Lords of Lorn.

It is an irregular oblong in floor plan, over sixty-five feet in length and about thirty-five feet wide. Split beach boulders were used in parts of the walls, and what remains of the dressed stonework indicates that a buff-colored sandstone was employed, perhaps quarried at Ardtornish.

Little remains of the courtyard or bailey. From this, the castle's first floor was entered through a series of defenses and a fore stair leading to a door in the northeast wall. A doorway in the southwest wall of the first floor still has its drawbar hole. This door provided communication from the landward side. Diagram 3 shows the position of the stairs that once led to the castle's second floor. A second staircase within the walls evidently led to the wall-walk that surrounded the roof. A short section of this stairway still survives.

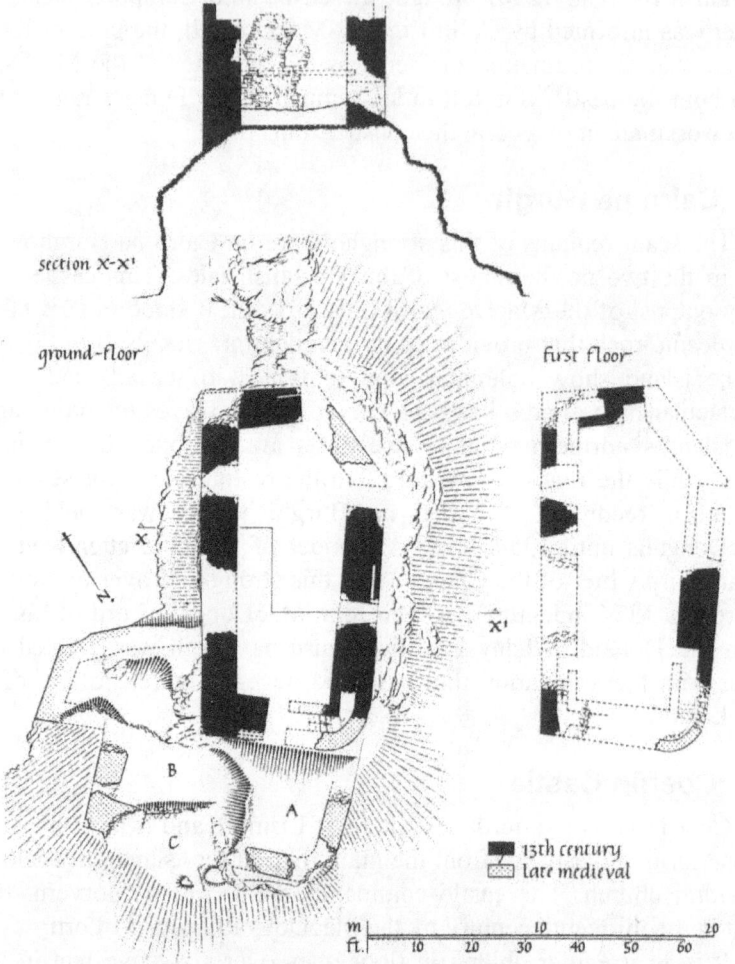

By permission of The Royal Commission On The Ancient & Historical Monuments Of Scotland.

Diagram 3. Coeffin Castle, Floor Plan

The remains of a tidal fish trap can be found in the small cove immediately southeast of the castle.

MacDougall possession of Lismore was lost following the defeat at Brander and was regained by the seventh Chief of the Clan in 1388 only to be sold to John Stewart of Innermeath.

It is likely that an early Norse fortification occupied the site of Coeffin Castle. Some three hundred feet northeast of the castle and on the top of a ridge above the coast are traces of a still earlier hill fort.

38. Degnish

Degnish is on the outer, north shore of Loch Melfort. The MacDougalls of Degnish[18] were an important cadet of the Clan; however, the present Degnish House was built by a Neil Campbell in 1786. The writer has no information of whether any structures remain of previous MacDougall occupation.*

39. Drissaig House

This house is on the north shore of Loch Avich and has a frosted glass MacDougall crest with the Clan motto in Latin as a part of its front door.

40. Duart Castle

Duart is on Mull, where it stands commanding the entrance to the Sound of Mull. This restored and impressive seat of the Chiefs of Clan MacLean has a high and massive curtain wall surrounding the keep. The curtain wall was built during the era when Mull was part of the realm of the MacDougall Lords of Lorn. Robert Bain† notes that the MacLeans were supporters of the Lords of Lorn until the rise of the MacDonald Lords of the Isles following the former's defeat by Bruce. The MacLeans continued to be often involved with the MacDougall Chiefs. Duncan of Dunollie, sixteenth Chief of the Clan, married Margaret, the sister of Sir Lauchlan MacLean of Duart.

When MacLean of Duart kidnapped Lord Neil Campbell's factor in 1681, the Lord asked Duncan MacDougall of Dunollie, twentieth Chief of the Clan, if he would go out to Duart Castle and fetch back the captured tax collector. MacLean greeted the MacDougall Chief as he landed on the shore and invited him to dinner, after which they would talk of business. Dinner over, Duncan asked where the Campbell's factor was. MacLean took Duncan across the room. "Here is his head," said MacLean, "but his body is out there." MacLean gave a wide sweep of his hand. MacDougall observed that as he had come to fetch the Campbell's factor, he would take what there was.‡

---

* See Chapter 14.
† Robert Bain, *Clans and Tartans*.
‡ Archibald Campbell, *Records of Argyll*. See also Chapter 31.

41. Dunach

This castle is on the north shore of Loch Feochan, a short distance off Route A816. The MacDougalls of Dunach[23] were an important branch of the Clan. The writer is unable to say what, if any, connection the present Dunach House or Dunach Farm may have with this cadet. Remains of an old dun or small hill fort are on the high ridge east-northeast of Dunach Farm and close to the shore of the loch. It may be this site that gives the name to the area.

42. Dunollie Castle

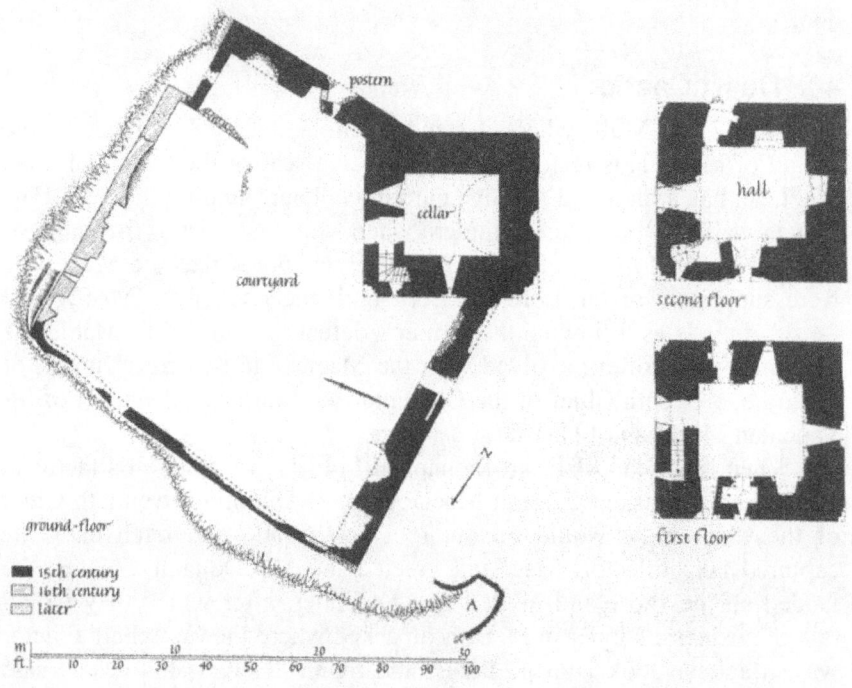

By permission of The Royal Commission On The Ancient & Historical Monuments Of Scotland.

Diagram 4. Dunollie Castle, Floor Plan

Dunollie stands upon a solid foundation—a great, exposed mass of lava, once part of a dike radiating from Mull's ancient volcano. The Iron Age dun builders may have fortified this promontory. The Scots of Dalriada erected a citadel, Dun Ollaigh, atop the cliffs, which became as important in the early realm of the Gaels as Dunadd.* The *Annals of Ulster* mention that Dun Ollaigh was burned by Tula Aman in 686 C.E. It was rebuilt only to be destroyed again twelve years later. In 701, Selbach (the seventeenth king of Dalriada, who belonged to the kindred of Lorn and who was a distant ancestor of the MacDougall Chiefs) destroyed Dun Ollaigh and then rebuilt it in 714. Dun Ollaigh is again mentioned in the warring annals of Angus MacFergus, King of the Scots and another ancestor of the MacDougall Chiefs.†

Encircling the present keep of Dunollie on the north and east are the buried remains of drystone ramparts dating from the early fortifications of Dun Ollaigh by the Scots. In 1978, Professor Leslie Alcock and a team from the University of Glasgow excavated a part of these ancient outworks. They found bone combs, pins, a glass shard from a Roman bowl, and the remains of a small bronze foundry.‡ Broken pottery suggests that the dwellers on Dunollie's rock were in contact with traders from western Gaul in the fifth to early eighth centuries.

While there would appear to be no references to Dunollie in the records from the early era of Clan MacDougall, Professor Alcock's excavations unearthed a silver penny dating about 1205–1218, which would indicate occupation of the promontory during the time of Duncan, second Chief of the Clan. Dunstaffnage was probably the principal residence of the powerful MacDougall Lords of Lorn; however, the strategic importance of Dunollie could not have been overlooked by the leaders of the Clan.

The date of the building of the existing keep and outer bailey remains unknown. The Royal Commission of Ancient and Historical Monuments of Scotland suggests a rather late date—the mid-1400s—and ties this assumption to the granting of Dunollie along with extensive holdings to Iain MacDougall, the eighth Chief of the Clan, by John Stewart, to whom the Lordship of Lorn had passed through the marriage of a MacDougall heiress. Other authorities have found evidence for a much earlier date. A part of the north curtain wall may represent the remains of a castle dating from the thirteenth century. Both Sir Iain Moncrieffe and Dr. W. Douglas Simpson note Dunollie's similarity to Bergen Castle in Norway, which dates from the era of Norse influence in Argyll.

The present keep is nearly square, measuring about forty feet on a side. The tower was expertly constructed, with good pinning inserted

---

* Graham Ritchie, *The Archaeology of Argyll.*
† *The Tartan*, Fall 1973.
‡ *The Tartan*. Fall 1979.

between the stones and the whole mass secured with a coarse lime mortar. Window and door openings are dressed with a greenish and gray-purple sandstone, probably quarried at Ardentallan or on the southern shore of Kerrera.

The cellar is entered through a portal in the tower's west wall. The barrel-vaulted cellar is dimly lit by two small windows inlet by deeply splayed "tunnels" penetrating the massive, nine-foot-thick walls. The impression of wicker centering used in the arch construction can be seen in the cellar's vault.

An unusually wide staircase leads from the portal-way, turning left in the thickness of the walls to reach the first floor above. The portal leading from the courtyard appears to be a later convenience, for the first floor was once entered through another portal in the west wall and on the first floor level. This portal must have been reached either by a draw-ladder or a fore-stair.

The stairs continue from the first floor, turning left within the wall to reach the now floorless hall lighted with large, arched windows featuring built-in window seats. "Corkscrew" stairs in the southwest angle of the keep mounted to the third floor, which was probably covered with a pitched roof of timber sheathed with slate (roof slates have been found in the rubble.) The roof was surrounded by a parapet walk with a turret in the southeast angle.

DUNOLLIE NORTH + WEST WALLS

The courtyard is about 576 square meters. The curtain wall, on the north and most vulnerable side, is seven and a half feet thick. In this wall there is an old postern with a "zigzag" design. This postern has been walled up at some later period of the castle's occupation. At the northwest angle of the curtain a height of wall remains, showing window openings and a possible fireplace serving a structure built against the internal face. Much of the remaining west curtain wall is of much later construction than the keep. Enough remains to show that this section also had outbuildings constructed against the wall.

The present gateway to the courtyard is in the east curtain wall. It has a bar-hole and remnants of corbels that once supported a projecting structure above the gate, thus providing a place from which sundry deterrents might be dropped on the heads of attackers.

43. Dunollie Castle Abandoned

Dunollie was besieged by Cromwellian troops under the command of Colonel Robert Montgomery in 1647. In 1686, King James VII of Scotland (James II of England) granted Allen MacDougall, the twenty-first Chief of the Clan, a greater part of Lorn for the Clan's support of the Royalist cause. That cause was to cost the Chiefs and the Clan dearly, including the temporary loss of Dunollie early in the eighteenth century, though at that time the castle was bravely defended by Mary of Sleat, the wife of the exiled Iain Ciar, twenty-second Chief of the MacDougalls.

The damage sustained by the castle during the troubled 1600s and early 1700s led to its abandonment by Chief Alexander MacDougall (Alastair Dubh) and the building of Dunollie House.

44. Dunollie House and Its Surroundings

This house has been the residence of the MacDougall Chiefs since 1764. The older portions of this house date from before the Chiefs moved down from the castle. In fact, the old kitchen may be part of the head keeper's cottage. In general plan, the house represents a two-storied "T" with a gable roof. To this central portion have been added south and west ranges, built about 1835.

Just to the northwest of the house is a quadrangle of single-story buildings surrounding a corbled yard. In the old days the carriage sheds were here (the Chief had his own carriage with his coat of arms emblazoned on the varnished door). Here too were the stables, where the help slept in the loft. A pump (probably a well in earlier times) is a feature of this yard. Across from these buildings was a barn, now converted into a cottage. Beyond these buildings, to the north and on the left of the roadway, were the dog kennels and the ferret cage. On the right was another barn, now fixed over as an attractive cottage for the caretaker and his wife.

The reader's attention is called to an excellent series of charming essays written by Jean MacDougall Hadfield, which recount her childhood in Dunollie House. These glimpses of a period from 1914–1920 have been published in *The Tartan*: "The Walled Garden," Spring 1992; "Spring Cleaning," Spring 1994; "Lighting and Heating," Spring 1996; "The Laundry," Winter 1998; and "Psychic Tales from Dunollie," Winter 2006.

DUNOLLIE HOUSE

45. Dunstaffnage Castle

Considerable description of Dunstaffnage has been given in the Journal text.[*] The site, situated upon a great mass of conglomerate rock, was an important seat of the Kingdom of Dalriada and the early Scottish realm. The existing castle, though much altered, was probably built by Duncan of Argyll, second Chief of the Clan. There is reason to suppose that Dunstaffnage was the principal seat of the MacDougall Lords of Lorn.

At the time this castle was built, its design included many state-of-the-art features such as the interconnection of the corner towers by the parapet walk, thus providing communications around the top of the walls. The fact that Duncan, the second Chief of the Clan, had been involved in one of the crusades may explain how advanced fortification designs came to the Highlands during the time when so many large castles were being constructed in mainland Lorn and the near islands.[†]

---

[*] Especially see Chapter 18 and Chapter 25.
[†] R. Andrew McDonald, *The Kingdom of the Isles*, pp. 234 ff.

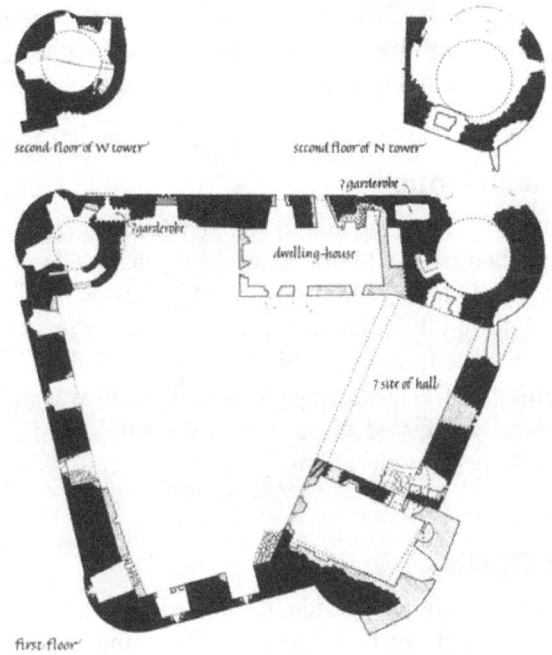

By permission of The Royal Commission On The Ancient & Historical Monuments Of Scotland.

Diagram 5. Dunstaffnage Castle, Floor Plan

46. Fraoch Eilean

The first mention of Fraoch Eilean is in a charter of custody granted to Gillechrist MacNachdan (MacNaughton) by Alexander III of Scotland in 1267. While this charter's authenticity has been questioned, there is no doubt that the MacNaughtons held this tower house. In the writer's opinion, and that of others, it is likely that the castle was built by the

MacDougalls (probably by Ewan, third Chief of the Clan) and given over to King Alexander as part of the established relationship between the Lords of Lorn and the Scottish throne. It is also likely that the MacNaughtons were chosen as custodians due to their close connections with the MacDougall Chiefs.[2]

The site of Fraoch Eilean was one of early habitation. Evidence of vitrified fortifications has been found, along with a fragment of glassware dating from the Roman era in Britain. (See also Note 71, "Fraoch Eilean's Dragon.")

47. Gallanach House

This mansion is on the mainland at the southern end of Kerrera Sound and reached by the Shore Road from Oban. The present mansion was erected by Dugald MacDougall of Gallanach[19] in 1814–1817, according to a design by William Burn. The house was extended in 1903 by the addition of a three-story block attached to the east corner. The original dwelling of the MacDougalls of Gallanach was a stone house of a design generally referred to as a "Laird's box"—a long two-storied building, unadorned, with chimneys at both ends and a projecting entryway.

48. Gylen Castle

The setting of Gylen, astride its clifted promontory on Kerrera's southern shore, could not be more ruggedly grand. The tower's height, rising fifty-six feet from the rock foundation to the crow-step gables, adds to its elegance in design. The cornices, corbels,[7] and Romanesque carvings contribute to its charm. Even the rocks of which it is constructed are a mosaic of beauty and represent a spectrum of Kerrera's geological past—greenish and pale purple sandstone (the former may have been quarried at Ardentallan on the mainland, while the latter came from Kerrera's own southern shore), banded limestones, slates, granites, and shales.

Altogether, one can only agree with MacGibbon and Ross who, in their *Castellated and Domestic Architecture of Scotland*, called Gylen "a little architectural gem." The construction of Gylen took several seasons and appears to have been completed in 1582. The builder was Duncan MacDougall of MacDougall. It is not clear whether this Duncan was a brother of Dougall, the fifteenth Chief of the Clan, or Dougall's son, Duncan, who became the sixteenth Chief. No record identifies the masons who wrought the carved moldings and who laid the fine arches, but there is a similarity in execution to work done in Galloway, from whence the craftsmen may have been imported. If the masons did come from Galloway, one wonders if they brought recommendations from the Macdowalls or MacDowells, who were kinsmen of the Lord of Lorn.

Whichever Duncan it was who had Gylen built, his decision to construct a substantial home of his own may have been influenced by strained relations with Dougall of Dunollie, the only MacDougall Chief to be charged with acting the part of a tyrant. In 1588, a "bond of caution" was drawn up at "The Gulinge" (Gylen) with the aim of circumventing a possible feud involving Duncan, Dougall, and Alan MacDougall of Raera.* An equally likely reason for the construction of Gylen is its strategic position on the old drove route across Kerrera. The collection of tolls on cattle passing across the island was an important source of income for the MacDougall Chiefs.

The descendants of Duncan were not to enjoy Gylen for long. In 1647, the tower house was captured and burned by a detachment from the army of the Covenanters. The loss of the tower's water supply, which apparently was a cistern located at the far end of the outer bailey and 160 feet from the tower, may have hastened the capitulation. The visitor to Gylen will sense the planning put into the tower house's defensive capabilities, including the positioning of gun loops to cover critical angles and the boat landings below the cliffs. However, Gylen did not have the massive strength of Dunollie and could not have withstood a large and determined force. Among the booty carried off from Gylen by the victors was the Clan's valued heirloom, the Brooch of Lorn.†

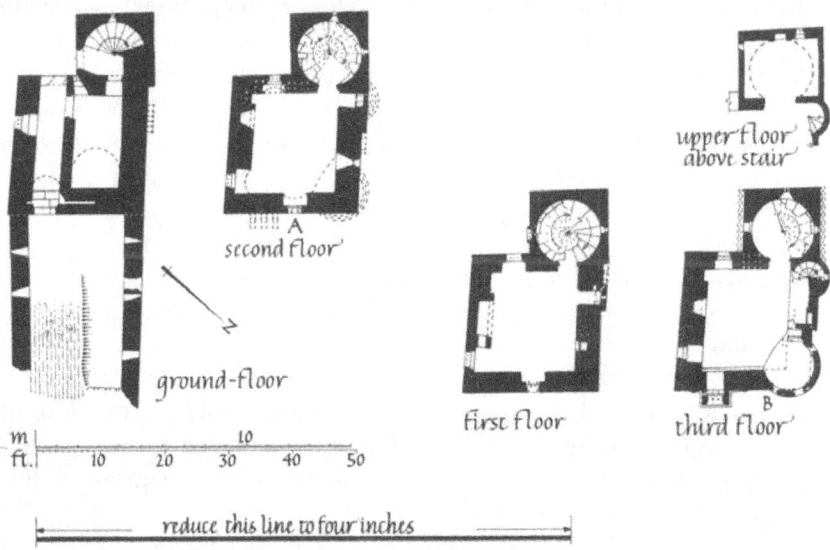

By permission of The Royal Commission On The Ancient & Historical Monuments Of Scotland.

Diagram 6. Gylen Castle, Floor Plan

---

* Michael Starforth's *An Official Short History of Clan MacDougall*, p. 27.
† *The Tartan*, Fall 1982. Also see Lore of Lorn, Note 73.

The tower house occupies the narrowest portion of the promontory upon which it stands. The tower itself divided the rather extensive outer bailey from the inner yard, which covers the outermost end of the clifted finger of rock. One passes from the outer to the inner yard through a passageway running through the vaulted cellar of the tower house. The outer portal of this passage is fitted for a heavy door, opening inwards from the carved, semicircular door jambs. The block of stone let in to receive the drawbar has a hole for a peg that, when inserted, would have secured the bar in its socket.

The main block of the castle is about twenty-one feet square with walls three feet thick at the cellar level. An unusually ample stair tower (twelve by nine feet) is attached to the main block of the tower and carries the circular stairs up to the three stories above. The first floor was a combination hall and kitchen with a large fireplace in the south wall that measures over five feet in width. Between the left fireplace jamb and an adjacent window opening are the remains of what was probably a salt box. A sink fills a recess in the northwest wall, and to its left is the now doorless garderobe, which has its own small window openings, grooved for a single glazing, along with a niche probably intended to hold a lamp.

The second floor accommodations (no longer floored) feature a small fireplace using the same flue as the kitchen fireplace, a garderobe in the northwest wall, a gun loop covering the boat landing far below, and windows let in to each of the other three walls. Like most of the window openings in Gylen, the windows in the second story are surmounted by a relieving arch over the lintel and have chamfered jambs fitted for wooden sashes and for vertical and horizontal iron bars.

The third floor is arranged much as the second, with three notable exceptions. A turret with a window and gun loop is beautifully corbeled outward from the north angle. A smaller stair turret projects from the west angle of the main tower block. And an oriel window projects out over the ground level portal, serving the dual purpose of a machicolation and a window. This oriel window with its "murder holes" in the floor of the projection is the only example of such contrivance in the western Highlands. Diagram 7 depicts the ornamentation that surrounds this window.

A fragment of faceted and corbeled cornice remains atop the north angle of the larger turret.

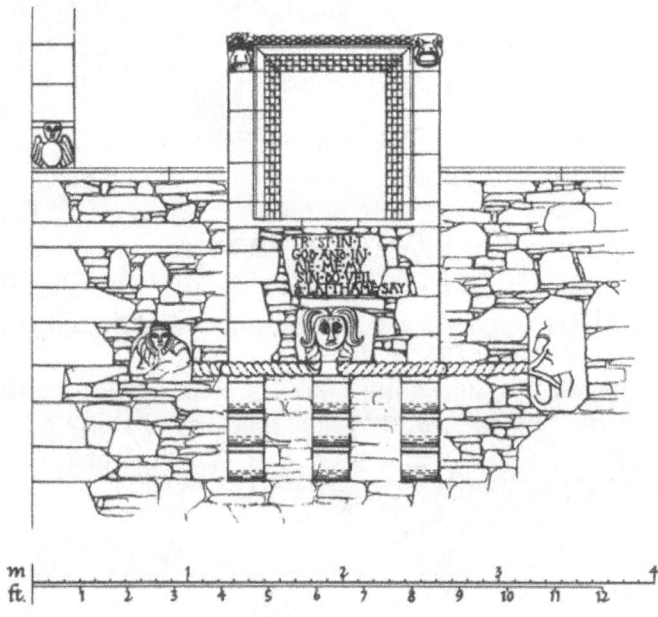

By permission of The Royal Commission On The Ancient & Historical Monuments Of Scotland.

Diagram 7. Gylen Castle, Oriel Window

For additional history and description of Gylen, the reader should consult Miss Hope MacDougall of MacDougall's excellent book, *Island of Kerrera: Mirror of History*. This book also contains drawings by Leslie Grahame MacDougall that depict Gylen as it probably looked before being captured and burned.

In 1915, there were still remains of fir beams that had escaped the fire when Gylen was torched. A builder, John MacDougall, made an old-style three-branched candlestick from this wood. He also drew up plans for the castle and was evidently employed in an attempt to make repairs on the castle.

In 1994, the MacDougalls of Dunollie along with the Ancient Monuments department of Historic Scotland and assisted by private donation and the Clan MacDougall Society of North America began an endeavor to consolidate the ruins of Gylen and to preserve this outstanding example of a tower house. This effort was concluded in May of 2006 with a ceremony conducted by Madam Morag MacDougall of MacDougall and other dignitaries before an attendance assembled at the castle. Every effort has been made to make repairs with authentic materials. In the course of clearing away rubble, roof slates were found lying on a bed of charcoal. The slates had beveled edges and holes for nails. Nails found that had secured the slates apparently had been fitted with washers. A coin from the reign of Charles II featuring a thistle was also discovered.

Preserved at Dunollie are the date stone from Gylen, a stone figure, and the fire basket from the large fireplace on the second floor.

49. Innischonnell Castle (Innis Chonnel)

Innischonnell rises with the massive strength of a true medieval fortress. It is located on an island mid-way up Loch Awe and just off the Loch's southern shore (Route B840). The castle is well placed to command the principal inland waterway of Lorn. The older portions date from the first half of the thirteenth century. As in the case of Dunstaffnage, there has been a great deal of remodeling, particularly during the fifteenth century. The earliest construction consists of split boulders roughly coursed, distinguishable from later building that is characterized by uncrushed flagstone rubble. In particular, the southeast tower has fine examples of arrow slits similar to those found at Dunstaffnage, along with gun loops that, of course, were added much later.

The Royal Commission on Ancient and Historical Monuments, in its *Argyll, Volume 2,* observed that "the castle has little recorded history." While the Commission expresses the opinion that the castle was built by a founder of the Campbells of Loch Awe, the text notes there is little known of the origins or activity of this family "prior to the appearance on record of Sir Colin Campbell at the end of the thirteenth century." This paucity of information has been confirmed through correspondence carried on by this writer with the present Duke of Argyll.

The question arises as to whether the Campbells of Loch Awe were in a position to build such a fortress as early as the accepted date for the building of Innischonnell and why, if they were, the MacDougall Lords Lorn would have permitted the erection of such a stronghold commanding the inner waterway of their realm. If the Campbells did construct Innischonnell, then there must have been an early period of amicable relations between the Campbells and the MacDougalls before the Battle of Allt Dearg.[10]

It is widely agreed that Innischonnell was in the hands of Alexander, Lord of Lorn, and his son Sir John MacDougall (Iain Bacach) at the time of Robert Bruce's victorious invasion of Lorn (1308). It is the opinion of this writer that R.W. Munro is correct in stating that this castle was a MacDougall fortress that passed to the Campbells following the battle in the Pass of Brander.*

It is hoped that future research will illuminate the early history of Innischonnell. In the meantime, the castle remains, in the words of the Royal Commission, "unusually well preserved and rates as one of the most outstanding monuments in the country."

50. Lunga House

Lunga House is an impressive mansion with corner turrets and crenelations in the "Baronial Style." It is built around an old tower house, whose presence can still be discerned. This house is reached by a road that leaves the newly built complex of condominiums called Crohaven, off A816 below Arduaine.

First associated with the Island of Lunga, this branch of the Clan[20] settled upon the mainland of Craignish by the mid-1700s. The house was originally called "Daill." The name was changed to "Lunga House" by Stewart MacDougall

LUNGA HOUSE

of Lunga, who greatly enlarged the mansion in the latter part of the nineteenth century.† On December 27, 2004, a fire at Lunga House caused extensive damage (thankfully, there was no human injury). These damages have now been repaired and the house is again open to guests.

---

* *Highland Clans and Tartans*, p. 20.
† *The Tartan,* Spring 1981.

51. Soroba House

This house is at the entrance to Glen Seileach, on the southern slopes and in sight of A816. It presents a well-balanced face toward Oban. The central door is flanked by two rounding bays, which rise to the roof and are topped with projecting eaves decorated by attractive wooden scrollwork. This house no longer remains in MacDougall hands and has been converted to a hotel. The interior of the house has been remodeled following a fire which occurred around 1970. Fighting the fire proved difficult due to the old walls being insulated with moss.

Soroba House has an interesting association apart from its MacDougall connections. The historian Thomas Babington Macaulay lived there for a time. His grandfather was a Presbyterian minister on Lismore.

Beyond Soroba House and higher up the south side of the glen is the shooting lodge that once belonged to the estate. Here Sir George Trevelyan, Macaulay's nephew, wrote his uncle's biography. He must have had a splendid view from that perch.

Churches and Burial Grounds

52. Ardchattan Priory

Ardchattan Priory was founded in 1230–1231 by Duncan of Argyll, ruler in Lorn and the islands just to the west as well as second Chief of the Clan. This priory stands upon the northern shore of Loch Etive about three miles west of Connel Bridge. Its name derives from Saint Cattan,[72] though it was dedicated (probably at a later date) to Saint Mary and Saint John the Baptist.

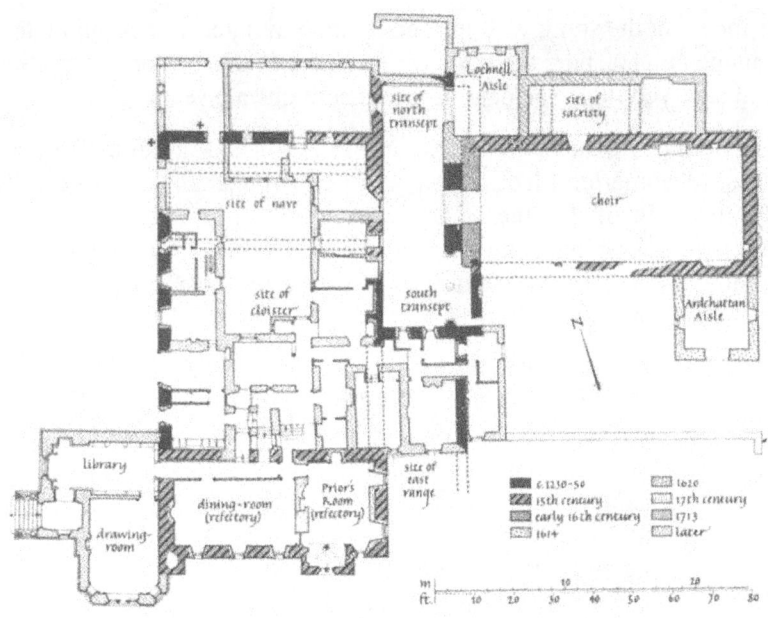

By permission of The Royal Commission On The Ancient & Historical Monuments Of Scotland.

Diagram 8. Ardchattan Priory, Floor Plan

In 1580, Alexander Campbell received the secular grant of this property. At that time, a domestic house was built around the old nave and refectory. The choir of the old priory, which had been enlarged during the 1400s, continued in use as a parish church perhaps as late as 1700. However, the structure had been damaged during the Religious Wars of the seventeenth century, then robbed of stone for building the domestic house, which incorporates parts of the ruins.

The thirteenth-century church was constructed mainly with local granite, having slate "pinnings" and dressed with a greenish-gray sandstone probably quarried on the island of Mull. In the fifteenth century, a buff sandstone, which may have come from a quarry in Morvern, was used in making additions.

The original church consisted of a choir, transeptal chapels, and a narrow nave (now incorporated in the private dwelling house). The other buildings of the priory were ranged from a cloister on the south side of the church.

Features of the choir dating from fifteenth-century reconstruction that can still be seen include:

- A recess in the south wall formed by three pointed arches, all under a rounded arch. There are traces of molding, foliaceous ornamentation, and a carved lion. The central recess contains a piscina.

- The remains of a mural recess in the north wall holding the tomb chest of Somerled MacDougall (Prior of Ardchattan) and his family. To the right of this recess and chest (now protected by a wooden box) are the remnants of a carved spray of foliage. To the left of the tomb chest, a door with a molded jamb is still in place. This door led to the sacristy.

The massive archway separating the choir from the transept is actually two arches, back to back. The arching on the transept side dates from the original church, as do a number of features in the south transeptal chapel, including the remains of two rounded pilasters and the stub of a freestanding column. The west wall of the north transeptal chapel has a round arched window dating from the 1400s and displaying dogtooth molding and carved foliage.[7]

The most interesting portion of the fifteenth-century priory is the refectory and refectory pulpit, which is now part of the private home. This alcove has an arcade of two pointed arches and a ceiling vaulted with crossing and molded ribs that spring from the central, filleted pier and from the corners of each of the two bays.

In addition to the monument stones mentioned in the Journal text, there is a notable stone dating from the early Christian era and displaying a wheel cross in relief along with intricate braids and symbolic figures. This stone has now been removed to the display area. It was probably brought to Ardchattan from some earlier holy place.

Alexander MacDougall, writing in *The Galley of Lorn* (p. 106), speaks of a conference held at Ardchattan by William Wallace following the invasion of the Irish mercenary, MacFadyan. According to the piece in *The Galley*, it was at this Ardchattan council that Duncan, the brother of Alexander (Lord of Lorn and fourth Chief of the Clan), was recognized as the head of his name and the sixth Chief of the MacDougalls. It is not clear just what sources were used to substantiate this statement, but the writer may have placed too much confidence in the works of Blind Henry the Minstrel and in *Barbour's Bruce*.* The invasion of MacFadyan is problematical, and the assertion that Wallace held a council at Ardchattan may be confused with the tradition that Robert the Bruce held a parliament at Ardchattan (perhaps in 1310). *The Galley* article also claims that the parliament held by Bruce was the last in which Gaelic was used as the official state language. It also asserts that Duncan was recognized as MacDougall of MacDougall and Dunollie at this parliament. (Compare with Starforth, *Official Short History of Clan MacDougall*, p. 21.)

In 1998 the author found that displays and informational boards had been erected for the benefit of tourists. It is possible that some of the items described here have been repositioned for safekeeping.

53. Cathedral Church of Lismore

This ancient seat of the medieval diocese of Argyll is on Lismore's main road, north of Achnacroish. It was built during the early fourteenth century on the site of a much earlier monastic center associated with Saint Moluag.[72] A little less than half the original fourteenth-century cathedral still remains, in the form of the much remodeled choir. The original length of the building was about one hundred and twenty-five feet and the width was a little over twenty-three feet. A wooden screen probably separated the nave from the choir; in its place now is found the west wall of the church with its massive pulpitum.

Removal of plaster from the south wall disclosed a piscina with its drain hole intact and a sedilia with three bays under rounded arches. The side pilasters show the remains of fillet rolls.[7] The medieval door to the choir (now blocked) is also in the southern wall and has a rounded arch. In contrast, the doorway in the north wall that led to the sacristy has a lancet arch springing from blocks bearing carved human heads. The left face is that of a bishop wearing a miter, while the face to the right is that of a cleric with tonsured hair.

Both within the church and in the yard outside there are some interesting grave monuments, many of which are done in the style of the Iona School.[9]

---

* John Barbour, *Barbour's Bruce*.

54. Dunstaffnage Chapel

Diagram 9 shows the fine workmanship of the masons who built this chapel. This chapel is considered the finest example of Gothic architecture in the west Highlands. (Also see Note 45.)

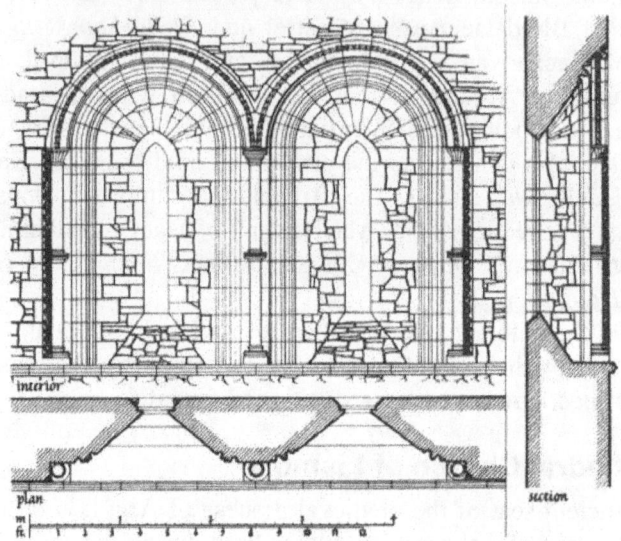

By permission of The Royal Commission On The Ancient & Historical Monuments Of Scotland

Diagram 9. Dunstaffnage Chapel, Windows

55. Inishail

This is an old church situated on an island in the north end of Loch Awe and southwest of Fraoch Eilean. A carved slab that probably was part of the altar displays two armored figures holding what may be a crown over a shield bearing a galley very similar to that used over the centuries as an emblem of the MacDougall Chiefs. If the interpretation of the object being held above the shield is correct, then it would be a fit symbol for the holding of nearby Fraoch Eilean by the MacNaughtens for the crown and the arrangements made by the MacDougall Chiefs. (See Chapter 34.)

56. Kilbride

The present ruins of the old parish church of Kilbride stand upon the site of a medieval church that is first mentioned in records dating from 1249. The existing church was built in 1706 and was revamped in the eighteenth and nineteenth centuries.

The MacDougall burial aisle is just southeast of the church. It is an unroofed enclosure built in 1786 by a mason from Barrachrail. Above the elliptical arch of the wide gateway is the armorial panel bearing the Arms of the MacDougall Chiefs.[59] Just inside the enclosure is the large slab covering the graves of Chief Iain Ciar and his wife, Mary MacDonald of Sleat. An opening at the rear and to the right of the enclosure leads to the memorials of succeeding generations of those who have been head of the children of Dougall.

The graveyard contains a number of tapered slabs that feature weathered traces of claymores, plant scrolls, and mythical beasts carved by workmen of the Loch Awe School in the fourteenth and fifteenth centuries.[9] There are also a great many grave monuments erected to the memory of later members of the Clan family.

Since the original writing of this note, Madam Coline MacDougall of MacDougall has been laid to rest in the enclosure with the other Chiefs of the Clan. Her grave and that of her husband is marked by a white Celtic cross. Greatly compounding the loss to the Clan, her two sisters Jean MacDougall Hadfield and Miss Hope MacDougall of MacDougall are now buried nearby. Recently Jean's husband, Dr. Stephen Hadfield, passed away and is also buried at Kilbride.

57. Kilchattan

The ruins of this church are northwest of the village of Toberonochy on the Island of Luing. The outer facing stones, especially on the north side to the left of an opening and on the south side near the center of the wall, bear graffiti predominated by representations of galleys—that ubiquitous symbol of the seafaring world of our Norwegian and Scottish ancestors.

These galleys, scratched into the slates, show high prows and sterns much like those found on the armorial seals of the MacDougall Chiefs. In the adjacent graveyard is the stone erected to the memory of Hugh and John Mac-Dougall of Lunga, which features the differentiated Arms of the MacDougall
Chiefs without the supporting lions. (See Chapter 17 for mention of other MacDougall families buried at Kilchattan.)

58. Kilmore

This church is located close to a cottage on the left beyond the crossroads (heading eastward) that once made this hamlet an important meeting place. The church appears in the records dating from early in the fourteenth century. As in the case of Kilbride,[56] this church was remodeled several times and finally abandoned in 1876 when a new church was built at Cleigh to serve the parishes of both Kilmore and Kilbride.

An arched tomb recess dating from late medieval times can be seen in the south wall. There are a few traces of filleted rolls and dogtooth ornamentation.[7] Lewis Spence in *The Magic Arts in Great Britain* speaks of a sacred well at Kilmore in which there were two black fishes. Placing fish in holy wells appears to have been a common practice. They were fed on red hazelnuts, which supposedly gave them both spots and oracular powers.

Chiefs of the Clan and Their Coats of Arms

By old tradition, the Highland clan is a tribal entity and the chief is the hereditary keeper of its well-being. A clan may be torn from its glens and so dispersed that it becomes a wanderer haunted by the memory of that place which once was home; but deprived of its chief, it becomes a "broken clan"—a house in which the chair at the head of the communal table is empty, upon whose central hearth the fire no longer burns, and whose ancient establishment, for want of renewal and continuation, is but a shadow retiring down the dim, cold corridor of the past.

Those whose quest it is to find the sapwood within their own branch of humanity may look with envy at the tokens of our clan belonging—the belted crest, the tartan sett, the plant badge, the rallying cry. Yet those who recognize these outward symbols of clanship and understand nothing more will find it difficult to reconcile the independence of the Scottish spirit with the devotion given to the chief of a clan by those who bear the same or an associated name. Yet the bonds of clanship are no mystery, nor is there any act of prostration in the respect so willingly given to the chief. The Highland clan is simply and powerfully an example of that most ancient and vital of human relationships—the extended family. At the head of this household of households and central within this confederation of mutual respect and this union of individual pride is the chief who is the representative of the clan's past and the trustee of its future.

Transcending older clan traditions is the influence of feudal law and practice, which entered the Highlands in the 1200s with the coming of powerful Norman families. Coats of arms (unlike, for instance, clan plant badges) are part of the feudal tradition. They do not belong to anyone simply because they have a certain surname, but identify and are granted to particular, landed gentry. Any use of coats of arms by anyone other that those granted these arms violates the context in which such heraldic symbols exist and is, in fact, illegal.

But again, in the Highland tradition a Celtic afterglow persists. Any member of a clan may wear his or her chief's crest (a key feature of that chief's arms) encircled with a belt symbolic of a bond of fidelity. Apart from heraldic and current law, there is a treasured relationship between a clan chief and his or her clanspeople. Coats of arms, clan seats, and remnants of old clan lands belong to the chief, but there lingers a sense of community—a sense of responsibility on the part of the clan member and of trusteeship on the part of the chief.

Families representing major branches or cadets of a clan often display a part of their chief's arms. Usually omitted in such representations are the supporters (in the case of the Arms of the MacDougall Chiefs, the crowned lions holding the shield), which are emblems of baronial standing or the position of head of the name.

59. Coats of Arms

Diagram 10. Arms of the MacDougall Chiefs

The quartered shield of the Arms of the MacDougall Chiefs feature the black Galley of Lorn, symbolizing descent from the Norse royal house of Man and the Islands,[*] while the lion displays descent from the Scottish kings of Dalriada. The Macdowalls and MacDowells of Galloway have long used a silver lion (white) on azure as their arms. The choice of symbol and colors indicates the interrelationship that has long existed between these two royal houses.

Interestingly, the Royal Commission on Ancient and Historical Monuments in *Argyll, Volume 2,* makes a mistake in recording the Arms

---

[*] *The Tartan*, Spring 1980, p.5.

of MacDougall of MacDougall and Dunollie. The arms described in that book were taken from the grave of Iain Ciar, where the MacDougall Arms are quartered with those of Iain's wife, a MacDonald of Sleat (a castle and a hand).

It is not certain how early the MacDougall Lords of Lorn combined the galley and the lion in their arms. Seals of the Lords of Lorn and Chiefs of the Clan dated 1292, 1296, and 1332 show only the galley, with its dragon head at both the high prow and stern. (These heads have been identified by some writers as being ravens—the raven being the Clan MacDougall bird.*) The earliest known representation of lion and galley in conjunction (but not quartered) is found on the remains of a stone cross at Ardchattan Priory that bears the date 1500 AD.†

The Clan Crest, found both at the top of the Arms of the MacDougall Chiefs and on the clansman's belted badge, features a right hand holding a "cross crosslet fitchy." This symbol may have been derived from the kindred of Saint Columba, from whom Somerled was descended. The elbow of the bent arm holding the cross rests upon an ermined "cap of maintenance," symbolic of baronial station. For more information on Scottish heraldry, see the *Scottish Clans & Family Encyclopedia* by George Way of Plean and Romilly Squire.

60. Investiture of Chiefs

The ceremonies of investiture were well established and drew from the Celtic past. For an account of these traditions, see Frank Adam's *The Clans, Septs and Regiments of the Scottish Highlands*, pp. 113 ff.

61. Somerled

The royal line of Somerled, Regulus of mainland Argyll and the western islands, intermingles the Norse and Scottish dynasties that long battled over this area.‡

Somerled appears as a leading figure in the western Highlands and islands in 1130, when he defeated the galleys of the Norse. He married Ragnhild, the daughter of Olaf, King of Man, by whom he had at least three sons. The eldest was Dougall, from whom the MacDougall Chiefs are directly descended. Somerled was killed at Renfrew in 1164. Tradition says that he is buried at Saddell on the east coast of Kintyre,

---

* *The Tartan*, Fall 1980, p.5.
† See Chapter 10.
‡ R. Andrew McDonald, *The Kingdom of the Isles*; Sir Iain Moncrieffe, *The Highland Clans*, pp. 117–118 and 56–60; and Michael Starforth's *An Official History of Clan MacDougall*, pp. 1–5.

but scholars doubt this. Ancient burial slabs preserved at Saddell depict in stylized images the warriors with padded surcoats and long claymores who populated the era into which Somerled was born.

62. Chiefs of Clan MacDougall

When known, the approximate year when a Chief attained the title appears after the name.

1st Chief—Dougall (1164)

Eponymous founder of Clan MacDougall. In 1164, upon the death of his father, King Somerled, Dougall received the mainland kingdom of Lorn from Morvern to Knapdale, along with the islands of Jura, Coll, Mull, Tiree, Kerrera, and Lismore and the surrounding smaller isles. He died in 1207. See McDonald's *Kingdom of the Isles* for Dougall's siblings.

2nd Chief—Duncan (1207)

Called King Duncan in the Sagas, second Chief of the Clan and son of Dougall. Ruler of Argyll (Ergadia) and Regulus of the Isles. Founded Ardchattan Priory. His major stronghold seems to have been Dunstaffnage, but he probably fortified Dunollie's promontory as well. He died in 1248.

3rd Chief—Ewan (1248)

Ewan or John of Argyll (de Ergadia), Lord of Lorn, third Chief of the Clan, and son of Duncan. For a time he was King of the Isles under the High King of Norway. There is evidence that Ewan had assumed the eponymic title of MacDhughaill (MacDougall). His sister was Gill of Argyll and wife of Brian O'Neill, the last king of Ireland. Ewan managed to maintain his position amidst the struggle between Alexander, King of Scots, and Haakon, King of Norway. His daughter Mary first married Magnus, King of Man, and then the Fifth Earl of Strathearn (c. 1268). He died in 1266.

4th Chief—Alexander (1266)

Alasdair de Ergadia, Lord of Lorn, fourth Chief of the Clan, and son of Ewan. Overlord of a large part of the western Highlands under King Baliol. Died in 1310. Married the third daughter of John Comyn and Marian, daughter of Alan of Galloway.

5th Chief—John of Lorn (Iain Bacach)

The fifth Chief of the Clan and son of Sir Alexander. Defeated Robert Bruce at Dalrigh and was himself defeated in the Battle of Brander. Became Admiral of the Western Seas under King Edward. Died in either 1317 or 1318. There is a tradition that Iain Bacach died while a prisoner in Dumbarton Castle; however, the records indicate that he was in London the year following and that he went on a pilgrimage to Canterbury. Dougal MacDowell or Macdowall was executor of his will. It is reported that his burial was paid for and his debts were squared with money from a grateful Edward III.

6th Chief—Duncan of Dunollie (1310)

The sixth Chief of the Clan and son of Ewan, the third Chief of the Clan. Duncan was a boyhood friend of William Wallace. He was granted Dunollie by Bruce (perhaps at the parliament held at Ardchattan Priory) after the defeat of the MacDougalls at Brander.

7th Chief—Ewan of Dunollie (1344)

Ewan or John, Lord of Lorn, seventh Chief of the Clan, and son of Sir John (Iain Bacach) of Lorn (5th Chief). (It is also possible that he was the son of Sir John's son, Alan.) Regained the Lordship of Lorn in 1344 through a marriage with Joan who was the daughter of Sir Thomas Isaac and Princess Matilda, the daughter of King Robert Bruce. Died around 1375. Had two daughters, Janet and Isabella, who both married Stewarts of Innerneath. Through Janet, the Lordship of Lorn passed to the Stewarts.

8th Chief—Iain of Dunollie (1375)

The eighth Chief of the Clan and the son of Allan who was the son of Duncan, the sixth Chief. He was granted large holdings in Lorn by John Stewart, Lord of Lorn, including Dunollie. Married Christina, the daughter of Sir Dougald Campbell of Craignish. Christina later married the second Chief of the MacNaughtens, and still later Ivor Campbell. Iain died around 1400. His second son was Allan of Raera (Rarray) and Ardmaddy.

9th Chief—Dougall of Dunollie (1400)

The ninth Chief of the Clan and the son of Iain (8th) of Dunollie. He married a daughter of MacDonnell of Isla, and was killed in a fight with the Campbells at Asknish.

10th Chief—Alan of Dunollie (??)

The tenth Chief of the Clan and son of Dougall (9th) of Dunollie. He married a daughter of Robert Stewart of Lorn.

11th Chief—Sir John of Dunollie (??)

The eleventh Chief of the Clan and son of Alan (10th) of Dunollie. Married Gyllis (Egidia) who was the daughter of Campbell of Glenorchy. Died in 1480.

12th Chief—Alexander of Dunollie (1480)

The twelfth Chief of the Clan and son of Sir John (11th) of Dunollie. Alexander's eldest son was killed in 1512. Alexander died in 1493.

13th Chief—John of Dunollie (1493)

The thirteenth Chief of the Clan and son of Alexander (12th) of Dunollie. Mentioned in a charter dated 1518; died around 1535.

14th Chief—John of Dunollie (1535)

The fourteenth Chief of the Clan and son of John (13th) of Dunollie. John quarreled with the Duke of Argyll and was imprisoned by the Campbells in Dollar Castle. Died in 1563. His son, Duncan, may have built Gylen Castle.

15th Chief—Dougall of Dunollie (1563)

The fifteenth Chief of the Clan and the son of John (14th) of Dunollie. Known as something of a tyrant. Mentioned in charters dated 1563 and 1567.[*]

16th Chief—Duncan of Dunollie (1591)

The sixteenth Chief of the Clan and the son of Dougall (15th) of Dunollie. Obtained a charter from King James VI in 1596. He may have been the builder of Gylen Castle. Married (1st) Margaret the sister of Sir Lauchlan MacLean of Dowart. His second son by this marriage was Allan of Torsay. The MacDougalls of Gallanach are descended from Allan's son John. Duncan married (2nd) Sibylla the daughter of Drummond of Cochyle. Simpson notes[†] that Duncan appears to have been a Protestant and in communication with agents of Queen Elizabeth.

---

[*] W. Douglas Simpson, *Dunollie, Oban, Argyll*, p. 74.
[†] W. Douglas Simpson, *Dunollie, Oban, Argyll*, p. 76.

According to a Gaelic manuscript,[*] Duncan died on the last day of August 1616, in the "speckled room at Dunollie." He is buried at Kilbride in the stone chest nearest the door at the back of the church.

17th Chief—Sir John of Dunollie (1617)

The seventeenth Chief of the Clan and the son of Duncan (16th) of Dunollie. He married in 1610 Katherine the daughter of Hector MacLean of Duart. In 1622 he was involved in complaints and counter-complaints dealing with cattle raids involving his father-in-law. Simpson says that there is some evidence that he practiced "robber baron tactics."[†] He died around 1634.

18th Chief—Alexander of Dunollie (1634)

The eighteenth Chief of the Clan and the son of Sir John (17th) of Dunollie. Chief during a period of relative peace. He married Katherine, the daughter of Sir Duncan Campbell of Glenorchy, and had three sons who became Chiefs of the Clan.

19th Chief—Ian (Iain) of Dunollie (1644)

The nineteenth Chief of the Clan and the son of Alexander (18th) of Dunollie. Ian became Chief at a young age sometime before 1644. He was Chief during the troubled times of the massacre at Dunaverty (some accounts say that he was the young MacDougall who alone was spared, but this is probably a case of mistaken identity), the burning of Gylen, and the taking of Dunollie by the Covenanter army. Married a daughter of Sir Roderick Mor MacLeod but had no children.

20th Chief—Duncan of Dunollie (??)

The twentieth Chief of the Clan and the second son of Alexander (18th) of Dunollie. He had a daughter who married Ian MacLean of Lochbuie in 1707.

21st Chief—Allen of Dunollie (??)

The twenty-first Chief of the Clan and the third son of Alexander (18th) of Dunollie. He received from James VII a charter to a greater part of Lorn in 1686. Married Mary, the daughter of Ian MacLachlan of Kilbride. He died in 1695.

---

[*] *MacDougall Collection*, collected by Hope MacDougall of MacDougall.
[†] W. Douglas Simpson, *Dunollie, Oban, Argyll*, p. 76.

22nd Chief—John of Dunollie (Iain Ciar) (1695)

Twenty-second Chief of the Clan and son of Allen (21st) of Dunollie. Joined the Rising of 1715 and led two hundred kinsmen at Sheriffmuir. After the failure of this rising, Iain Ciar was in exile for eleven years. He was known for his swordmanship and bravery, and his name is associated with many bold tales, especially the "Red Robber" stories that appear in Archibald Campbell's *Records of Argyll*. He married Mary, the daughter of William MacDonald of Sleat. Mary bravely defended Dunollie during her husband's exile. His second son, Allan, went to the East Indies. His third son joined the Rising of 1745.

23rd Chief—Alexander of Dunollie (Alastair Dubh)

The twenty-third Chief of the Clan and the son of John (22nd) of Dunollie. Alexander did not join the Rising of 1745. He built the manor house below the castle and raised a large family. Married Mary, the daughter of Patrick Campbell of Barcaldine, in 1737. His first son, John, married the daughter of Lord Ruthven and died in 1775 at Bombay without issue. Alexander died in 1801.

24th Chief—Patrick of Dunollie (1801)

The twenty-fourth Chief of the Clan and the second son of Alexander (23rd) of Dunollie. Patrick was nearly sixty when he became Chief. He had a reputation of being frugal, which is small surprise considering the size of the family he raised. Married Louisa Maxwell, the daughter of Campbell of Achalader. He was born in 1742 and died in 1825. His first son, Captain Alexander, was killed at Ciudad Rodrigo in 1810 and died without issue.

25th Chief—Sir John of Dunollie (1825)

The twenty-fifth Chief of the Clan and the second son of Patrick (24th) of Dunollie. Sir John rose from a midshipman to the rank of Vice Admiral, R.N., K.C.B. He was known for his courageous seamanship and for his consideration to his tenants as Chief of the Clan. In 1826, he married Elizabeth Sophia, the daughter of Captain Charles Timins of the East India Company. Sir John was born in 1789 and died in 1865. His portrait appears in Starforth's *An Official Short History of Clan MacDougall*, opposite p. 15.

26th Chief—Captain Alexander John of Dunollie (1865)

The twenty-sixth Chief of the Clan and eldest son of Sir John (25th) of Dunollie. He was a captain of artillery in Crimea. He married Anna, the daughter of Thomas Barclay. He was born in 1827 and died in 1867, seven weeks after his marriage.

27th Chief—Lt. Colonel Charles Allan of Dunollie (1867)

The twenty-seventh Chief of the Clan and the third son of Sir John (25th) of Dunollie. He was a member of the Bengal Staff Corps. He was active in the local government of Argyll and encouraged the formation of Clan MacDougall societies. Married Harriet Elizabeth, the daughter of Charles Munro of Ingsdon. He was born in 1831 and died without issue in 1896.

28th Chief—Deputy Surgeon General Henry Robert Lawrence of Dunollie (1896)

The twenty-eighth Chief of the Clan and the fifth son of Sir John (25th) of Dunollie. Received an M.D. from the University of Edinburgh and made a career in India, where he was a member of the Bombay Medical Service. He married Caroline Harriette, the daughter of James Forsyth of Glengorm on the Island of Mull. He was born in 1835 and died in 1899.

29th Chief—Colonel Alexander James of Dunollie (1899)

The twenty-ninth Chief of the Clan and the son of Henry Robert Lawrence (28th) of Dunollie. Received an M.B. and Ch.B. from the University of Edinburgh and became a colonel in the Royal Army Medical Corps. He was a member of the first expeditionary force in 1914. He was twice mentioned in dispatches and was made a Commander of Saint Michael and Saint George. Served in the Home Guard and as a welfare officer in World War II. He was a supporter of youth organizations and greatly interested in the heritage of the Clan. He married Colina Edith, the daughter of Alexander MacDougall of Soroba. He was born in 1872 and died in 1953. He had three daughters: Coline Helen Elizabeth; Jean Louisa Morag, who married Dr. Stephen Hadfield; and Margaret Hope Garnons MacDougall of MacDougall.

30th Chief—Coline Helen Elizabeth MacDougall of MacDougall and Dunollie (1953)

The thirtieth Chief of the Clan and daughter of Colonel Alexander (29th) of Dunollie. In 1949, married Leslie Grahame-Thomson, a member of the Royal Society of Architects. Madam MacDougall of MacDougall served in the armed forces during World War II and was actively interested in preserving the heritage of the Clan. She was born in

1904 at Blackheath, England, where her father was stationed, and she died in May of 1990.

31st Chief—Morag MacDougall of MacDougall and Dunollie (1990)

It is a privilege to bring this list of MacDougall Chiefs to the present with an autobiographical sketch of Morag MacDougall of MacDougall, thirty-first Chief and daughter of Jean MacDougall of MacDougall (the 30th Chief's sister) and Dr. Stephen Hadfield. In July of 2006, she wrote:

> I was born just after the start of the 2nd World War in 1939 in the village of Beer in Devon where my father was the local Doctor in practice. When he was called up we moved around to various places, including Dunollie, Oban, where my grandparents lived. From Beer I went to a Convent school near by for 2 years before moving to Surrey in 1948 as my father had a job in London with the British Medical Association.
>
> We lived in Surrey for 15 years during which time I went to Boarding School at Sherborne' Dorset (1951–58). I then trained for the Licentiate of the College of Speech Therapists in London for 3 years. After qualifying I took a Speech Therapy job in Cardiff, where I met my husband, Richard.
>
> We were married in St Columba's Church at Argyll Square, Oban, on 30th July 1966 and celebrated in Dunollie House. Forty years later we celebrated our Ruby Wedding at Dunollie. Our son, Robin, was born on 18th March 1970, and our daughter, Fiona, on 31st May 1974. Having worked in Wales from 1961–1999 (with some gaps) we share our time between Herefordshire and Oban, the home of my ancestors and the home of my parents since 1977. My mother, Jean, died on New Year's Day, 1999, and my father, Stephen, still lives in an old people's home in his late 90s.*
>
> My main interests are walking; wildlife, including Bird watching; and Music of various kinds—I play the organ and am a member of a Recorder group, a Handbell group, and a Choir—and I enjoy Scottish Dancing. In recent years we have taken several holidays in Europe and particularly enjoy exploring Alpine regions both on foot and on cross-country skis.

---

* Dr. Hadfield died February 5, 2007.

Flora and Fauna

63. Flowers

One's enjoyment of a journey through the countryside of Lorn will be greatly enhanced by a guide to the flowers of the Highlands. A fairly comprehensive book and easy to carry is *Wild Flowers*, a Collins Gem guide. The writer's sister, Leah Macdougall Rawding, greatly enriched one of our visits to Scotland by identifying 73 species of wild flowers and shrubs.

Heather

Of special interest to the members of the Clan MacDougall family is the bell heather (*Erica cinerea*), which differs markedly from the common heather (*Calluna vulgaris*) or ling. The bell heather is the MacDougall Clan badge and perhaps the oldest of all the clan's emblems. The bell heather has dark green, needle-like leaves growing in whirls on wine-red stems. The flowers are individually larger than those of the common heather, are a crimson-purple growing in terminal clusters, and blossom in July.*

The common heather has dull-green leaves and dense flowering spikes that bloom in late August and September, turning the moors lavender.

The diminutive member of the Highland heathers is the bog heather (*Erica tetralix*), which blossoms amidst the lichen of wet areas. Its blossoms grow in terminal clusters and are individually larger than those of the common heather. In color the blossoms are more pink than the crimson bell heather.

Fireweed

The fireweed is also known as the rosebay willow-herb. While it may not be indigenous, it now adds its lavender beauty to the Highland roadsides. The writer was told that this first made its appearance along the margins of airstrips where the seeds were introduced by planes returning from missions over the Continent. However, Miss Hope MacDougall of MacDougall notes that this plant is mentioned in Johns' *Flowers of the Field* (1888) as being present though "scarcely in Britain." She remembers seeing this plant in 1928 growing profusely in

---

* *The Tartan*, Fall 1981, p. 7.

the Loch Avich area. Evidently the seeds of this lovely flower spread rapidly on their airborne silk during and following World War II.

Foxglove

The foxglove, mentioned several times in the journal text, has a delightful Gaelic name: *miaran na sith*, "thimbles of the fairies."

Public Gardens

One of the joys of traveling anywhere in Scotland are the public gardens. In these flowing precincts, exotic plants brought home from the far empire bloom beside indigenous species. Close to Oban, the following public gardens deserve special mention: the gardens at Auchnacloich and Ardchattan, both on Loch Etive, and Arduaine Garden on Asknish Bay, south of Melfort on Route A816.

64. The Caldonian Forest

SCOTS PINE

The natural forest that once covered the glens and hillsides of the Highlands has long since disappeared, with the exception of scattered remnants such as the Black Wood of Rannoch. The great forests were the victims of climatic changes and the ravages of man. In an increasingly delicate ecological balance due to greater rainfall, the leaching of minerals, the development of peaty and acid soils, and the matting of surface areas by moss and lichen, the natural processes of reforestation were unequal to the rate of man's destruction.

Beginning as early as the invasion by the Norse and likely long before, large tracts of woodlands were burned in the constant warfare. Such destruction continued through the medieval period. For example, Robert the Bruce destroyed the forests of Inverary in his campaign against the Comyns. At the same time, the demands for timber increased—a need that culminated in the rapid growth of the population and the demand for such products as charcoal. The exploitation of the land for the grazing of sheep added a final blow to the old wildwood.

The natural forests contained both deciduous and coniferous trees. The former (oak forests with a hazel and holly understory) predominated on the southern slopes, while the coniferous woods (typified by Scots pine with its great spreading branches) tended to survive best on the northern slopes and in areas of peaty soils.

Some examples of natural forestation can still be found in Lorn. For example:

- **Clais Dearg Forest** with oak and birch—on the west of Black Loch and reached from A85 at Stonefield on the south shore of Loch Etive.

- **Black Mount's old pine woods**—on Loch Tulla, south of the Moor of Rannoch, off A82 from Tyndrum to Fort William.

- **Coille Leitire and Coille Driseig** with oak, birch, ash, and wych elm—at the entrance to the Pass of Brander on Route A85.

- **Scattered Scots pine**—west of Dalrigh below Tyndrum, on Route A82.

65. Heaths

The heaths are a study in themselves and are hardly as "barren" as often supposed. The flora varies a great deal with altitude. However, many of the heaths on exposed headlands have the character of habitats much higher in elevation. The high heaths are characterized by blueberry, mountain azalea, lichens, hard fern, wavy-hair grass, heath bedstraw, mosses, sedges, and rushes. In the mountains such as those of Glencoe, the heaths display beautiful alpine flowers—purple saxifrage, starry saxifrage, alpine forget-me-not, and rock speedwell.

66. Birds and Animals

Those devoted to bird identification will find ample challenge in MacDougall Country, which provides many habitats: coastline, island cliffs, woods, and high heaths. For the casual observer, *A Handguide to Birds of Britain and Europe* by Martin Woodcock is a useful companion. The writer's sister recorded 47 species of birds in one brief visit in Argyll.

On the other hand, the writer saw very few species of wild animals in his tramps. This fact may indicate a lack of observation or may be due to having walked primarily upon open heaths rather than in wooded areas.

The following notes refer to some of the birds and animals mentioned earlier in this book.

Buzzards

For many Americans, the word "buzzard" will call to mind the image of the turkey buzzard rather than a mental picture of the great Highland hawk. The Highland buzzard is related to the eagle, for which it is often mistaken. It has a wide variation in the shades of brown and buff that are the predominant colors of its plumage. There is considerable white upon its breast. Its black, sharply hooked bill gives the impression of a predator, and this impression is correct.

Deer

Perhaps no other animal is more closely associated with our romantic impression of the Highlands than the red deer: "The stag at eve had drunk its fill..."[*] The very name "stag" or "hart" brings a mental image of proud racks of antlers spreading up and outward from a head held high upon a massive and shaggy neck. Red deer may grow to a weight of four hundred pounds and, for all that size, is capable of great agility and speed in rugged country. Time, patience, and a good pair of field glasses are a great help in seeing these deer in the wild. Deer appear to be on the increase; however, the surest way to see this animal is to visit one of the many deer farms. The much smaller roe deer are often seen feeding close to Dunollie House.

---

[*] Sir Walter Scott, *The Lady of the Lake*.

Golden Eagle

There are strict laws protecting the golden eagle and programs intended to encourage their increase. The mountainous country of upper Glen Etive provides a chance of seeing this rider of the thermals. It is larger than the buzzard, golden brown in coloration with a mottling of white, and has a more massive beak than its relative. It nests at about fifteen hundred feet, preferring a ledge, though it does nest in trees. The author was told by a veteran who had been stationed at the seaplane base on the island of Kerrera during World War II that the airmen shot eagles—they were death to the pigeons that were used to carry messages from the patrolling planes to shore.[*]

Herons

Reports show that the heron has made a comeback in the Highlands. Wading on its yellow, stilt-like legs, this bird carries its wings folded like a great feathered cloak upon a hunched back. Its long, straight bill was certainly fashioned for utility and not good looks. A sparse crown of long dark feathers draping back over its head appear as if they had been purposely combed to cover a bald spot. In flight, however, the heron assumes a slow, beating majesty.

Raven and Hooded Crow

Considered by many to be the most intelligent of all the birds, the raven deserves a special note as it is the Clan MacDougall bird.[†] The raven's wing span can reach a length of four feet, making it a larger bird than its close relative, the crow. It has a heavy black bill, and its throat feathers tend toward iridescent hackles. Unlike the gregarious crow, the raven is usually seen flying alone or in the company of its mate.

Among the raven's Highland cousins is the hooded crow, the only member of genus *Corvus* that is not completely black. While the "hoodie crow" is often described as having patches of white plumage, gray would be more descriptive. This bird's reputation is also more gray than white. The hooded crow is said to be a good parent, but it is a menace to the nestlings of other species and a bother to lambs.

---

[*] See Chapter 42.
[†] *The Tartan,* Fall 1980, p. 5.

Swans

The mute swan is the common white-plumed galley of the lochs of Lorn. This bird has an orange and black bill in contrast to the yellow and black beak of the whooper swan. The latter is a winter visitor.

Wildcats

A British postage stamp was issued that featured this animal (*Felis silvestris*) as a species at risk. Rare as it may be, it deserves note as many place names derive from associations with the wildcat. The Gaelic for cat is *cat* and even the diminutive *cattan* is close enough to the English to catch one's eye. The wildcat of the Highlands is smaller than the American bobcat but larger than a domesticated cat, with which it is closely enough related to interbreed. The coloring resembles the "tiger" variety of housecats, including the stripes on the forehead between large and pointed ears. The tail has a black tip.

Wolves

The last sighting of this prowler in Scotland was recorded in 1743. However, Scottish heraldry bears witness that the wolf was well known to our Highland ancestors. There may be an association between the name of this animal and the word "Lorn." It may be a wolf represented on the base of a broken stone cross that displays the early heraldic symbols of the MacDougalls at Ardchattan. There has been a heated debate concerning the reintroduction of wolves into Scotland as a means of controlling the expanding deer population.

Physical Geology

67. Rocks

Five hundred million years ago, deep layers of sediments and sedimentary rocks in Lorn were subjected to great pressure, heat, and folding. They were thus metamorphosed into slate, gneiss, and schists. Mixed with black limestone, these rock stratums now often lie exposed.

New mountains were pushed upwards during the period in which the early metamorphosed rocks were being formed. Erosion produced sand, gravel, and cobbles which, in turn, were cemented during the Devonian and Ordovician periods (400–495 million years ago) to form red sandstones and conglomerates. These newer sedimentary layers now lie on top of the older metamorphic layers. Unlike the still older and barren Torridonian sandstones, these newer sedimentary stratums contain fossilized proof of life, in the form of plants and primitive fish.

Much later, during the Tertiary Period (30–70 million years ago), the forces of vulcanism changed the face of Lorn. A great volcano, whose much eroded heights still dominate the Island of Mull, sent lava flows across the landscape, and intrusive dikes radiating outward through the older rock strata. This igneous rock material joined in forming the ramparts of Lorn. They include the great granite batholiths, basaltic lava flows cooling with characteristic columnar formations, and the fine-grained dolerites of the spreading dikes.

Examples of rock layers and formations from all these periods can be seen in the Oban area. A few examples are given below.

Granite

The high cliffs of Mull's southern shore are a most striking display of fine red granite. Stone from quarries along this shore was widely used in London and other major cities. Granite of this type was, and still may be, used extensively for imported gravestones found in cemeteries of the eastern United States.

Lava Escarpments and Exposed Dikes

Good examples are on Mull and on Kerrera. Dikes are a major geological feature of the northern end of Kerrera and below Gylen Castle.

Conglomerates

The Ardbhan Craigs along the west margin of the Shore Road to Gallanach are composed of this "pudding stone," as is the rock upon which Dunstaffnage sits. Bedrock on Kerrera also contains conglomerates.

Sandstones

The "freestone" of the operative masons, which they carved and formed into moldings and decorated window jambs, was quarried from a number of sites close to Oban. Quarries can be seen at Ardentallan and Barnacarry Bay on Loch Feochan and at the Bridge of Awe.

Slates and Limestones

While outcroppings of slate and limestone are encountered on Kerrera and elsewhere about Oban, limestone is particularly associated with Lismore, and slate with Luing.

Glaciation

All the above rock types have been cut, scoured, and exposed by the coming and going of the glaciers, which once covered Scotland and which kept out human habitation until relatively late in prehistoric times. Much of the rugged countryside—the corried and truncated mountains, the sweep of U-shaped valleys, the long and deep lochs running generally northeast to southwest, and the many boggy areas—are the result of glaciation. So too are the podsoils, whose poor drainage has resulted in the formation of peat and heaths.

68. Raised Beaches, Stacks, and Caves

Observing the west coast of Scotland, it is evident that either the level of the sea has receded or the land has risen. One theory claims that the entire plate of which Scotland is the abovewater manifestation is tipping, with the west side rising and the east dipping downward. Whatever the cause or combined causes, the sea once scoured the headlands of the west Highland coast as much as thirty feet above the present high tide. Where the Atlantic once rolled in, there now runs shelves of old terraced sea beaches. Behind these old beaches are cliffs that, though no longer pounded by waves, show the effect of ancient seas.

The formation of caves is one feature of special importance to early inhabitants and later secretive uses. One macabre find consisting of a quantity of human bones, a gold-headed cane, and a silver brooch was discovered in a cave upon the Shore Road to Gallanach called Uamh nan Claigionn, "the Cave of Skulls."

Columns of more resistive rock once washed around by the sea stand high and dry along the coast, such as the famous Clach na Choin or "Dog Stone" just south of Dunollie Castle.

69. Islands of Nether Lorn

These islands were the home of many MacDougall families or families of those associated with the Clan. Booklet numbers three and five of the *West Highland Series*, "The Islands of Nether Lorn" and "Walking in South Lorn," provide much fascinating information, although the material on Glen Dubh Leitir on Luing may be confusing.* Two delightful and informative books are Marion Campbell's *Argyll: The Enduring Heartland* and Garth and Vicky Waite's *Island: Diary of a Year on Easdale*. The latter features the island of Seil.

Torsa

This island is closely associated with Clan MacDougall. It lies east of Luing in Seil Sound. The passage between Luing and Torsa is fordable at low tides. It has fertile land and was once covered with run-rig farms (joint use of land).

Lunga

The name of this island is derived from the Norse word meaning "long" or "longship." Lunga is said to be haunted by a phantom drummer whose ghostly tattoo is still heard. At the north end of the island is a source of water that has never gone dry known as Tobar Chalumchille or "Saint Columba's Spring." The MacDougalls of Lunga take their name from this island.†

Scarba

Separating Lunga from Scarba is Bealeach a' Choin Ghais, the "Straight of the Gray Dog," which, like so many of the channels between the island of Nether Lorn, churns with tidal rips and powerful currents. Scarba is the top of a seamount—rugged and no longer permanently inhabited. Its high top is a landmark along the coast of Lorn.

The Garvellachs

This four-island group (not counting the smaller fragments of rocks) is in a line west of Lunga. The name comes from *garbh aileach*, meaning

---

* See Chapter 39.
† See Chapter 15.

"rough rock." Other names for this group are "The Islands of the Sea" and "The Holy Islands." These high-clifted confronters of Atlantic storms were once the havens of Saint Brendan and Saint Columba. On the southernmost isle, Eileach na Naoimh, are the remains of an extensive monastery where Saint Columba may have buried his mother. At the other end of the island chain is Dun Chonnel, the site of an ancient stronghold said to have been erected by Conal, King of Dalriada. Starforth in his *Official Short History of Clan MacDougall* gives Dun Chonnel as one of the early strongholds of the MacDougall Lords of Lorn. Later the castle became part of the realm of the Lords of the Isles, and under their control the MacLeans became the keepers of this fortification.

70. Kerrera

Despite centuries of vicissitudes, Kerrera (except for the northern point) still belongs to the Chiefs of Clan MacDougall. Through their stewardship and insistence, Kerrera remains unspoiled by resorts and condominiums. It is still farm, moor, and miles of spectacular coastline. The history of this island and the portrayal of Highland life lived by its inhabitants has been delightfully and minutely recorded by Hope MacDougall of MacDougall in her book *Island of Kerrera: Mirror of History*.[*] With such a source book available, the present writer will include only those few notes of immediate assistance to the reader of this journal.

Horseshoe Bay

This bay is on the Sound of Kerrera, directly below the ferry landing. In the spring of 1249, King Alexander of Scotland, intent on regaining the Hebrides from the King of Norway, anchored his fleet here and, upon the seaside field still called Dalrigh or "the King's Field," he parleyed with Ewan, Lord of Argyll, the third Chief of the Clan. In July, still encamped on Kerrera, Alexander was taken with a fever and died.[†]

In 1263, King Haakon of Norway arrived off Kerrera with a large fleet and anchored in Horseshoe Bay. At this time, Ewan made a complete break with his Norwegian affiliations and, raising the full strength of the Clan from his widespread realm, fought for the King of Scotland.

---

[*] In 2002, Hope MacDougall's book was republished in a most attractive third edition by the publishing firm House of Lochar.

[†] Starforth, *An Official Short History of Clan MacDougall*, pp. 6–11; Hope MacDougall of MacDougall, *Island of Kerrera: Mirror of History*, pp. 3–5.

Slaterach Farm

This farm is on the west shore of Kerrera, overlooking Slaterach Bay and the Firth of Lorn. Closer to the shore and beyond the present farm buildings are the ruins of an eighteenth-century meal mill once powered by a large water wheel. Between the farm and the water is also the ruined cottage in which Chief Iain Ciar's wife lived after the death of her husband. This cottage was the last building on Kerrera to have a thatched roof. A food vessel and cinerary urn, now at the National Museum of Antiquities of Scotland, were found near Slaterach Farm in the remains of a Bronze Age cairn.

Lochan na Circe

This is a lovely little loch deserving of its name—"little loch of the water lilies." It is also known as Lochan of the Seven Boundaries. It is just east and above the road to Barnabuck Bay. The point at which one should begin the climb from the road is marked by a small burn that crosses under the road. (See Chapter 41.)

Barnabuck (Bar nam Boc)

This was once an important harbor for the flow of goods out to the islands beyond Kerrera and for the landing of cattle droves headed to mainland markets. Among the cluster of houses was an inn (changehouse). This was one of three that once welcomed travelers to this island. The inn at Barnabuck, now a cottage, still has a window at the rear where drinks were passed out to customers.

71. Legends

Many of the old legends of Lorn are recorded in *A Lorn Miscellany* which was edited by Màiri MacDonald, published by the Lorn Archeological Society, and printed by the *Oban Times*. This book, by the way, has a foreword by Coline MacDougall of MacDougall, the thirtieth Chief of the Clan. The following notes give a brief resume of those tales either referenced in or related to places mentioned in this book.

Beothail and Castle Coeffin

In the days when Coeffin was a Norse stronghold, Beothail of the golden hair lived there. She was very much in love with a young Viking warrior. When in far-off Lochlann this warrior was killed, Beothail grew pale with her grief and died. Then in the wind that buffeted the walls of Coeffin came the pleading voice of the dead maiden begging her father and brother (whose name, by the way, was Caiffen or Coeffin) to carry her bones to Lochlann. Finally, her bones were washed in the sacred spring of Saint Moluag (still called Tobar Cnamh Beothail, "Well of Beothail's Bones") at Clachan and, thus blessed, were carried to where Beothail's lover lay buried. Still the voice came upon the ceaseless winds of the Lynn of Morvern. A bone was missing, left behind in the well. A search was made, and the bone was found. It too was carried to Lochlann. Then the pleading ceased, though the restless winds often sound a maiden's sigh around the walls of Coeffin.

Deirdre

The story of Deirdre strikes a resonance in our lives. It touches our own secret "might have beens."

Deirdre was born under the prophecy of both the morning and the baleful star. She would become the most beautiful woman in all the world, and she would be the cause of the House of Ulster's fall. Conchobar, King of Ulster, hid the fair baby, planning to marry her when she came of age, but Deirdre and the young warrior Naoise fell in love. Together they fled from Ireland to Glen Etive—that place apart from the scheming world. In a bower thatched with royal fern and by tradition located by the waterfall of Dalness on River Etive, the two lovers felt the gentle touch of joy until Conchobar in his wrath and deceit lured them back to Ireland. Naoise was murdered with his own sword, and Deirdre took her own life, falling into the grave of her warrior.

Fingal or Fionn

The stories of Fionn and his warrior band, the Fianna, linger thoughout the Celtic world of Ireland and the western Highlands. As in the case of all folklore, "there were giants in those days." The stronghold of the Fianna warriors is said to have been in Sgurr nam Fiannaidh, close by Glencoe. Some say that Fionn and his heroes sleep beside their hounds and their arms, in a cave somewhere in the mountains. In the day of Scotland's greatest need, they will arise.

Formation of Loch Awe

There was a spring high on Cruachan from which welled the waters of youth. It was in this spring that Cailleach, the Winter Hag, bathed to keep from growing old. (It was this hag who bid the Faoilteach, the "Storm Wolves," to bare their cold fangs and breathe the howling gales.) Each night, Cailleach covered the spring with a great rock, until one evening when, with other matters upon her mind, she forgot to do so. All night the waters gushed upwards and fell down the sides of the mountain.

In the morning, there stretched from the foot of Cruachan, the long, shining waters of Loch Awe.

Fraoch Eilean's Dragon

One does not think of the Highlands as one of the mythical habitats that bred dragons. In fact it would seem there was little spare room for dragons with all the *kelpies, bean-nighe,* and *glaistigs,* but perhaps these specters of the fairy mounds and the desolate glens moved in after all the dragons had ceased to lick their chops with tongues of fire. Be this as it might have been, a dragon once lived on the island of Fraoch spending its days coiled about the base of a magic rowan tree. (All rowan trees are, of course, the source of some magic.) There is more to this story: a lovely princess, a brave prince named Fraoch, and the princess' jealous mother, who really made a mess of things. No one is sure whether Fraoch Eilean is named for this prince, who was killed by the dragon as he attempted to get magic rowan berries for his princess (which she really didn't need), or whether the name is derived from the Gaelic word for heather.

John Maol MacDougall and His Wives

John Maol ("the Bald") MacDougall of Raera and Ardmaddy married a sister of the Earl of Argyll. It was said that she was bewitched and that even as John Maol looked upon his wife (whom he truly loved) there would appear above her head the apparition of a gray goat chewing its cud. Evidently this sight got on John's nerves. He built a house at Bamaghearry and put both his wife and her goat away from his sight.

Then John of Raera met Donald Dubh of Calder, a suave Campbell, in a public house at Kilmore. Donald inveigled John to marry Donald's sister who, instead of a goat, would bring the Pass of Brander as her dowry. John agreed, which was a bad mistake, for now the Campbells had John Maol of Raera charged with bigamy.

Accounts differ as to what took place once John had signed the contract to marry Donald Dubh's sister. Some say that the Earl of Argyll had John turned out of Ardmaddy Castle forthwith. Some say that a settlement was made that John could not pay, and that even as John lay dead in his own hall the Campbells arrived to take possession. Another version states that, in 1648 or 1649, the aged John Maol was imprisoned at Inverary by the Marquis of Argyll and forced to give up Ardmaddy. It is a fact that in 1661, the seizure of Ardmaddy Castle by the Campbells was condemned by Parliament, yet the Campbells' possession was confirmed by Charles the Second.

72. Saints and Place Names

Saint Bride

There seems to be no evidence that this saint was ever in Lorn, and this being the case, one is left to wonder why his name is found so often attached to churches and sacred places. An interesting answer has been suggested. His name was close enough to that of the pagan Celtic goddess, Brigid, to allow the early Christians to make the substitution, thus renaming, with far more acceptable association, the older places of veneration. There are several "Kilbrides" in Lorn, including the burial place of the later MacDougall Chiefs.

Saint Cattan

This saint was held in special veneration by the descendants of Lorn, one of the three sons of Erc who founded the Scottish Kingdom of Dalriada and from whom the MacDougall Chiefs are descended. As representative of this royal line, Duncan of Argyll, the second Chief of the Clan, built the Priory of Ardchattan upon a site hallowed to the memory of this saint. Cattan is said to have been a great scholar. He must have been well liked by the masses, for he is remembered by his nickname, Cattan, the "Little Cat."

Saint Conan

This holy man came to Lorn in the sixth century. He settled in the area of Dalmally, where there is still a spring associated with his name. Eventually he became Bishop of Man. Innis Chonain, an island in Loch Awe, bears his name. Saint Conan Church at Lochawe, built in 1881, gives testimony that this holy man has been long remembered. As Saint Conan is said to be the patron saint of Lorn, it is fitting that the carved stalls of the chancel in this church bear the arms of the chiefs of all the clans who have figured in the annals of this land.

Saint Fillan

The chapel of Saint Fillan is located on the east of the road, a mile south of the the site of the Battle of Dalrigh. The site is within a grove of trees some distance beyond the railroad tracks and away from the highway, and approached by a road that leads to nearby Kirkton Farm. There is little left of the chapel. A informative sign tells of the Saint's life, his crosier, his bell, and many miraculous things, including the story that the Saint's left elbow gave off light sufficient for him to write by. Bruce is said to have attributed his escape from the MacDougalls to the fact that he had prayed at this chapel and to Saint Fillan. The silver shrine holding the Saint's arm bone was reportedly brought to Bruce's tent on the eve of Bannockburn.

Saint Muire (Mary)

Kilmore and Corranmore (in Craignish) are English renditions that contain *Muire*, the Gaelic form for "the Virgin Mary." Kilmore, therefore, derives from Cille Mhuire, meaning "the church dedicated to Saint Mary." Dedications to Saint Mary appear to be relatively late in Lorn. Kilmore was originally dedicated to Saint Bean, who may have succeeded Columba as Abbot of Iona. When Roman Catholicism became victorious over the Celtic Church, names were changed. It was a practice to "bury" not only the older pagan deities but also the older saints, who likely thought that Rome did not know how to determine when to celebrate Easter.

Saint Moluag

Born in 489 of the Cruithne Tribe of Irish Picts and educated in the Monastery of Bangor in Ireland, this man dedicated himself to the brave task of spreading Christianity through the pagan Highlands. (Like Saint Brendan, he is also credited with sailing far to the west—perhaps as far as Greenland.) He landed on the shores of Lismore and there set up his base of operations at about the same time that Saint Columba arrived on Iona.

A very old man, but still at work, Saint Moluag died at Rosemarkie, another monastery, which he had established on the Black Isle north of Inverness. Tradition says that his body was borne back to Lismore and laid to rest close to the present cathedral church. It was on Lismore that his most famous relic, the Bachuil Mor, the "Great Staff," was kept for centuries by the MacLeays (the Livingstones of Lorn).[26] This staff was carried before the forces of Lorn as a symbol of consecration and the continuation of power and faith.

Only two feet and nine inches of this staff remains, but this portion is remarkably sound—a miracle of preservation—for it has been one thousand four hundred years since Saint Moluag raised his crosier in blessing over Lorn.*

---

* *The Tartan*, Fall 1981.

Other Lore

73. Brooch of Lorn (Bràiste Lathurna)

This brooch was taken from Robert the Bruce at the Battle of Dalrigh.* It was taken from the Clan when Gylen was plundered in 1647 and returned by the Campbells in 1824. The brooch is not Celtic in design but, rather, similar to Continental work of the early medieval period. It was probably a family heirloom of the Bruces that came to them through their Norman ancestors.†

74. Snuff

In 1736, Iain Ciar, Chief of Clan MacDougall, was bartering the then new wonder crop, potatoes, with his "tobacco spinner" in Oban for snuff. Evidently the novelty of potatoes passed, for Iain's son had to pay cash for the snuff he ordered from a merchant in Glasgow.

75. Professor Blackie

John Stuart Blackie held the Chair of Greek at Edinburgh University. He was an enthusiastic researcher of Highland lore and a prolific writer, and spent his summers in his Oban home of Alt na Craig until 1881.

76. McCaig's Tower and the Oban Hydrophathic Sanitarium

Oban has had its share of grand schemes. Among these (one might say over all of them) is McCaig's Tower. In erecting this huge structure, McCaig seems to have had mixed motives. One of his aims was to provide much-needed work for Oban's unemployed; however, he also planned to set up statues of himself and his family throughout the tower. McCaig died before these statues became a reality, and litigation brought by citizens of Oban blocked the fulfillment of the dead benefactor's intent. In 1983, an observation platform was added to McCaig's Tower, quite appropriately, to provide work for the unemployed.

Evidence of another grand scheme can be seen in the remains of what nearly became a health spa of two hundred rooms for Victorians, who were to be hoisted on lifts from the railway station, dined in three luxurious dining rooms, and bathed in healing waters. This was the proposed Oban Hills Hydropathic Sanitorium, upon which some fifty

---

* See Chapter 10.
† *The Tartan*, Fall 1982, p. 5.

thousand pounds was expended before the project was abandoned. These "new ruins" stand just south of McCaig's bid for immortality.

77. Lazybeds
A method of planting in contoured strips upon the hillsides. The main purpose of these laborious hand-dug furrows was to achieve better drainage.

78. Carding Mill Bay and the Brandy Rock
This is a small bay just below Dungallan Parks, on the Shore Road to Gallanach. The bay, now used as a yacht anchorage, gets its name from a small tweed mill that once stood on the east side of the Shore Road. A prominent feature on the north of the bay is Brandy Rock, which probably has some association with smuggling.

79. Eilean Musdile Lighthouse
This lighthouse is on a small island just off the southern tip of Lismore and is plainly seen from Oban. It was built in 1833 under the supervision and by the design of Robert Stevenson. Instead of following the family tradition, Robert's grandson, Robert Louis Stevenson, was to light the beacons of adventure in such splendid books as *Kidnapped*, which takes place, in part, in the western Highlands. The lantern of the lighthouse is one hundred feet above ocean level.

80. Beacon Fires on Cnoc Carnach
The practice of lighting beacon fires atop Cnoc Carnach has been carried on in celebration of major national events. At the time of the writer's first visit in 1981, plans were being made to light a fire atop this hill in honor of the wedding of Prince Charles and Lady Diana.

81. Burial of the Chiefs at Ardchattan
While it is known that Ardchattan was the burying place for the MacDougall chiefs until 1737, the exact location of their graves within these precincts has been erased by time. Despite family intentions, it is unlikely that all the early chiefs of the Clan were laid to rest at this sanctuary. Both the fourth chief, Alexander of Lorn, and his son John, the fifth chief, died outside of Lorn and under conditions that would have made the return of their bodies to Ardchattan very difficult.

Iain Ciar, who died 1737, was the first chief to be buried in Kilbride rather than Ardchattan. The story is that a severe and prolonged storm prevented carrying his body across the Falls of Lora, but there may have been more than storm involved in this departure from tradition. Through his mother, Iain Ciar had strong connections with Kilbride. One record says that he had been born in a house located on high ground near the old church at Kilbride.

82. Robber's Waterfall

The topographical map (1:50,000 Ordnance Series) has the following notation placed midway up Allt Mheuran: Eas nam Meirleach, the "Robber's Waterfall." A study of this map adds anecdotal mystery to any journey.

83. The String of Lorn

This name is a literal translation of the Gaelic *Sreang Lathurnach*. Some sources make the String of Lorn the natural boundary of Lorn and of MacDougall territory, which is an understandable mistake—the "string" follows a prominent watershed. However, the boundary of Lorn lays well south and across Loch Awe. Those who were to become the Campbells of Lochawe settled within Lorn and within MacDougall Country.

84. Cas Chrom

This is a hand and foot tool (the name means "crooked foot") used for centuries in the Highlands to turn the sod. It has a long, bent handle, a cutting blade, and a peg above the blade upon which one would place one's foot. Both foot pressure and the leverage of the handle were used to cut and turn the sod.

85. Diarmid and the Boar

This legend is also recounted as having taken place upon Bein an Tuirc in Kintyre. There really may have been a man by this name around whose memory the myths grew. This Diarmid is said to have been part of the Campbells' ancient lineage.

86. Rush Lamps and Rush Thatch

Stripped of its outer sheath, with the exception of a strip left for strength, and dipped in tallow, the pith of the rush may be burned as a candle. It may also be used as a wick in cruse lamps. The old Highland lamps burned either tallow or fish oil. They were open dish-type lamps with a protruding lip that made a cradle for the wick. Before the door at Dunollie House is a stone found by Madam MacDougall of MacDougall in which has been cut a mold for just such a "rush lamp."

Rushes were also used as thatch. The cottage near Slaterach Farm on Kerrera where Iain Ciar's wife lived following the death of her husband had a roof of rush thatch until the early 1900s.

87. Dunollie Gates

The drive to Dunollie Castle and Dunollie House joins the road from Oban (on the way north to Ganavan) and stands at a point opposite a narrow seaside park with a small lighthouse. This is a "new" entrance and much to be regretted, as Madam MacDougall explained to this writer. The drive used to continue its pleasant, tree-arched way to the head of George Street within the burgh, beginning rather more regally in what older maps of Oban labeled "Dunollie Gates." The change came when the new seaside road was built to reach the bathing sands of Ganavan as Oban, itself, continued to grow as a resort town. And so a lovely bit of Dunollie's precincts were sacrificed to pale Glasgow shopkeepers searching for the sun and to women challenging Victorianism in swimming bloomers.*

88. Achnacree

Three thousand years ago, before the layers of peat began to form, men tilled the level fields of Achnacree. Archaeologists have discovered the wall that once marked the boundaries of these plots.†

---

* See Chapter 26.
† Graham Ritchie, *The Archaeology of Argyll* and the Royal Commission on Ancient and Historical Monuments' *Argyll, Volume 2, Lorn.*

Bibliography

Adam, Frank, *The Clans, Septs, and Regiments of the Scottish Highlands 1934*, Kessinger, Whitefish, MT, 2004.

Annals of Ulster, translated by Mac Airt and Mac Niocaill, Dublin Institute for Advanced Studies, [Dublin], 1983.

Argyll: An Inventory of the Ancient Monuments, Volume 2, Lorn, with the Nineteenth Report of the Royal Commission on the Ancient and Historical Monuments of Scotland (RCAHMS), HMSO, [Edinburgh], 1975.

Baigent, Michael and Richard Leigh, *The Temple and the Lodge*, Arcade, New York, 1989.

Bain, Robert, *Clans and Tartans of Scotland*, Collins, [London], 1999.

Barbour, John, *Barbour's Bruce I, II, III*, edited by Matthew P. McDiarmid and James A. C. Stevenson, Scottish Text Society, Edinburgh, 1980-1985.

Black, J.W.N., *MacDonald's Guide to Oban and the District Around*, Hugh MacDonald, Oban [Scotland], [c. 1950].

Black, Nancy, *From a Hollow on the Hill*, Nancy Black, Oban, Argyll, 1999.

Burke, Bernard, *Landed Gentry*, Volume 1, Burke's Peerage, London, [various editions].

Campbell, Archibald, *Records of Argyll*, W. Blackwood and Sons, Edinburgh, 1885.

Campbell, Archibald, *Waifs and Strays of Celtic Tradition*, Vol. I, David Nutt, London, 1889.

Campbell, J.E., *Popular Tales of the West Highlands, Vol. 4*, Alexander Gardner, Paisley, 1890.

Campbell, Marion, *Argyll: The Enduring Heartland*, House of Lochar, [Isle of Colonsay, Argyll], 2001.

Dwelly, Edward, *Illustrated Gaelic-English Dictionary*, Birlinn, [Edinburgh], 2001.

Fisk, Robert, *Scotland in Music: A European Enthusiasm*, Cambridge, 1985.

Gillies, H. Cameron, *The Place-Names of Argyll*, D. Nutt, London, 1906.

Haldane, A.R.B., *The Drove Roads of Scotland*, Birlinn, Edinburgh, 1997.

Hensel, Sebastian, *The Mendelssohn Family (1729-1847) From Letters and Journals*, Greenwood, New York, 1968.

Highland Papers, Vol. ii, Edited by J.R.N. Macphail, Edinburgh University, Edinburgh, 1916.

Hunter, Charles, *Oban—Past and Present*, C. Hunter, Oban [Scotland], 1993.

Jenks, David and Mark Visocchi, *Mendelssohn in Scotland*, Chappell, London, 1978.

Johns, Rev. C.A., *Flowers of the Field*, Society for Promoting Christian Knowledge, London, 1888.

Lay of Deirdre, traditional Highland poem, www.scottishradiance.com/galcol/galcol9801.htm and www.electricscotland.com/history/literat/lamentof.htm.

MacDonald, Màiri, *The Islands of Nether Lorn*, West Highland Series, No. 3, [unknown], [c. 1980].

MacDonald, Màiri (Ed. and illus.) *A Lorn Miscellany of History and Tradition*. Lorn Archaeological and Natural History Society, [unknown], [c. 1980].

MacDougall Collection, collected by Hope MacDougall of MacDougall, Oban, Scotland, www.friends-macdougall.co.uk.

MacDougall of MacDougall, Hope, *Island of Kerrera: Mirror of History*, House of Lochar, [Isle of Colonsay, Argyll], 2002.

MacDougall, Alexander, *The Galley of Lorn*, A. MacDougall and Son, 21–23 North Church Street, Sheffield, n.d.

MacDougall, Dugald Gordon, *Bràiste Lathurna (The Brooch of Lorn): A Memorial Volume of Gaelic Poems and Songs*, K&R Davidson, Glasgow, 1959.

MacDougall, Elizabeth, letter to Sophie MacDougall, 1908.

MacDougall, Jean, *Highland Postbag: The Correspondence of Four MacDougall Chiefs, 1715–1865*, Shepheard-Walwyn, London, 2004.

MacDougall, William L., *Kings in the West Beyond the Sea*, n.p., Moncton, New Brunswick, 2001.

MacGibbon, David and Ross Thomas, *Castellated and Domestic Architecture of Scotland*, Mercat Press; Edinburgh, 1971.

MacPhail, J.R.N. (ed.), *Highland Papers*, Vol. ii, Scottish History Society, Edinburgh, 1916.

McDonald, R. Andrew, *The Kingdom of the Isles: Scotland's Western Seaboard c.1100–c.1336*, Tuckwell, East Linton, 1996.

McDonald, R. Andrew, *The Kingdom of the Isles: Scotland's Western Seaboard in the Central Middle Ages*, Tuckwell, East Linton, 1997.

McKerracher, Archie, "The Battle at the Red Ford," *The Tartan*, Winter 2002, reprinted from *The Highlander*, May/June 2000.

Moncrieffe, Sir Iain of that Ilk, *The Highland Clans*, Clarkson N. Potter, New York, 1982.

Morton, H.V., *In Search of Scotland Again*, reprinted in *The Splendors of Scotland*, Dodd Mead & Company, [New York], 1977.

Muir, Richard, *Riddles of the British Landscape*, Thames and Hudson, New York, 1981.

Munro, Neil, *Para Handy Tales*, Birlinn, Edinburgh, 2007.

Ordnance Survey, United Kingdom, *Topographic Maps, 1:50000 Series*, www.ordnancesurvey.co.uk.

Pearson, Joan, *Kilmartin: The Stones of History*, Famedram, Aberdeenshire, 1975.

Piping Times, The College of Piping, Glasgow, November, 1978.
Popular Tales of the West Highlands, Vol. 4, edited and translated by John Francis Campbell, Kessinger, Whitefish, MT, August 2003.
Ritchie, Graham, *The Archaeology of Argyll*, Edinburgh University, Edinburgh, 1997.
Ross, William, *Ross' Collection [of] Pipe Music*, Wood & Co., Edinburgh, 1885.
Scotland Magazine, March 1968.
Scots Kith and Kin, Collins, London, 1989.
Scott, Sir Walter, *The Poetical Works of Sir Walter Scott*, Vol. III, Nichol, Edinburgh, 1857.
Simpson, W. Douglas, *Dunollie, Oban, Argyll*, University of Aberdeen Center for Scottish Studies, Aberdeen, 1991.
Spence, Lewis, *The Magic Arts in Celtic Britain*, Rider, London, 1945.
Starforth, Michael, *An Official Short History of Clan MacDougall*, Scotpress, Morgantown, WV, 1983.
Stevenson, Robert Louis, *Kidnapped*, [various editions since 1886].
Tabraham, C.J., *Scottish Castles and Fortifications: An Introduction to the Historic Castles, Houses and Artillery Fortifications in the Care of the Secretary of State for Scotland*, Edinburgh, H.M.S.O., 1986.
Tennyson, Alfred Lord, "The Princess," [poem in various editions since 1847].
The Highlander, May-June 1983.
The Steam-Boat Companion, or Stranger's Guide to the Western Isles and Highlands of Scotland, Lumsden & Son, Glasgow, 1831.
The Tartan, newsletter of the Clan MacDougall Society of North America, www.macdougall.org.
Waite, Garth and Vicky, *Island: Diary of a Year on Easdale*, Mainstream, Edinburgh, 1995.
Wallace-Hadrill, David and Janet Carolan, *Turner in Argyll in 1831: Inverary to Oban*, Turner Series, Vol. II, No. 1, Summer 1991.
Way, George of Plean and Romilly Squire, *Scottish Clan & Family Encyclopedia*, Barnes & Noble Books, New York, 1999.
West Highland Series, #5, West Highland Publications, Oban, Argyll, n.d.
Wild Flowers, Collins (Gem), [London], 2004.
Woodcock, Martin, *A Handguide to the Birds of Britain and Europe*, Treasure, London, 1985.
Wordsworth, William, and Dorothy Wordsworth, *The Letters of William and Dorothy Wordsworth: Volume V: The Later Years: Part II 1829-1834*, edited by Alan G. Hill, Oxford University, USA, 1980.

Contact Information

Oban Tourist Information Centre
   Argyll Square
   Oban, Argyll, PA34 4AN Scotland
   Tel: +44 (0)1631 563122
   www.oban.org.uk

The MacDougall Collection
   Dunollie House,
   Oban, Argyll, PA34 5TT Scotland
   www.friends-macdougall.co.uk

Clan MacDougall Society of North America, Inc.
   www.macdougall.org

Clan MacDougall Society (Great Britain, Eire, Europe)
   www.clanmacdougall.co.uk

Maps

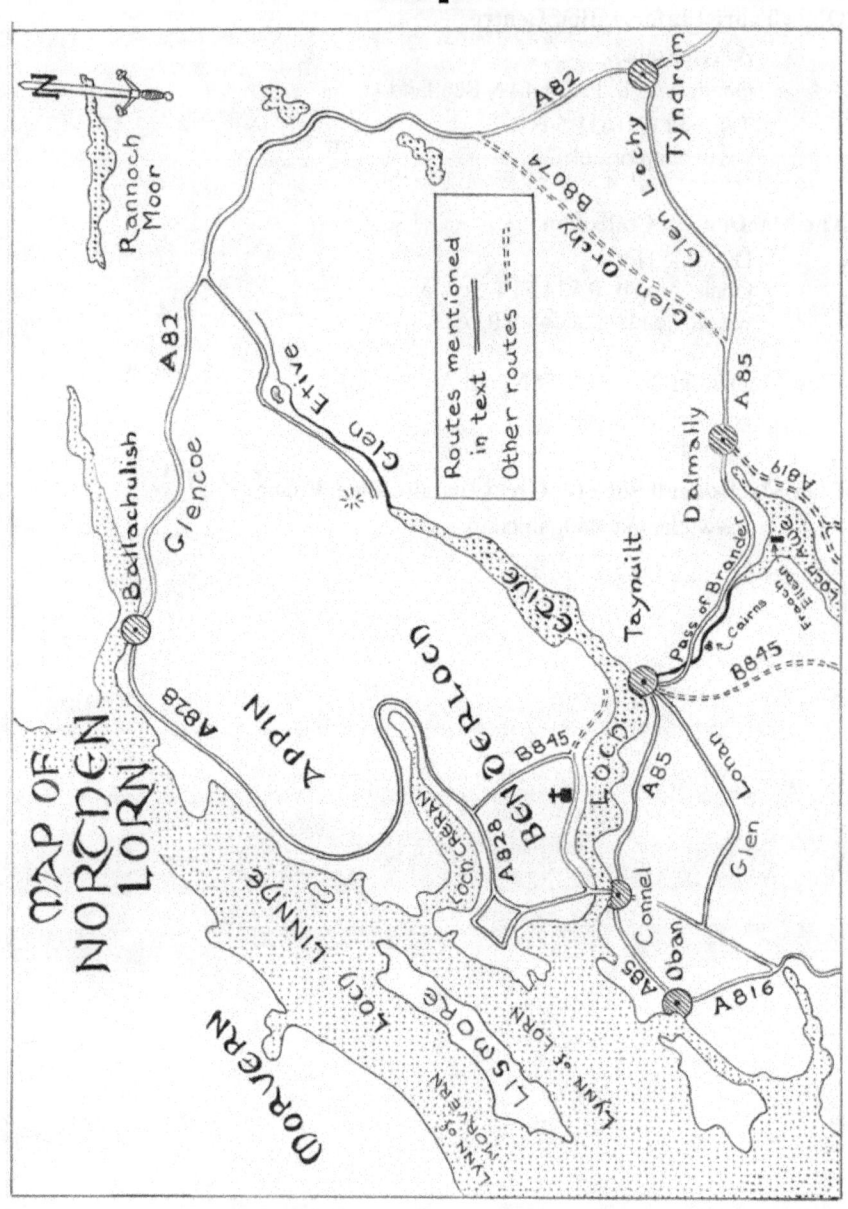

Map 1. Northern Lorn

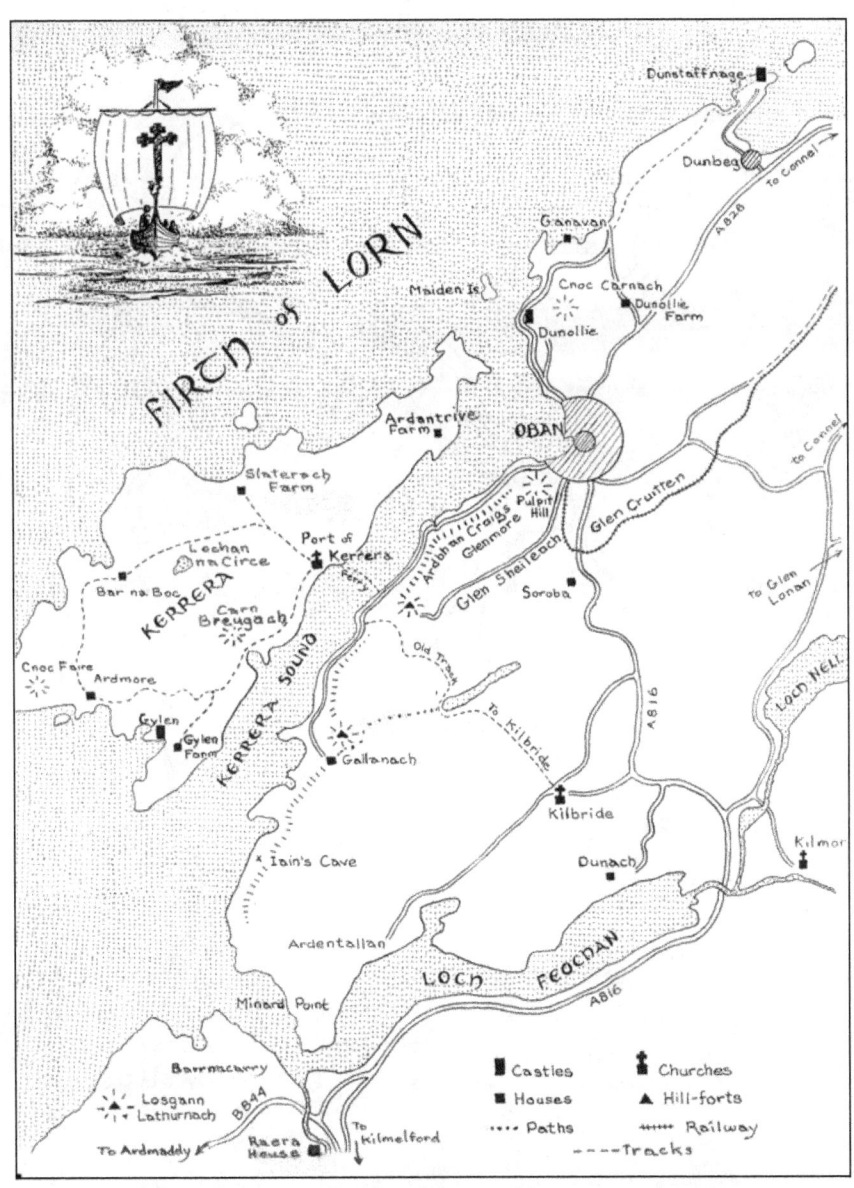

Map 2. Central Lorn

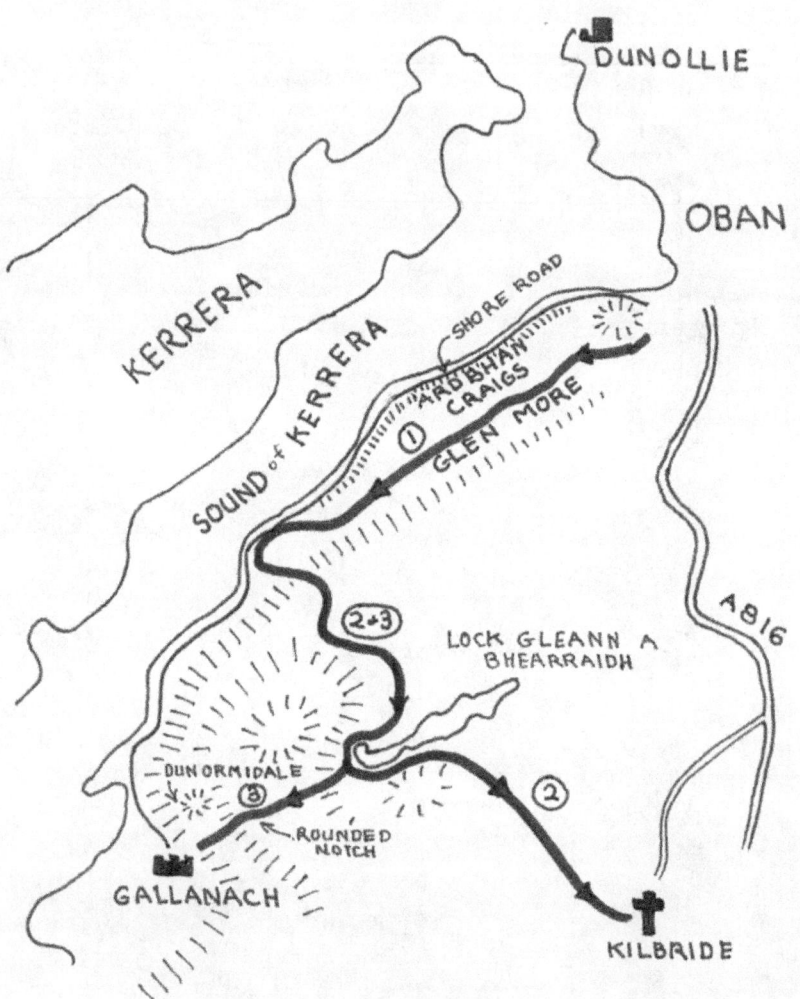

Map 3. Oban Area

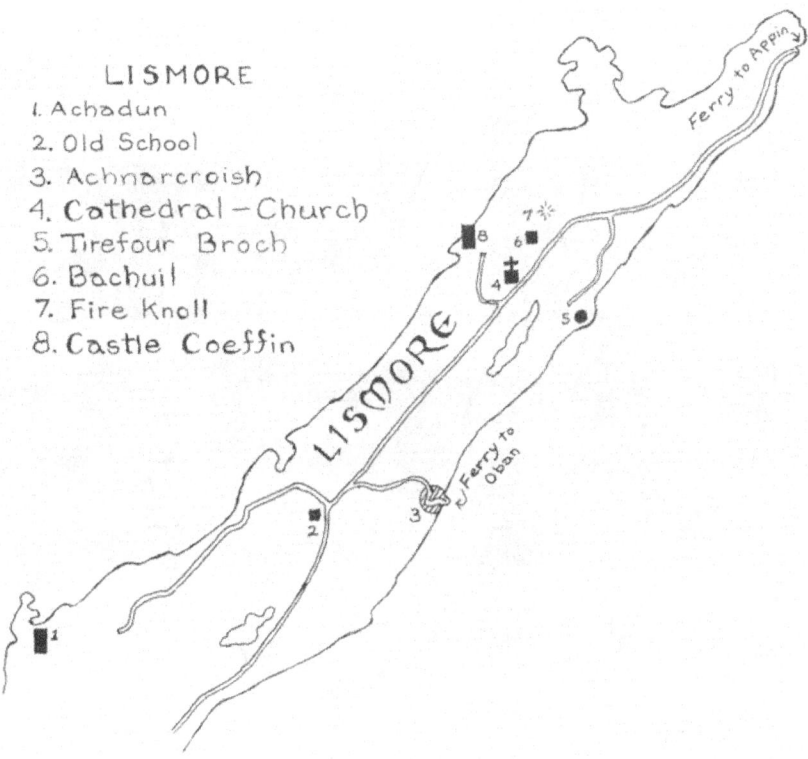

Map 4. Lismore

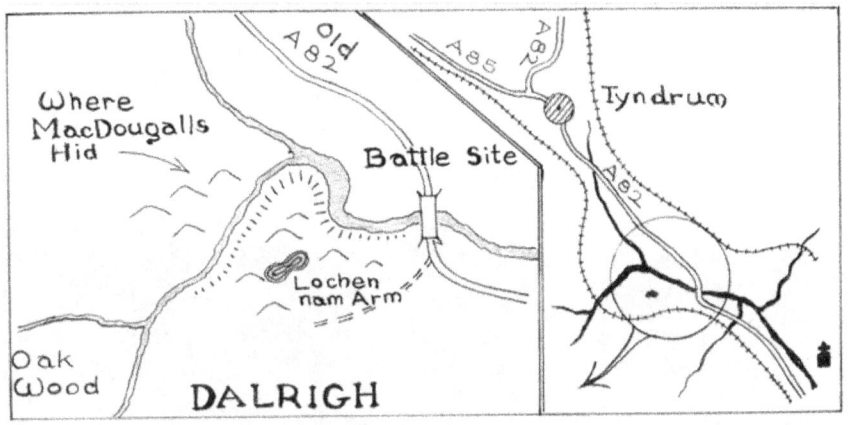

Map 5. Dalrigh

Map 6. Southern Lorn

Index

Achadun Castle (Lismore), 23, 213
Achafolla (Luing), 166
Achnacree, Moss, 111, 113, 189, 192, 267
Achnacroish (Lismore), 22
Alexander, King, 28, 91, 188, 258
Allt Dearg, 64, 196
Am Maolan (Kerrera), 88
Aoineadh Mor (Mull), 41
Appin, 134
Ard na Cuile, 138
Ardantrive, 204
Ardbhan Craigs (Oban), 27, 174
Ardbrechnish, 71
Ardchattan Priory, 47, 187, 209, 233
Ardencaple, 84, 163, 203, 213
Ardfad Castle (Lismore), 85, 163, 214
Ardfern (Craignish), 73, 76, 160, 162
Ardlarach, 166, 204, 214
Ardmaddy Castle, 82, 83, 163, 165, 186, 215
Ardmore, 89, 205
Ardnahoy, 205
Arms of the Chief, 10, 240
Aros, 38, 146, 215
arrest of island chiefs, 216
Arrow Rock, 65, 70
arrow slits, 96, 195, 230
Asknish, 197
Awe, 67, 70, 81, 128, 153, 185, 186, 188, 260
Bachuil Mor (crosier), 24, 26, 209, 263
Balichun, 205
Balliol, King, 187, 188
Balure (Oban), 106
Barcaldine, 216
bards, 113, 196, 208
Baregonium. *See* Barr nam Gobhan
Barnabuck (Kerrera), 87, 88, 126, 176, 259
Barnacarry, 82, 168
Barr nam Gobhan, 111
Barranrioch Farm, 106
beaches, raised, 7, 256
beacons, signal, 134, 265
Benderloch, 111
Beothail (Legend), 259
birds, 73, 252

buzzards, 179, 252
eagle, 177, 180, 253
heron, 98, 253
hooded crow, 175, 253
raven, 138, 241, 253
swan, 254
Black Mill Bay (Luing), 167
Black, Nancy, 27, 88, 103, 111, 130, 145, 148, 159, 174, 209
Blackie, Prof. John Stuart, 32, 264
Blacksmith of Taynuilt, 16, 22
bonfires, 178
Braes of Lorn, 67, 205
Brander, 5, 49, 92, 154, 200, 205
Bridge of Awe, 50
Bronze Age, 172, 259
Brooch of Lorn, 123, 264
Bruce, Robert, 50, 185, 188, 264
Buachaille Mor and Beag (Etive), 59
burial of MacDougall Chiefs, 47, 107, 237, 242, 265
Burns, Robert, 59
Cailleach (Winter Hag), 77, 260
Cairn na Burgh, 38, 217
cairns, 49, 53, 65, 70, 107, 113, 134, 172, 178, 189, 196, 259
Cairns of Brander, 49
Caisteal na Nighinn Ruaidhe, 69, 216
Caisteal nan Con, 216
Campbells, 50, 64, 65, 67, 71, 82, 94, 163, 167, 185
Cailein Mor, 65, 70, 185, 196
Carding Mill Bay (Oban), 126, 174, 265
Carmichael, 208
Carn Breugach, 177
cas chrom, 23, 87, 266
castles, 25, 38, 70, 83, 91, 146, 163, 193, 213–32
cathedrals
 Lismore, 23, 193, 235
 Oban, 17
cattle, 11, 18, 24, 28, 32, 86, 88, 153, 165, 259
caves, 16, 22, 27, 38, 39, 41, 124, 138, 140, 151, 189, 256
Chiefs of MacDougalls. *See* MacDougall Chiefs

chief's role, 239
Christ Church (Oban), 17
Christina, wife of 8th Chief, 199
chronological chart, 185
church designs, 192
Clach na Choin. *See* Dog Stone
Clachan Bridge (Seil), 69, 84, 163
Clan Crest, 241
Clan Dougall's Incitement to Battle, 65
Clan Society, 53, 99
Cnoc Carnach, 43, 265
Cnoc na Faire, 81, 88
Cobblers of Lorn (Luing), 167, 215
Coeffin, 217, 259
Coline, 30th Chief. *See* under MacDougall Chiefs
Coll Island, 38, 152
Columba (ship), 37
Columba, Saint, 81
Connel, 49
Conocher, 209
Cononish, Glen, 50
Corranmore (Craignish), 76
Corrielorne, 67, 205
Covenanter Army, 12, 90, 198, 227
Cowan. *See* MacCowan
Crag of the Wild Cat (Oban), 36
Craignish, 73, 81, 162
Creag nam Marbh, 82
Crianlarich, 5
Crinan Canal, 80
Crosier of Moluag. *See* Bachuil Mor
cross, 13, 36, 48, 76, 77, 78, 79, 81, 154, 234, 237, 254
Cruachan, 187, 205
Cruitten, 36, 105, 115
Crystal Talisman of MacDougalls, 63
Cuan Sound, 69, 165
cup and ring, 190
Cutter Island (Sound of Kerrera), 27
Daileag, 197
Dalriada, 53, 73, 80, 92, 186, 220, 224
Dalrigh, 50, 258
deer, 252
Degnish, 67, 165, 203, 219
Deirdre (Legend), 61, 119, 260
Diarmid (Legend), 107, 266
Dochart, 50, 188
Dog Stone (Dunollie), 7, 123, 126, 257
Dorus Mor (Craignish), 74
Dougall, 241

Dowacha, 205
Dragon (Fraoch Eilean), 261
Drissaig House (Loch Avich), 70, 219
Druimnean, 67, 199
Duachy Farm, 171
Duart, 219
Duart Castle, 37, 145, 188
Dubh Leitir, 166
Dubh, Loch, 172
Dumbarton, 3
Dun. *See* hill forts
Dun MacSniochan. *See* Barr nam Gobhan
Dun Ormidal, 29
Dunach, 206, 220
Dunadd, 34, 73, 80
Dunaverty, 12, 51, 67, 198
Dunbeg, 93, 98
Dunollie, 7, 43, 55, 94, 98, 101, 125, 174, 267
  Castle, 10, 123, 180, 220–23
  House, 7, 8, 99, 129, 130, 223–24
duns, 191
Dunstaffnage, 43, 125
  Castle, 92, 224
  Chapel, 95, 236
Easdale (Seil), 164
Eilean Musdile, 265
Elizabeth Sophia (25th Chief's wife), 9
Etive, 56, 59, 61, 187
Euchar, River, 168
fairies and fairy stories, 37, 47, 78
Fairy Knoll, 166
Falloch, Glen, 50
Falls of Lora, 47, 111
Feochan, 81, 109
Ferlochan, 206
ferrys, 18, 22, 26, 28, 62, 86, 123, 134, 153, 165, 174, 213
Fillan, Chapel, 51, 262
Fingal, Fionn, 7, 39, 58, 107, 151, 260
Fire Knoll (Lismore), 24, 134
Firth of Lorn, 37, 54, 126
flowers, plants, and trees, 32, 68, 73, 74, 87, 98, 130, 134, 138, 140, 154, 155, 162, 164, 165, 170, 177, 249
forests, 51, 60, 69, 74, 112, 142, 159, 250
Fraoch Eilean, 50, 155, 188, 225
Gallain, Glen, 67

Index

Gallanach, 27, 28, 29, 30, 136, 139, 141, 203, 226
Galley of Lorn, 48, 240
Ganavan, 14
Garvellachs (Holy Islands), 41, 257
geology of Lorn, 255–56
glaciation, 256
Glen Lyon, 206
Glencoe, 56, 57, 123, 158
Glenmachrie, 108
Glenmore (Oban), 18
goat, spectral, 29, 261
graffiti (galleys), 237
gravestones, 35, 79, 82, 188, 205, 237, 255
gristmills, hand, 15
gun loops, 195
Gylen Castle, 41, 89, 126, 178, 226
Haakon, King, 28, 242
Hadfield, Dr. Stephen, 62, 248
harp, 11, 99
Hayfield, 206
heather, 60, 105, 109, 115, 123, 141, 160, 162, 249
heaths, 74, 79, 108, 169, 251
Hebrides, Inner, 74
heraldry, 10, 254
hill forts, 111, 191
Hope (sister of 30th Chief). *See* under MacDougall of MacDougall
Horseshoe Bay (Kerrera), 28, 91, 258
Hounds of MacDougall, 71
Inishail, 153, 154, 236
Innis Chonnel, 70, 230
Innisaig, Dower House of (Lunga), 74, 162
investiture of Chiefs, 241
Iona
  Island, 39, 148
  School of Sculpture, 48, 78, 195
Iron Age, 29, 31, 82, 165, 172
Jean Hadfield (sister of 30th Chief). *See* under MacDougall of MacDougall
Johnson, Samuel, 86, 119
Jura, 41, 160
Keil, 57, 112
Kerrera, 19, 27, 32, 37, 41, 81, 174, 258
Kilbride, 236
  Old Track to, 31
  School of Piping, 207
Kilchattan (Luing), 160, 166, 237
Kilmartin, 79
Kilmore, 31, 81, 238
Kilmun, 70, 206
Kintraw, 70, 79
Knapdale, 81
Lagna an Phail (Appin), 202
lazybeds, 265
Leccamore, Dun (Luing), 166
legends, 144, 259
Leslie, General, 90
Leven, 81, 123, 158
Lindsay-MacDougall
  Colin of Lunga, 74, 79, 82, 153, 203, 216, 217
  Katherine, 70, 74, 76, 162
Linnhe, 123
Lismore, 22, 134, 235
Livingstone, 105, 209
  Alastair, Baron of Bachuil, 22, 24, 134
Lochan
  Craig na Cailleach (Etive), 58
  na Circe (Kerrera), 259
  nan Arm (Dalrigh), 50
  nan Seachd Crioch (Kerrera), 176
Lochbuie (Mull), 144
Lochy, Glen, 50
Lonan, Glen, 105
Lords of Lorn, 186, 224
Lorn, geographic extent of, 38, 43, 56
Losgann Lathurnach (Toad of Lorn), 82, 171
Luing, 41, 165, 166
Lunga, 167, 203, 231, 257, *See* also Lindsay-MacDougall
  burials, 76
  House, 71, 74, 77, 160
  Iain MacDougall, 77
  John MacDougall, 76
  Mary Bheg, 78
  Stewart MacDougall, 78
MacArthur, 186
MacCoul, Alan, 94, 201
MacCowan, 170, 209
MacCulloch, 210
MacDill, 210
MacDonald, 57, 186
  Dunollie Gatekeeper, 129

Mary of Sleat (wife of 22nd Chief), 237, 241
MacDougall. *See* also under Lunga
   Ailean Dall (Bard), 208
   Alan Miles, 204
   Bishop Martin, 23
   Captain, Alexander, 7
   Charles Williamson, 203
   Colina, wife of 29th Chief, 10, 54
   Donald, 97
   Dugald Gordon (Bard), 208
   Elizabeth, 181
   Gordon (Bard), 196
   Iain of Degnish, 67
   James Williamson, Major, 28, 136
   John Maol, 204, 205, 215, 261
   John of Lunga, 76
   John of Raera, 84
   Leslie Grahame, 9, 17, 216
   Mary (last birth at Dunollie Castle), 12
   Robin (Morley), 156
   Sandy, 98
MacDougall Cadets and Branches, 203–7
MacDougall Chiefs, 242–48
   Alexander, 29th, 13, 54, 188
   Alexander, 4th, 92, 185, 186, 200, 211
   Allen, 21st, 57
   Coline, 30th, 9, 10, 19, 36, 39, 45, 47, 53, 98, 108, 129, 180, 207, 210, 216, 229, 237
   Dougall, 1st, 210
   Duncan, 16th, 188
   Duncan, 2nd, 47, 48, 93
   Ewan, 3rd, 28
   Ewan, 7th, 92, 93, 111
   Iain Ciar, 22nd, 11, 12, 15, 16, 34, 35, 41, 47, 138, 140, 176, 264
   John (Iain) Bacach, 5th, 49, 50, 51, 187, 200
   John, 11th, 94
   John, 25th, 9, 98
MacDougall of MacDougall
   Coline. *See* under MacDougall Chiefs
   Hope, 14, 41, 46, 47, 49, 50, 51, 52, 86, 90, 91, 99, 108, 130, 140, 177, 178, 201, 237, 249
   Jean Hadfield, 18, 62, 237

Macdowall/MacDowell, 210
MacEachan, 211
MacEwan, 211
MacFadyan, 234
MacFergus (King), 221
MacIntyre, 187
MacKichan, 211
MacLaren, 94
MacLean, 163, 188
MacLeay. *See* Livingstone
MacLeish, Archibald, xiii
MacLucas, 212
MacNab, 188
MacNamell, 212
MacNaughten, 188
Maid of Lorn, 53, 54
Maiden Island (Oban), 7, 14, 22, 98
McCaig's Tower (Oban), 20
Melfort, 67, 69, 76
Methven (Battle), 51
mills, milling, 23, 36, 106, 126, 166, 259, 265
Minard Point, 81
Mingary MacDougalls, 204
Morvern, 25, 37
Mull, Island, 28, 37, 143, 146
Narrachan, 206
Nell, 106, 109
Nether Lorn, 63, 81, 82, 257
Oban, 3, 43, 53, 93, 115, 129, 264
Ossian Legend, 112, 113, 114, 122, 191
peat, 14, 68, 113, 141, 177
pipe music, 197
pipers, 75, 136, 197, 206, 207
plants. *See* flowers
Port Mor (Oban), 7
Port nan Cuilc (Sound of Kerrera), 31, 32
Pulpit Hill (Oban), 19, 126
quarries, 47, 81, 82, 135, 164, 234, 255
Raera, 24, 82, 168, 186, 203
Rannoch, 58, 159
Red Comyn, 51, 92, 188
Religious Wars, 81, 203, 206, 233
Rising of 1715, 12
Road of Kings, 81, 106
Robber's Waterfall, 266
Royal Cause in 1600s. *See* Religious Wars
run-rig farms, 257
rushes, 109, 159, 164, 267

Saint Michael's Craig (Dunollie), 7, 16, 22
Saint Oran's Chapel (Iona), 40
Saints, 262–63
   Columba, 23, 39
   Fillan, 188
   Moluag, 23, 209
   Muire (Mary), 81, 263
Scammadale, Loch, 63, 67, 70
Scarba, 81, 257
Scots pine, 60, 74, 98, 106
sea beaches, 7
sea stacks, 7, 139, 167, 256
sea wolves, 26
Seil, 41, 81, 84, 163
Seileach, Glen, 20, 32
Selbach, King, 221
Shore Road (to Gallanach), 18, 27
Slaterach Farm (Kerrera), 87, 175, 189, 259
snails, 34
snuff, 15, 264
Somerled, 38, 53, 90, 186, 210, 241
Soroba, 9, 20, 36, 54, 207, 232
Spanish Armada, 97, 146
Staffa Island, 38, 41, 123, 128, 149
Stalc, 201
standing stones, 79, 82, 107, 172, 190
Stewart Lords of Lorn, 94, 186, 201
stone circles, 107, 159, 190

Strath Fillan, 50, 51
String of Lorn (Sreang Lathurnach), 63, 266
Strontoiller Farm (Lonan), 107
Swallow Rock, 27, 174
swans, 106
Table of Lorn, 98
Tartan, Clan, 10, 15, 34, 75, 76
Taynuilt, 16, 22, 49
thatch, 106, 112, 267
Tigh an Truish, 84
Tigh Cuil, 168
Tir nan Og, 39, 113
Torsa, 69, 204, 257
Torthain Mor (Kerrera), 88
tower houses, 193
trees. *See* flowers *and* forests
Turnberry Band, 187
Tyndrum, 5, 50
Uamh nan Claigionn, 256
Vikings, 25, 40, 80, 185
Wallace, William, 234
weather, highland, 17, 26, 37, 43, 54, 65, 67, 85, 93, 100–104, 115, 119, 120, 122, 156
windy corner, 8, 130, 181
wolves, 254
Wordsworth, William, 180

About the Author

Walter Marshall Macdougall's lifelong fascination with Clan MacDougall heritage ultimately led him to serve as newsletter editor, board member, and president of the clan society in North America. He worked tirelessly to organize the society into regions, recognize the clan's Macdowall and MacDowell heritage, and strengthen clan connections between the United States, Canada, and Scotland. In 1998, he was appointed Torsheadeor (Commander) for the Macdowalls of Garthland by Fergus Macdowall of Garthland in recognition of his service. This book is a testimony to the deep and lasting friendships, joy, and pride of belonging that his association with Clan MacDougall has brought to his life. A retired public school science teacher and college professor with academic interests in philosophy, Walter completed his teaching career in the Honors College at the University of Maine. During his career he received a Doctor of Education degree. He lives with his wife Judy in Milo, Maine.

www.ingramcontent.com/pod-product-compliance
Lightning Source LLC
Chambersburg PA
CBHW022106150426
43195CB00008B/285